THE IMAGINARY WAR

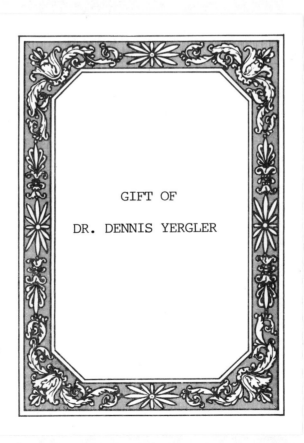

To Joshua and Oliver

THE

IMAGINARY

WAR

Understanding the East-West Conflict

Mary Kaldor

Basil Blackwell

Copyright © Mary Kaldor 1990

First published 1990

Basil Blackwell Ltd
108 Cowley Road, Oxford, OX4 1JF, UK

Basil Blackwell, Inc.
3 Cambridge Center
Cambridge, Massachusetts 02142, USA

British Library Cataloguing in Publication Data

A CIP catalogue record for this book is available from the British Library.

Library of Congress Cataloging in Publication Data

Kaldor, Mary.
  The imaginary war: understanding the East–West conflict
Mary Kaldor.
    p.   cm.
  ISBN 1–55786–180–3
  1. Europe–Politics and government–1945– 2. Cold War.
3. Detente. I. Title.
D1053.K35 1990
327–dc20   90–494
                                                                           CIP

Typeset in 11 on 13 pt Sabon
by Wearside Tradespools, Fulwell, Sunderland
Printed in Great Britain by TJ Press Ltd, Padstow, Cornwall.

Contents

Acknowledgements

Much of the research for this book was undertaken while I was West European Coordinator of the United Nations University subprogramme on Peace and Global Transformation. I am grateful to the UNU for financial and intellectual support, to all those people who participated in the European part of the subprogramme, and to Richard Falk, Giri Deshingkar and Rajni Kothari for a fruitful and stimulating collaboration. During this period I was also a fellow of the Transnational Institute, and co-convenor of the TNI's New Europe project with Fred Halliday. I want to thank the TNI and the Cadbury Trust for financial support and for hosting a series of meetings under the auspices of the UNU Peace and Global Transformation subprogramme and the New Europe project, and also Fred Halliday for an enjoyable and productive controversy about the nature of the cold war.

I also want to thank my friends in European Nuclear Disarmament, and especially the *END Journal* collective, for an intensive discussion that has lasted ten years, and Edward Thompson who inspired so much of our work. And I want to thank my friends in the West European peace movement and in East European peace, green and human rights groups who taught me so much about Europe, both East and West. I owe a special debt to Mient Jan Faber of the Dutch Inter-Church Peace Council – many of the ideas in this book emerged from political projects on which we worked together.

Finally I am very grateful to all those people who helped with the preparation of the book. Roy Bhaskar, Anthony Giddens, Chris Freeman, Gerard Holden, Judit Kiss, Robin Murray, Kate Soper, Romesh Vaitilingam, Hilary Wainwright and Nancy Wood read various parts of the manuscript and provided invaluable comments. The Armament and Disarmament Information Unit helped me a great deal with source material. The Rowntree Charitable Trust provided financial support while I was writing the book. Claire Trevelyan, Cecily Collingridge, Janet French, Chris Gaterell, Sarah Hannant and especially Jane Scroggie typed and retyped the manuscript. Everyone involved with the book at Basil Blackwell was very helpful, particularly my copy-editor Ann Bone. And last but not least, as always, my family, especially Julian Robinson, gave me much needed and practical encouragement.

PART I
Argument and Method

1
Introduction

The post-war period is over. The international political order that came into being during and after the Second World War is disintegrating. Changes that were unthinkable only a few years or even months ago have taken place so thick and fast that it is impossible to keep abreast of them. The Berlin Wall is breached, Germany is unifying, communist regimes have toppled throughout East Central Europe. The Soviet Union is engulfed in unpredictable struggles for democracy and national self-determination.

But it is not only the East that is changing, although the changes are more dramatic there. Gorbachev's disarmament initiatives, especially the INF (Intermediate Nuclear Forces) treaty, revealed a growing distance between the United States and Western Europe and a new political outlook among large sections of West European opinion, especially but not only in Germany. Preparations for the single West European market, due to come into effect in 1992, and for the unification of Germany have provided a new impetus for political integration.

This is a time of political spontaneity, when real choices can be made about the future. It is a time of fluidity, when established political alignments are breaking down, and when new ideas expressed by individuals, social movements, political factions, etc. can really influence the situation. All the same, it is also a time of risk. Choices that are made on the basis of narrow, particularist interests, or of inherited theories that no longer fit the current conjuncture, could have dark consequences.

This book is an attempt to describe the post-war political order so as to help inform these choices. It explores the assumptions that underlie conventional interpretations of the post-war political order and offers an alternative interpretation based on alternative assumptions. It is impossible to predict the outcome of the present changes but it is possible to suggest what kind of future is implied by different understandings of the immediate past.

The post-war political order was dominated by the conflict between East and West. In this book, I use the term 'imaginary war' to describe the East–West conflict in Europe. It is often said that we in Europe have enjoyed 'peace' during the last 40 years. Quite apart from the fact that there have been real wars in Eastern Europe, in Greece and Turkey, or in Northern Ireland, the word 'peace' seems to be a misnomer. What we actually experienced was a state of imaginary war. Over and over again, in military exercises, in the scenarios of military planners, in the games and stories of espionage and counter-espionage, in the training of millions of men, in the hostile rhetoric of politicians and newspapers, we have fought out an imaginary war between East and West. We have lived with the permanent anxiety of war, with many of the forms of organization and control that are characteristic of war. Except for the fact that people are no longer actually killed (and that is, of course, a big difference) we have lived as if the Second World War had not really ended.

The imaginary war could be viewed as a 'disciplinary technology', to use Foucault's term. It is a discourse which expresses and legitimizes power relationships in modern society.[1] It serves to maintain social cohesion. The rise of the nation state was accompanied by the rise of nationalism, conjuring up an imagined community around which the people living in a given territorial area could coalesce, and which provided legitimacy for the nation state. In much the same way, the consolidation of blocs of nations in the aftermath of the Second World War was accompanied by an imaginary war which specified the character of blocs and gave meaning to the sense of belonging to East and West. Each bloc of nations identified itself in terms of a shared social system and set of values, democracy or socialism, which was contrasted to an opposing system, totalitarianism or imperialism. Each system, at least in the imagination, threatened the very existence of the other. It was a struggle between good and evil of epic proportions. And it was substantiated by a real military confrontation and, indeed, real wars in remote parts of the world.

The imagery was so powerful, at least in the first two post-war decades, because it drew on ideas that had inspired millions of men and women, and on actual experience, particularly the experience of the Second World War. Moreover, an identity based on abstract values, freedom or equality, seemed more progressive than an identity based on racial or cultural characteristics, which had been so discredited in two world wars.

It is true, of course, that the two blocs of nations that came into being in the post-war period were characterized by two quite distinct social systems. And it is true that one could be termed capitalist, although the state played an increasingly important role, as well as democratic, at least in a formal sense; while the other could be termed socialist depending on how socialism is defined, and totalitarian, at least in the early years. But it does not follow that the existence of each system threatened the other.

In this book, the two systems are termed Atlanticism and Stalinism and/or post-Stalinism. (Thus Atlanticism is used to refer to a social system and not a geopolitical entity.) Atlanticism and Stalinism constitute specific variants of capitalism and socialism, which came into being before and during the Second World War in the United States and the Soviet Union respectively. They were also associated with a new phase of industrial development characterized by mass production and the intensive use of energy, especially oil. The wartime experience seemed to provide a successful formula for coping with different deep-rooted problems that had confronted both societies in an earlier period. (It was not necessarily the only formula, but it was the only formula which had been proved in practice.) The imaginary war replicated that Second World War experience and provided a mechanism for imposing or spreading the two systems to groups of nations, particularly in Europe. Hence, far from threatening each other, the two systems reinforced each other through their shared need for an imaginary war. It was not exactly a collusion, for that implies foreknowledge and consciousness of what was happening; rather it was a fortuitous complementarity. Nor was the evolution of the two systems symmetrical, except in so far as the imaginary war itself injected a kind of symmetry. By and large,

Atlanticism was accepted in Western Europe, at least in the north-west, on the basis of popular consent and even enthusiasm; Stalinism was a tragedy for the peoples of East Central Europe which will have ramifications for several generations.

For the first 20 years or so, the imaginary war seemed to work, in the sense that it served to consolidate and reproduce the two social systems; how this happened is developed in part II of this book. In the 1970s, new problems began to confront both systems – economic stagnation, environmental degradation, social and cultural aliena-tion. Détente and new cold war, described in part III, can be viewed as ways of adjusting to these new pressures for change. Both failed, it is argued, because the two systems remained bound together in their conflictual embrace and their stockpiles of weapons and this impeded change. Part IV traces the role of the military confrontation in both systems through the whole post-war period.

Today, there is a possibility of peace. The ideas and institutions of the imaginary war are being dismantled and this could permit a progressive evolution of both systems, an emancipation from the current social, political and economic status quo. There is also a danger of new imaginary and real wars.

The idea of the cold war as a 'joint venture' is not new.[2] It has become widespread in Europe, both East and West, during the 1980s primarily as a result of the dialogue between the Western peace movement and independent peace, green and human rights groups in the East. The idea has been expressed eloquently by others, especially E. P. Thompson and George Konrad.[3] This book is an attempt to elaborate and systematize the argument, so as to contribute to current debates about foreign policy and about the study of interna-tional relations.

A central theme is the way in which certain mindsets create myopia with respect to areas outside those mindsets. This is a crucial factor in explaining the East–West conflict in Europe. Historians and political analysts simply did not see certain uncomfortable facts which contradicted the inevitable clash hypothesis. This is not an accusation although some of the omissions were glaring, such as the way in which policy-makers treated nuclear weapons like any other weapons and stockpiled tens of thousands of warheads, enough to destroy humanity several times over, or such as the way in which the left, for the most part, failed to appreciate the realities of socialism as it actually existed.

The point about any explanation of natural and social phenomena is that it *is* partial. It has to be partial if it is to be useful or comprehensive. Every generation has its own interpretation of history and its own interpretation of nature. From time to time, especially during moments of change, the very partiality of those interpretations becomes an obstacle, instead of an aid, to action.

In order to offer a different interpretation of the post-war political period, a few preliminary remarks are required about the method of analysis and how this differs from existing approaches. This method is also partial. But I hope that a different mindset, a different set of partialities (and myopias) will enable people to envisage alternative futures for Europe.

Notes

1 Michel Foucault says:

> In a society such as ours, but basically in any society, there are manifold relations of power which permeate, characterize and constitute the social body, and these relations of power cannot themselves be established, consolidated nor implemented without the production, accumulation, circulation and functioning of a discourse. There can be no possible exercise of power without a certain economy of discourses of truth which operate through and on the basis of this association. We are subjected to the production of truth through power and we cannot exercise power except through the production of truth. ('Disciplinary power and subjection', in Steven Lukes, ed., *Power* (Basil Blackwell, 1986), pp. 229–30.)

2 The term used was used by Giangiacomo Migone, in a lecture given at the seminar on *Arms Control and East–West Relations*, Moscow, 10–24 July 1989, organized by the Moscow State Institute for International Relations (MGIMO), the Institute for Global Conflict and Cooperation (IGCC) of the University of California and the Armament Disarmament Information Unit (ADIU) at the University of Sussex. His arguments are set out more fully in 'The nature of bipolarity: an argument against the status quo', in Mary Kaldor and Richard Falk, eds, *Dealignment: A New Foreign Policy Perspective* (UNU/Blackwell, 1987), and in 'The decline of the bipolar system, or a second look at the history of the cold war', in Mary Kaldor, Gerard Holden and Richard Falk, eds, *The New Détente:*

Rethinking East–West Relations (UNU/Verso, 1989). His argument emphasizes the importance of the cold war as a way of ensuring the hegemony of the United States and the Soviet Union in Europe.
3 E. P. Thompson, 'Notes on exterminism', in *Exterminism and the Cold War* (New Left Books, 1982); George Konrad, *Antipolitics* (Quartet, 1984).

2

States and Blocs

This chapter is intended to define the terms used in the rest of the book. It describes the basic concepts through which the analysis of the post-war order is developed and it relates these concepts to the broad schools of thought in international relations. The focus is on the relationships between political, economic and military power.

A useful starting point is the distinction, made by Anthony Giddens, between what he calls allocative and authoritative resources.[1] Allocative resources refer to 'dominion over material goods and energy', that is, economic power or property. Authoritative resources refer to the 'means of dominion over human beings themselves', that is, political power. An organization is political if it is capable of mobilizing authoritative resources. According to this definition, all organizations are political. What distinguishes the state from other political organizations is its sovereignty within a given realm, be it a community or territory; that is, its capacity to act as the ultimate form of authority, to enforce laws which all those who are part of the realm of the state must respect, its dominance over other political organizations. Historically, an important feature of most states has been their reliance on military power, which can be defined as organized violent means of dominion over human activities; a particular type of authoritative resource.

The state can be described as the dominant agency for the reproduction of a specific type of resource, namely authoritative resources, within a given realm. The state is treated not so much as an institution but as a set of social relations, an overlapping subset of the social relations that constitute society as a whole – but one with unique properties, that is to say a dominant capacity to mobilize political power. The economy is distinguished from the state in terms of the type of resources it produces and reproduces.

Clearly, the reproduction of allocative and authoritative resources is by no means an exhaustive description of the social relations that constitute society. A fuller analysis would need to take into account, for example, domestic reproduction (housework, childrearing, etc.) or the reproduction of cultural and intellectual resources.

There are many different ways in which authoritative resources can be reproduced. States can be classified according to the form of reproduction. In this chapter, I describe the typical characteristics of the modern state, how these have influenced thinking about international relations, and what has changed since the end of the Second World War.

The modern state

Giddens sharply distinguishes between a modern and a traditional state. The modern state emerged in the sixteenth and seventeenth centuries and accompanied the rise of capitalism. What are the distinctive characteristics of the modern state?

Territoriality

First of all, the modern state is territorially ordered. Territoriality, rather than kinship or religious allegiance, defines the administrative reach of the modern state. The modern state raises taxes, recruits soldiers and acquires legitimacy from the inhabitants of a particular territory. State activity may spill over beyond the confines of its territory but state power is reproduced domestically. Modern states have borders, says Giddens, rather than frontiers. A frontier can be rather a vague term denoting the peripheral regions of a state, its boundary with other states or with uninhabited areas over which the state has minimum control. A border is a clearly demarcated division between the administrative reach of one state as distinct from that of another.

The states system

Secondly, the modern state is part of an international states system, one divided into multiple centres. Territorial definition only becomes possible when it is recognized by other states. Hence the existence of borders implies the existence of an international states system.

A states system, or collectivity of states, came into being in Europe in the sixteenth and seventeenth centuries during the period of absolutism and was later described by Edmund Burke as the Diplomatic Republick of Europe. It expanded after the emergence of the nation state in the eighteenth and nineteenth centuries, and since 1945 it has been generally considered to be a world system covering the entire globe. The term states system is said to have been given currency after the treaty of Westphalia by Grotius and Pufendorf, who were professional Swedish diplomats. The term refers to a system of states which have relations between them based on mutual recognition and accepted norms and rules of behaviour. It was associated with the rise of professional diplomacy, the establishment of regular congresses, a plethora of treaties and agreements, and concepts of sovereignty, territoriality and international order, especially balance of power concepts.

The states system was always unequal. Political and military power was distributed unequally among individual states within the states system. The rules and norms of behaviour were generally shaped by a group of dominant world powers – known as the great powers. Although *de jure* sovereignty within a given territorial space is a basic *a priori* assumption of the states system, *de facto* sovereignty is limited by those same rules and norms. Self-determination is only possible to the extent that an individual nation has a role in shaping those rules and regulations or has the right to dissent or withdraw from a particular form of the international states system. In the post-war period, Nicaragua and Poland constituted examples of the way in which self-determination is constrained by the international states system.

Martin Wight distinguishes between a states system and a suzerain state system. A suzerain state system, like the Roman empire or imperial China, is one in which a dominant imperial power has relations with smaller tributary states. A states system, like the city states of Greece and Italy or the modern states system, is characterized by the fact that political and military hegemony can pass from one state to another. This process does not occur smoothly. It involves war, revolution, economic or social dislocation.[2]

Political and economic relations

A third feature of the modern state is the distinction that emerges between the political and the economic. This distinction arises not out of the difference between types of resources but because the rise of capitalism and the modern states system involves a clear differentiation in the way that these different types of resources, allocative and authoritative, are reproduced. In other words, relations of authority become differentiated from relations of property. This point requires further elaboration.

In any system of production in which producers and consumers are separated and in which production and consumption are each collective, some sort of relationship has to be established between producer and consumer and among producers and consumers in order to reconcile needs and resources, demand and supply, to decide how much to produce and by what method. In other words, production and consumption have to be organized in order to produce appropriate quantities for consumption and reproduction. An economic and political organization can be classified according to its organizing principle, the specific characteristics of the relationships of reproduction. In this book, the term *regulation* is used to describe this organizing principle, the specific relationship between production and consumption. It is important to note that this is different from the normal usage of the term regulation, which tends to mean government intervention in the economy and has more of a purposive and exact character than is intended here.[3]

Capitalism can be described as the system of property relations that displaced feudalism in Western Europe as the dominant mode of material production. Under capitalism, regulation takes the form of the market. Capitalism is based on the exchange of equal values represented by prices and wages. The existence of markets for labour and for material goods and energy means that a process of social bargaining can determine price, representing, in the case of goods and energy, the resources required to produce them efficiently and, in the case of labour, a wage which reflects the resources required to produce efficiently the goods and energy needed for the workers' subsistence. The worker becomes 'free' in the sense that he or she owns his or her own labour. But since workers own no capital to buy land or tools or machines, they are forced to sell their labour, which yields a surplus controlled by the capitalist. The behaviour of the capitalist in turn is constrained by the cut-throat competition with other capitalists. Thus the market can be described as a form of economic coercion. What distinguishes capitalism from previous modes of production is the removal of physical violence from the labour contract.

Capitalist regulation is dynamic. Changes in profit rates, reflecting changes in prices and wages, are signals for rapid adjustment in methods of production, quantities and types of output. Decisions about what to produce and by what method are taken by the individual enterprise on the basis of its relationship with other enterprises, with its customers and relationships within the enterprise (between workers and managers). These are expressed in the movement of prices and wages, at any rate in a pure market system.

In contrast to capitalist regulation, the relationship through which authoritative resources are reproduced are non-economic, or to use Claus Offe's term, decommodified.[4] A point made by state theorists like Offe and Habermas is that the wage relationship requires that non-economic forms of regulation are separated off from the sphere of material or allocative production so as to guarantee the conditions for the free exchange of goods and labour. This is an analytic description of a historical process associated with the emergence of capitalism. Means of dominion over human beings or forms of social control, such as the police force or legal services, are financed by taxation on the basis of a variety of relationships ranging from consent, through the political process, to coercion, both ideological and physical. Decisions about state behaviour are taken by individual states, which are constrained by the relationship with other states, with citizens, and by their own internal mechanisms – the bureaucracy, the structure of the legal system, the role of the legislature, etc.

Unlike the economic sphere, resources and requirements cannot be assessed with numerical precision. Adjustments or changes in the pattern of state behaviour may evolve perhaps slowly through votes or political parties or media criticism, or may be brought about abruptly through war or revolution.

Capitalism was always an international system. In contrast to the state, capitalist reproduction was never territorially bounded. Capitalist accumulation was always concentrated in one or two core countries – Holland in the seventeenth century, Britain in the eighteenth century, Britain and later Germany and America in the nineteenth century, America and later Japan and West Germany in the twentieth century. But it always depended on trade and overseas investment.

Thus, the emergence of capitalism and the modern state system marked a separation of the political and the economic in the sense that the social relationships through which economic and political power were reproduced became mutually distinct. Nevertheless these two forms of reproduction are mutually dependent.

The capitalist economy requires the state to guarantee capitalist property rights, to ensure free markets for labour and material goods, to issue currency and credit, to provide what might be described as techno-material infrastructure – facilitating internal and international transportation and communication, access to raw materials and so on – and to provide for internal pacification. The modern state requires the economy to provide taxes, loans, labour and technology for expanded administrative and military power, and as a source of legitimacy.

Likewise, the development of the states system provided the conditions for the expansion of international economic relations, especially trade. And by the same token, the development of a states system was made possible because economic expansion was no longer tied to territorial annexation. Under earlier economic systems, technical progress was extremely slow and economic expansion was brought about through the acquisition of land and slaves or other types of dependent labour generally tied to land. Under capitalism, land was no longer so important. What was important was the availability of 'free' labour (achieved through the decline in infant mortality and expulsion from the land, and based on the wage relationship), technical progress, the growth of markets at home and abroad, and access to natural resources used in industrial production such as coal, cotton, or iron.[5]

Because authoritative and allocative resources are produced through distinct social relationships, they evolve at different rates. Change can be viewed as a form of experimentation. Under capitalism, economic change is more or less continuous. Because changes in taste and changes in productive techniques are more or less continuous, individual enterprises have to experiment in order to survive (although their experimentation is always confined by the cultural, social, architectural and political parameters of a given historial moment).

Political experimentation is much riskier. The survival of states, or more specifically particular ruling groups and forms of governments, is really only challenged in periods of major political upheaval, including revolution and war. Hence political change tends to be discontinuous. A period of political transition is a period in which different political approaches are tried out, for better or for worse, eventually settling down to some form of political compromise which seems to provide political stability, that is, that can be reproduced.

Because the economy and the state are mutually dependent, the evolution of one stimulates the other. In periods of political inertia, economic change generates new social pressures, new conflicts, or changes in the resource base of state activity, thus constituting a pressure for political change. In periods of political transition, political change may redirect economic change.

Civil and military relations

A fourth feature of the modern state that usually receives less emphasis than the distinction between the political and the economic is the distinction between the civil and the military – a distinction between types of authoritative relationships.

Giddens says that a defining characteristic of the modern state is the claim to a monopoly of the means of violence within the territorial sway of the state.[6] This means the elimination of independent forms of military organization within the territory of the state. This involves a twofold process: on the one hand, the organization of violence by the state, the development of regular armed forces as an established component of the state apparatus; and, on the other hand, internal pacification. Internal pacification has been characterized by the removal of violence from the labour contract, the decline of violent and public forms of punishment like hanging and public flogging, and the withdrawal of the use of military power in the internal affairs of the state. According to Giddens:

What it involves, however, is not the decline of war, but a concentration of military power 'pointing outwards' towards other states in the nation-state system. The consolidation of the internal administrative resources of the state dislocates administrative power from its strong and necessary base in the coercive sanctions of armed forces ... In the nation-state, as in other states, the claim to effective control of the means of violence is quite basic to state power. But the registering of the more or less complete success of this claim, made possible by the expansion of surveillance capabilities and internal pacification radically lessens the dependence of the state apparatus upon the wielding of military force as the means of its rule. The distinction between the military and civilian police is a symbol and material expression of this phenomenon.[7]

The concept of peace came to prominence in the sixteenth and seventeenth centuries. This was not only because of the process of international pacification. It was also because the emergence of a states system led to an increase in non-military methods of regulating interstate relations, such as by treaties, congresses and diplomatic activity. Wars became less frequent (although more destructive and total). In place of generalized and more or less continuous violence comes discontinuous organized violence in which periods of peace alternate with periods of war.[8] Hence the role of military power in regulating political relations through direct physical coercion is increasingly confined both in space (to international and not domestic affairs) and in time (because war is periodic).

This does not mean that the military do not intervene in politics. But they do so as political actors in their organizational self-interest rather than as direct agents of coercion – by and large, they continue to rely on the civil police for physical control of citizens and, in international affairs, they are not necessarily more likely to resort to war than other agencies of the state. The term militarism, which generally refers to the intervention of the armed forces in politics, has come to mean an interruption in the normal forms of political reproduction. An authoritarian government, that is, a government which depends on various forms of coercion to maintain its rule, is not necessarily militaristic, but a military government or a militarized government, by which I mean a government in which the military constitute an important component of the state apparatus, tends to be authoritarian.

This arises from a special characteristic of the military as an institution, as an agency for the reproduction of military power. This is the fact that war represents the main stimulus to change in military organizations. War is a kind of test of utility for the military. It is a way of reconciling resources to requirements, of adapting organization to new tactics and technology. In between wars, the way in which resources are mobilized for warfare tends to depend on subjective assessments about what might happen in a future war. The assessments are shaped by past experience and by institutional self-interest. Both these factors imply inertia, a tendency for the military to replicate themselves in their past image, to 'fight the last war'. For this reason, in peacetime, a militarized state – a state in which the military represent an important and influential component of the overall social relationships that constitute the state – tends to be rather rigid, resistant to change and unresponsive to social pressures.

The origins of the imaginary war can be traced to the separation of the civil and the military. The concurrent process of internal pacification and the externalization of violence implies a tendency to channel domestic tensions outwards, against some external enemy. The need to establish some common identity as a basis for legitimacy within implies the existence of an 'other', for instance, England versus France. Rousseau saw the link between domestic order and international anarchy quite explicitly:

If the social order were really, as is pretended, the work not of passion but of reason, should we have been slow to see that . . . each one of us being in the civil state as regards our fellow citizens, but in the state of nature as regards the rest of the world, we have taken all kinds of precautions against private wars only to kindle national wars a thousand times more terrible?[9]

The existence of an external threat is substantiated by military preparations. Once regular armed forces are established, they need to be occupied in the absence of war. The elimination of idleness is important for domestic peace, for the disappearance of private wars, as well as for long periods of international peace. Soldiers traditionally prepared for forthcoming confrontations. They were drilled and trained, they dug trenches and built fortifications (military innovations such as drill, military academies, permanent staff, date from the seventeenth and eighteenth centuries). In this way, they acted out an imagined confrontation which often tended to resemble the last war. Such behaviour actually serves to substantiate an idea of conflict, which also tends to uphold the status quo. As war became industrialized towards the end of the nineteenth century, peacetime military preparations became more expensive and visible because it was not only soldiers but also factories and shipyards that had to be kept busy.

These four features of the modern state have certain implications for any analysis of the international behaviour of states. First of all because state power is territorially bounded, the behaviour of states is primarily determined by the domestic political process. Politicians want to hang on to their political power and this depends on votes, money, newspapers, or alternatively, the party or the security apparatus. Secondly, because the modern state is part of a states system, state behaviour is constrained by the rules and norms of the system in any given period, which reflect the power relations among states. Thirdly, state behaviour is distinct from but dependent upon economic behaviour (and vice versa). Finally, state behaviour depends on how the state is constructed, the methods, including both consent and coercion, through which state power is reproduced. In particular, state behaviour is influenced by the balance between civil and military power.

Differing approaches to the study of international relations

The main traditions of thought in the study of international relations have to be understood in their historical context. The differences between these traditions can be traced to the rise of the modern state.

Because there have been significant changes in the characteristics of the modern state and the states system in the post-war period, to be described in the next section, each of these traditions are, in some degree, inadequate as a method of analysis of the current period.

The distinction between realism and Marxism can be traced to the distinction between the political and economic that arises with the emergence of capitalism. The realist tradition, which is the dominant tradition in modern international relations, focuses on states and the states system. States are treated as the main unit of analysis, as subjective agents characterized by a drive for power, or, alternatively, compelled to maximize power because of the competitive nature of the states system. Power is primarily, although not exclusively, conceived in military terms.

Economic developments are relevant only in so far as they contribute to or detract from national power. Some realist writers, most notably those preoccupied with the decline of empires, do, of course, deal with interaction of the economic and the political. But whereas for Marxists, political power is functional (or dysfunctional) for capitalism – the unit of analysis being the capital relationship – for these realists, economic developments are functional (or dysfunctional) for political power – the unit of analysis being the state.

According to the Marxist tradition, political struggles and the vicissitudes of the state system can ultimately be explained in terms of the evolution of capitalism. Properly speaking, it is difficult to speak of a Marxist tradition of international relations because there is no Marxist theory of the state as such. There are Marxist international theories (Lenin on imperialism, Luxemburg on militarism, Wallerstein on the world system), but they are not theories of interstate relations. This is not to say that Marxists have not developed theories of the state. In these theories, however, the state tends to be treated either as a dependent variable, the neutral instrument of the ruling class, the 'executive committee of the bourgeoisie', or as 'relatively autonomous', free floating, and hence not clearly distinguishable from realist assumptions about the state.

For Marxists, a given social formation is defined in terms of its mode of production, the way in which allocative resources are reproduced. What is important about the Marxist approach is the analysis of relationships and how they are reproduced, that is to say, the notion of a mode of production. However, the limitations of Marxism stem from the almost exclusive focus on economic relationships. If the state is defined not as an institution but as the way in which authoritative resources are reproduced, that is, as a set of social relationships, a mode of authoritative production, then it becomes apparent that there is no *a priori* reason why special analytical weight should be attached to the reproduction of a particular type of resource, namely allocative or material resources. The Marxist approach does largely hold for capitalism because of the dynamic nature of capitalist relations – although war has also provided an important impulse for economic and political change. But the inadequacy of its treatment of the state is more evident in relation to other social formations. This is particularly important in the current epoch when Marxism fails to provide an adequate description of the social formation that characterizes Eastern and Central Europe.

It is worth noting that there are many similarities between Marxism and classical realism. Classical realism, whose exponents can be traced back to Thucydides, through Hobbes and Machiavelli, to more recent writers such as E. H. Carr or Raymond Aron, was an historical approach and was concerned with conflict and change. Marxists shared the view of classical realists that force was a primary instrument of change, as Marx put it, the 'midwife' of a new society. Modern realists, especially the so-called neo-realists,[10] have a much more static analysis in which key concepts are 'balance', 'equilibrium' and 'stability'. There is a strong parallel with neo-classical economics, in which the independent units of analysis are firms or entrepreneurs (an abstract prototype approach much scorned by E. H. Carr[11]).

If the Marxist/realist distinction arises from the separation of the economic and the political, the distinction between idealism and realism can be derived from the modern distinction between the civil and the military. The idealist tradition, which can be traced to political philosophy of the seventeenth and eighteenth centuries (Locke, Rousseau, Kant, for example), is concerned with the construction of international peace projects, democratic methods of regulating relations between states. The argument is that if a civil society can be created within a nation state, then this should be possible internationally.

It should be stressed that this distinction is quite different from the distinction between idealism and realism in philosophy or social science.[12] Broadly speaking, in international relations, the distinction between realism and idealism is a distinction between a conservative *realpolitik* approach and a liberal approach. As expounded by E. H. Carr, the distinction has some similarities to the philosophical distinction between realism and idealism, in that he conceived the idealists to be utopian, that is to say, he presented them as thinkers who believed that their peace projects could be achieved merely through the strength of ideas. In contrast, realism for E. H. Carr meant recognizing the reality of the structures of power in international relations. He did not reject the possibility of peaceful change in international relations but he thought that this was only possible if predicated on reality, which, in his view, was a world of nation states and national armies.

In fact, those philosophers who are considered to be idealist in international relations are not necessarily philosophical idealists. Rather, their interpretation of reality differs from that of E. H. Carr. Their concern is with the way in which state power is constructed, the nature of the political process. Typically, idealists argue that state power in democratic societies does not rest on violence, even though violent methods may be used and even though the state may originate in some act of violence, war or revolution.[13] In other words, state power is, in effect, treated as a relationship which has to be reproduced.

Realists, on the other hand, treat the state as an agent with certain properties, for instance, military strength, and therefore they are less able to offer insights into the possibilities for alternative non-military ways of regulating relations between states. Realists sometimes talk about international society but, by this, they mean a society of states. People, domestic political struggles, or transnational social movements are largely bypassed or treated as contingent developments. Similarly, even though many realists are concerned with non-military forms of power, it is very difficult for realists to cope with the growing impotence of military capabilities in the nuclear age.

The approach of this book draws on both the Marxist and the idealist traditions. The method of analysis is Marxist, with the emphasis on relationships and how they are produced and reproduced, as opposed to the reification of the state, an analysis centred around the state as a subjective entity. Likewise, the concern with socio-economic change is also Marxist, although a socio-economic determinism is not presumed. On the other hand, the emphasis on domestic political processes and the possibility of bringing about non-violent change through domestic and international political processes is idealist (although not necessarily idealistic). Some kind of new synthesis is required in order to explain certain novel features of the post-war political order that cannot be fully captured by any of the prevailing approaches to international relations because they are rooted in an earlier historical period.

The post-war period

After 1945, a global states system came into being which displaced the nineteenth-century European states system. The entire world was parcelled off into nations and the privileges of the former great powers were passed to an extra-European power, the United States, together with the Soviet Union. For reasons elaborated in chapter 4, the socialist states could perhaps be said to constitute a separate states system, a sort of suzerain states system. Having reached what might be described as its apogee, the states system began to mutate and to demonstrate features that depart significantly from those described above.

First of all, with the Russian revolution of 1917 and the emergence of social democracy in Western Europe after the Second World War, the distinction between the political and the economic began once more to blur. Significant segments of the economy were taken over by the state. Or put another way, the relationships which characterized the reproduction of allocative resources were replaced, or partially replaced, by the relationships which had previously characterized the reproduction of authoritative resources. Marxists have tended to assume that the replacement of capitalist relations by statist relations, of the market by planning, is a 'progressive' development. But the assumption results from an inadequate understanding of state relations. A militarized authoritarian state relies on more primitive forms of coercion than the wage relationship and, indeed, this proposition forms the basis of the liberal critique of statism. On the other hand, the replacement of economic coercion by democratic consensual relationships is clearly a progressive development.

The development of statism has important implications for the relationship between political and economic change. In societies in which there is no or virtually no private sector, economic change is almost entirely an outcome of political change. A militarized authoritarian state tends towards stagnation and hence undermines the conditions for its own reproduction. For such a state, war is one important mechanism for change.

In Western countries, the private sector remains an important and dynamic component of society. Nevertheless, the state plays an increasingly important role as consumer (for welfare or warfare), as supplier (of infrastructures, transportation, a legal system, education and training, fiscal and monetary regulations, etc.) and, in Western Europe, as producer. Hence economic change is shaped, encouraged or constrained, to a much greater degree than formerly, by state behaviour. Whether or not it is possible to establish a more or less harmonious process of adjustment depends primarily on the nature of power relations, the form of authoritative reproduction. A state, such as the United States, in which the armed forces are an important component of the state apparatus is less able to respond to new social pressures than other less militarized states.

An important feature of the post-war period was the development of more consensual forms of regulating relations among advanced capitalist countries, within a military-political framework dominated by the United States. Organizations like the General Agreement on Tariffs and Trade (GATT), the International Monetary Fund (IMF) or the European Economic Community (EEC) have been able to settle the most acute economic conflicts among advanced capitalist countries, including those respecting their spheres of influence in the Third World. The development of more consensual forms of reproduction both between and within states lessened the social impact of the major economic restructuring experienced by Western countries during the 1980s. On the one hand, this meant that the economic problems of Western countries – mass unemployment, international economic imbalances, environmental deterioration, etc. – experienced during the 1980s cannot be described as a 'crisis' in the same sense as that experienced in the 1930s or currently in Eastern Europe and the Third World. On the other hand, the continued political dominance of the United States impeded an effective response to these problems.

Two conclusions can be inferred from this argument. First, the economic crisis in the East and the economic problems in the West were both crises of power relations. In resolving these economic problems, therefore, the key issue is not market versus state (capitalism versus socialism) but the form of state relations – consent versus coercion, or civil versus military forms of power. Secondly, this issue of state relations is not an East–West issue, even though the Soviet Union and East Central European countries were, during the post-war period, undemocratic and more militarized. It is an issue for the West as well.

The second novel feature of the post-war period was the rise of blocs of nations pushing the military further 'outwards'. Within Nato and the Warsaw Pact, countries continued to possess national armed forces but these were integrated into the alliance command structures. Even in the case of Britain and France, which possess national nuclear weapons and which have engaged in unilateral interventions in the Third World (Falklands/Malvinas or Chad), their military apparatuses remain highly dependent on technical and infrastructural support from other members of the Western alliance, particularly the United States. Even though bloc forces were used internally, as in Hungary and Czechoslovakia, or for conflicts between members of a bloc, as between Greece and Turkey, the ostensible purpose of the armed forces was defence against an enemy external to the bloc, primarily but not exclusively the opposing bloc.

Nato and the Warsaw Pact were quite different from the nineteenth-century alliances, or from the wartime alliances of the twentieth century, in that they were rigid and institutionalized. In practice, through strategies, integrated command systems, the supply of equipment, joint exercises, etc., if not in theory, there were no really independent European armed forces within the blocs. Individual European countries retained their sovereignty, in the sense of administrative power over their citizens and their mutual recognition of each other, without the need for national military power. The

British and French nuclear forces and imperialist interventions have to be understood in terms of an obsolete determination to cling to earlier conceptions of national identity.

Internal pacification was achieved among advanced industrial countries, more successfully in the West than in the East, through the fostering of a bloc identity, which can be termed blocism. This came to augment, if not displace, nationalism. Rousseau's point about solving private wars only to encounter far more terrible national wars can be rephrased. Quarrels between and within nations were turned against bloc enemies. Blocism was based around abstract ideals like 'freedom' or 'socialism' rather than history or culture or race and therefore appeared to be a more progressive mobilizing concept.

The rise of blocism was accompanied by preparations for warfare on a scale never before witnessed in 'peacetime'. The integration of armed forces entailed the creation of a (cumbersome) joint staff, joint exercises, training schools, etc. The growth of science and technology meant that laboratories and test facilities had to be occupied, as well as factories and men, and this gave rise to a technological arms race and to an uncomprehendable level of destructiveness.

Blocism and continuous preparations for war were the main ingredients of an imaginary war far more pervasive than any of its earlier anticipations. It could be said that the advanced or semi-advanced industrial nations insulated themselves from the real violence and poverty of the rest of the world. There have been many violent forays into the Third World, the most notable being Vietnam and Afghanistan, and it can be argued that their purpose was to substantiate the imaginary war, to uphold perceptions of military power. (Their failure has helped to undermine the imaginary war.) These took place outside what Robin Luckham has called the 'Cold War quarantine' of the bloc system.[14]

The concept of imaginary war should be distinguished from the theory of deterrence. The argument that deterrence has kept the peace in Europe is based on the assumption that the only possible conflict was between the blocs. The concept of imaginary war presupposes that the fear of an external enemy is used to deal with conflicts *within* the blocs. The integration of armed forces prevents, or minimizes, national or domestic conflicts. The absence of interbloc war is explained by the absence or unimportance of conflict between the blocs.

Are blocs here to stay? It could be that the current political transition is merely a way of reorganizing the bloc system, a prelude to a new global ordering of the blocs. One scenario for the future is a world of competing blocs, consisting of the United States, Western Europe or more particularly Germany and Japan. The Soviet Union (and China) might also constitute blocs, or alternatively, all of Eastern Europe might disintegrate and rejoin the realm of national and civil wars. Bloc enemies might be transposed to the fanatics and fundamentalists of the world outside the blocs. Such a scenario could bring about a redistribution of power among advanced capitalist countries and hence make it possible to resolve, for a while, Western economic problems. It would carry with it not only the unspeakable risk that imaginary wars might (by mistake) become real, but also the prospects of periodic economic 'crises' because of the rigidity of the bloc state form.

Alternatively, blocism could be a transitional state form, just as absolutism can be regarded as a transitional state form between traditional states and the nation state.

Blocism and statism imply militarism and rigidity, but they also anticipate the removal of military power as a way of regulating relations between states, just as military power was removed from relations within states. Indeed, the emergence of a bloc identity has also, to some extent, given rise to a bloc public opinion, as became evident for example in the emergence of a Western peace movement in the early 1980s or an Eastern democracy movement in the late 1980s. It has become possible to envisage a future international system that is still unequal and anarchic, in the sense of having no single world government, but in which military force plays a less important role in settling disputes. In other words, it *is* possible to conceive of blocism not as a more or less permanent feature of world affairs, but as heralding a transition from the nation-states system to an international civil society.

Notes

1 Anthony Giddens, *A Contemporary Critique of Historical Materialism*, vol. 1: *Power, Property and the State* (Macmillan, 1981) and vol. 2: *The Nation-State and Violence* (Polity, 1985). The description of the state put forward in this section should not be confused with Giddens's analysis. Although I draw heavily on his work, my points about relations of authority and reproduction and the way I treat the role of military power are different from although not inconsistent with Giddens's argument.

2 Martin Wight, *The System of States* (Leicester University Press, 1977).

3 The term *regulation* is used in much the same way by the so-called regulationists in France. See Michel Aglietta, *The Theory of Capitalist Regulation, The US Experience* (New Left Books, 1979; revised edn, Verso, 1987). The regulationists characterize different phases of capitalist development in terms of different forms of regulation. A recent article suggests that because of the ambiguity of the term in English, a better translation would be 'tuning'. See Robert Boyer, 'Technical change and the theory of "regulation"', in G. Dosi, C. Freeman, R. Nelson, G. Silverberg, and L. Soete, eds, *Technical Change and Economic Theory* (Pinter, 1988).

4 See Claus Offe, *Contradictions of the Welfare State* (Hutchinson, 1984).

5 Territorial annexation, whether in Europe or elsewhere, came to be seen by liberals in the early nineteenth century as a regressive and defensive form of political expansion. Of course, territorial annexation was still important in the formation of nation states, as became apparent in the European wars of the mid-nineteenth century and in the 'scramble for colonies' in the late nineteenth century and in German irridentism in the twentieth century. But it was no longer a necessary condition for economic expansion. In the post-1945 period, decolonization can be viewed as a way of creating a global states system and hence as a form of international integration. Writing in 1833, Thomas Macauley argued:

It would be, on the most selfish view of the case, far better for us that the people of India were well-governed and independent of us, than ill-governed and subject to us; that they were ruled by their own kings, but wearing our broadcloth, and eating with our cutlery, than that they were performing their salaams to English collectors and English magistrates, but were too ignorant to value, or too poor to buy, English manufactures. To trade with civilized men is infinitely more profitable than to govern savages. (Quoted in James Kurth, 'The political consequences of the product cycle: industrial history and political outcomes', *International Organisation*, Winter 1979, p. 10)

6 This point is derived from Weber's definition of the state. According to Weber, a 'compulsory political association with continuous organisation will be called a "state" if and in so far as its administrative staff successfully upholds a claim to the *monopoly* of the *legitimate* use of physical force in the enforcement of its order.' Quoted in Robert Dahl, 'Power as the control of behaviour', in Steven Lukes, ed., *Power* (Basil Blackwell, 1986). For Giddens, unlike Weber, this definition only applies to the modern state. It is a definition that implies *both* a monopoly over the means of violence and the use of violence by the state to enforce order. Crucial to the rise of the modern state was the elimination of legally independent forms of organized violence within the territory of the state – this is what is meant by the monopoly of violence. Clearly, also, all modern states are violent to some degree. But whereas the elimination of independent forms of organized violence is a necessary basis for the rule of the modern state, is this also true of the use of violence by the state to enforce order? There are modern states which have more or less eliminated violent forms of punishment and for whom, it could be argued, the use of violence would undermine authority. This point is relevant when trying to understand the process of democratization in Eastern Europe, for example, or when considering possible new forms of political order.

7 Giddens, *Nation-State*, p. 192.

8 See Michael Howard, 'The concept of peace', *Encounter*, 61:4, December 1983.

9 Quoted in Ian Clark, *Reform and Resistance in the International Order* (Cambridge University Press, 1980), p. 62.

10 For an excellent analysis of the differences between classical realism and neo-realism, see Robert W. Cox 'Social forces, states, and world orders: beyond international relations theory', in Robert Keohane, ed., *Neo-realism and its Critics* (Cambridge University Press, 1986).

11 E. H. Carr, *The Twenty Years' Crisis* (Macmillan, 1940).

12 Philosophical idealism has to do with the importance of ideas in natural science or history: whether 'facts' are merely human constructions or whether ideas are the agent of change in history, as for instance in Hegel. In constrast to idealism, the various versions of realism recognize reality independent of ideas, that is to say the natural world or social structures, but, unlike empiricism or historical determinism, they also recognize the importance of ideas in interpreting or transforming reality. Hence, in philosophical terms, the approach in this book is

realist rather than idealist or determinist. See Roy Bhaskar, *Reclaiming Reality* (Verso, 1989).

13 The argument that democracy cannot be reproduced internationally presupposes *either* that democracy within a nation state requires an exclusive identity, that is to say, democracy is based on the social cohesion, which can only be achieved through having an enemy, or else that some societies are inherently violent, for racial, cultural or economic reasons. If it is the former argument, then one could make a further idealist point – namely that an exclusivist identity is a form of ideological coercion designed to conceal unpopular policies. A truly democratic society rests on consent and therefore does not require an enemy.

14 Robin Luckham, 'Operation El Dorado Canyon: globalising the cold war', in E. P. Thompson, Mary Kaldor et al., *Mad Dogs: The US Raids on Libya* (Pluto, 1986).

PART II
The Cold War

3

The Debate about the Origins of the Cold War

The term 'cold war' was first used by Bernard Baruch in 1947. It usually refers to the East–West conflict in general. In this book, the term is used in a more precise sense to refer to the most conflictual mode of the imaginary war, in contrast to détente which is a more cooperative mode. This part of the book covers the period 1947 to the mid-1960s, in which the blocs were established and in which the ideologies of the East–West conflict were institutionalized. (Some would argue that the cold war, as defined above, only lasted from 1947 to 1953).

The period of the cold war was probably the most dangerous phase of the imaginary war, at least up to now – a period when the two sides seemed closest to real war. Both sides could be said to have been testing out the boundaries of their systems, exploring limits, feeling their way towards a set of rules and regulations which would govern their behaviour. Dulles, who was Eisenhower's Secretary of State, described it as a period of 'brinkmanship'.[1]

Most studies of the cold war, in the general sense, are historical and they have been undertaken largely in the United States. They focus on the origins of the cold war in the 1940s, and on the preoccupations, motivations and inclinations of the key political figures of the period. They tend to presuppose a fundamental conflict between East and West and they seem mainly concerned to assign responsibility to one side or the other. Basically, they seem to be interested in the question of who started the cold war.

My concern is somewhat different. Politicians are necessarily imperfect. They cannot, *a priori*, comprehend fully the realities of power, the consequences of any particular policy or action, although some may have a better grasp of what can or cannot be done than others. What they achieve is very often different from what they intend. Politics, as argued in the previous chapter, is a kind of experiment. Policies succeed when they last, when they bring about stability at least from the point of view of the ruling institutions, when they seem worth repeating.

It is in this respect that the relationship between politics and economics and between domestic politics and foreign policy has to be understood. The definition of the state as a set of relationships for authoritative reproduction entails a focus on the domestic political process – the process whereby the domestic institutions of the state are sustained and reproduced. An understanding of this process has to take into account the internal structures of government (the relationship between, say, the executive and the legislature, the nature of bureaucratic infighting, party politics, the role of the military or the police apparatus), the relationship between state and society (the electoral process, say, or police coercion) and the relationship with other states. Economic factors and foreign policy concerns are mediated through this domestic political process.

Politicians may or may not have economic motivations, for example 'grand designs' or merely greed, but what is important is how their policies affect the economic conditions within which the state operates, whether they yield resources with which they can be carried out, whether they satisfy citizens and so enhance legitimacy. On the whole, periods of economic growth are periods when more competing social demands can be met, and so policies which contribute to economic growth tend to be successful. But even though this seems to have become a generally accepted political assumption in the post-war period, it is by no means necessarily so. From the point of view of the ruling group, what is more important is its own survival and not the well-being of society as a whole, although, especially in the case of democracies, the well-being of society probably contributes to the survival of the ruling group. (The well-being of society as a whole may not, however, include marginal groups.)

A similar argument can be advanced with respect to foreign policy questions. Politicians may have their own particular theories about the international situation and their own particular strategies for dealing with that situation. But what matters is the way in which the relationship with other states directly or indirectly impinges on the domestic political process (through war, economic interdependence, or institutional ties and alliances) and how that relationship is perceived by different participants in the domestic political process. A foreign policy is likely to succeed, that is to say, to be worth repeating, if it accords with a range of domestic political perceptions, which may or may not be influenced by the actual behaviour of other states.

Given these considerations, therefore, my primary interest is to discover why the fundamental elements of the East–West conflict – the military confrontation, the hostile rhetoric, the games of diplomacy and espionage – persisted for so long, why the structures and institutions established during the cold war period were reproduced, why it was so difficult to introduce policies which departed significantly from those of the cold war period. The starting point is less important than the question of why it continued.

During the Second World War, rather different political models for the post-war period were envisaged. Roosevelt and the New Dealers espoused an idealist vision of the world expressed in the Atlantic Charter in which global collective security arrangements and international economic liberalism would respect the self-determination of peoples. The European resistance movements hoped for a united socialist Europe which would banish for ever European nationalism and imperial ambitions. And Churchill and Stalin, in their different ways, dreamed of a relative harmony between competing spheres of influence – the American, the Russian, and the British empires. None of these aims or anticipations were entirely fulfilled, although the international political system came close to the spheres of influence concept both immediately before the onset of the cold war and during the détente period. How was it, therefore, that Truman and Stalin chanced on a formula in the late 1940s that was to dominate international politics, to a greater or lesser degree, up to the present day?

Even though the answer does not lie in the story of the origins of the cold war, the debate about the origins of the cold war is instructive for what it reveals about the differing assumptions of historians as to the nature of the underlying conflict. Just as politicians can never know enough to gauge fully the effect of any particular policy or proposal, so historians can never tell the full story of a set of events. Their choice of relevant events is shaped by a set of presuppositions about the story they expect to tell. Their presuppositions can be proved wrong – they do not fit the evidence. But they can never be proved right because there is always other evidence, lost or unsought. Or rather, to be right means telling what actually happened, which is physically impossible – it would take as long as the events themselves, and any one person can, in any case, experience only a part of what happened. Some historians may be more right than others as they accumulate evidence which is consistent with their story, but there is always the possibility of alternative interpretations.

The strength of the story each historian has to tell lies therefore either in its intrinsic interest, its aesthetic qualities perhaps, or else in its power to legitimize or delegitimize present political postures. In the case of the origins of the cold war, it is this last aspect which is obviously of relevance. And this is why a few comments about the debate are a necessary preliminary to an analysis of the cold war period.

Orthodoxy, revisionism and post-revisionism

The notion of assigning responsibility to one side or the other implies a non-deterministic view of history. It suggests that there were moments when different behaviour might have produced a different outcome. Most literature on the origins of the cold war focuses on the closing years of the Second World War. But there are some histories which start with the Bolshevik revolution in 1917.[2] And, from the point of view of missed opportunities, this may be a more appropriate time-scale. It can, for example, be argued that it was Western intervention in the Russian civil war, 1918–21, that created war communism, the model for the Stalinist system that came later.[3] Alternatively, the blame for the cold war might be laid at the door of the appeasers. Had the British and French been willing to join

Litvinov, the Soviet foreign minister and representative at the League of Nations after 1934, in a genuine collective security effort, by reacting forcefully to the Italian invasion of Abyssinia and Hitler's occupation of the Rhineland, the Second World War, some would argue, might have been avoided. Russia would have remained behind the borders agreed at Brest-Litovsk in 1918 and a Wilsonian international policy might have come into being.

Be that as it may, the story, as it is usually told, focuses on the 1940s and the story is mainly told by Americans. There are a few European histories,[4] but most European discussions of the cold war tend to be more analytical than historical in approach.[5] There are, roughly, three types of story:[6] the orthodox versions, which initially appeared only in the statements of politicians and memoirs;[7] the revisionist versions, which gained in acceptance during and after the Vietnam war;[8] and the self-styled post-revisionist histories,[9] which appeared in the 1970s and early 1980s, although, for reasons I will explain, they are more accurately described as neo-orthodox.[10]

The orthodox story largely deals with the early 1940s and Stalin's occupation of Eastern Europe. The orthodox view holds that once the Red Army was installed in these territories there was nothing much the West could do except to halt further expansion. The containment policy, the Marshall Plan, the creation of Nato, it is implied, all follow from Stalin's actions during this earlier period. The orthodox historians emphasize the nature of the Stalinist system and Stalin's basic insecurity and concern with establishing a defensive perimeter, although, of course, defensive obsessions may become expansionary. Less sophisticated variants of the argument that were current at the height of the cold war period in the early 1950s tended to equate all totalitarian systems, and assume that Stalin had a master plan just like Hitler.[11] Some of the orthodox historians also argue that it was Anglo-American tolerance in that early period, and also the failure to open a second front earlier, that allowed Stalin to get away with his sphere of influence in Eastern Europe. Litvinov told Edgar Snow in an interview in 1945: 'Why did you Americans wait until now to begin opposing us in the Balkans and Eastern Europe? ... You should have done this three years ago. Now it's too late and your complaints only arouse suspicion here.'[12]

The revisionist historians tell a different story. They concentrate on the period immediately after the Second World War. They assume that, at that point, some kind of agreement was possible on Germany and on troop withdrawals from Central Europe. However, a series of American actions prevented such an agreement and sealed the division of Europe. These actions included the Marshall Plan, the Truman doctrine of 1947, the West German currency reform and later (after the Berlin blockade) the introduction of the Basic Law which established a West German state, the formation of Nato and the subsequent military build-up. The refusal to provide economic assistance to Eastern Europe, the trade embargoes, the atmosphere of hostility, forced Stalin to tighten his grip on Eastern Europe and adopt an equally hostile posture.

The revisionist historians explain American behaviour in terms of the inner dynamic of American society. William Appleman Williams was the first revisionist historian to relate the cold war to the frontier thesis: the notion that American political cohesion and stability had stemmed from the continuous possibility of westward expansion. When the Pacific Ocean had been reached, the United States economy had to expand overseas and this gave rise to the 'open door' policy of the 1890s. National economic rivalries in the 1930s, especially the creation of the sterling bloc in 1931, resulted in a new version of the open door: the New Dealer's conception of an international liberal economy which was incorporated into the Atlantic Charter and in conditions attached to lend-lease and subsequent American loans. This conception was, however, thwarted by the socialist ideas and policies in Europe in the last years of the war. The next best thing was to push the socialist countries out of the states system so that an international liberal economy could be realized in the rest of the world. The Marshall Plan and high levels of military spending both served to expand American markets.

The post-revisionists cover both the early and late 1940s and assign some degree of responsibility to both sides. They deplore the excessive militarization of the cold war but they see no alternative to the balance of power system and the coexistence of spheres of influence. John Lewis Gaddis elaborates this position in his essay 'The long peace' and concludes that historians in the future might look back on 'our era, not as "the Cold War" at all, but rather, like those ages of Metternich and Bismarck, as a rare and fondly remembered "Long Peace".[13] And Daniel Yergin ends his fascinating and detailed account of the diplomatic and bureaucratic complexities of the period with a plea for détente, in the sense of an uneasy but somewhat less dangerous coexistence, within the framework of the balance of power.[14]

The post-revisionists tend to see a sharp break between Roosevelt and Truman, what Yergin calls the Yalta and Riga axioms. Roosevelt was pursuing at that time a policy of cooperation with Stalin, which involved mutual respect for spheres of influence.[15] Truman broke with that policy and adopted an openly confrontational approach. The post-revisionists seem to imply that the period of the cold war, the period of confrontation, could have been avoided, and that a continuation of Roosevelt's policies would have led to a more or less permanent détente.

The post-revisionists consider themselves close to the later views of George Kennan. Kennan, it will be remembered, is generally credited with the doctrine of containment, both as a result of his famous 'long telegram' to Truman in 1946 when he was based in Moscow and the anonymously authored 'X' article which appeared in the journal *Foreign Affairs* in 1947. Kennan has subsequently made it clear that he never meant containment to be interpreted as a military response to the Soviet threat. Indeed, he saw the Soviet threat as political and not military.[16] He supported the Marshall Plan and Truman doctrine (although not the universalist language in which the doctrine was presented) because he believed that economic aid to Western Europe and military aid to Greece and Turkey were ways of combating the internal communist threat. But he was doubtful about the West German currency reform and opposed the formation of Nato because he believed that these would preclude any possibility of agreement about overcoming the division of Europe in the future.

My own view, coming from a European perspective, is that both the orthodox and the revisionist versions are partly right. The orthodox historians were probably right in arguing that once the Soviet Union had occupied Eastern Europe, there was nothing much the West could do to prevent communist takeovers within those countries. Even though bourgeois parties participated in coalition governments up to the winter of 1947–8, the communists from an early date took charge of the ministries of the Interior and controlled the police apparatus. They also became, presumably on instructions from Moscow, the most dynamic agents in the process of reconstruction. For a variety of reasons, having to do with the sense of insecurity and paranoia built into the Stalinist system, it was likely that, sooner or later, the Soviet Union would impose more direct forms of control.

On the other hand, there was no obvious reason why the West should have reacted to the occupation of Eastern Europe through such devices as the Truman doctrine or the formation of Nato. The explanation given by the revisionists for the American policy of confrontation is much more convincing. Moreover, the failure to offer economic aid to Eastern Europe on purely humanitarian grounds (without political strings)[17] and the subsequent trade embargoes, undoubtedly hastened the process of Stalinization and left less room for possible autonomous development. This was certainly a widespread view in Europe at the time and is illustrated by a Polish joke circulating in the spring of 1947: 'What is it that is red and eats grass?' Answer: 'Us, next year.' Subsequently, the formation of Nato, the military build-up and all the paraphernalia of the early post-war years undoubtedly fed Stalin's megalomania and provided a perfect legitimation for Soviet behaviour in Eastern Europe.

Paradoxically, this view is closer to both the orthodox and revisionist historians than to the post-revisionists. The post-revisionists tend to play down both the logic of the Soviet role in Eastern Europe and the internal dynamic of American policy, even though they ascribe some responsibility to both sides. They would not agree with this assessment, I hasten to add. On the contrary, Gaddis concludes his book on containment with the following reflection:

George Kennan made the point in both the Long Telegram and the 'X' article that Soviet foreign policy was the product of internal influence not susceptible to persuasion, manipulation, or even comprehension from outside. Without pushing the point too far, the same might be said of American foreign policy during the thirty years that separated Kennan's appointment as Director of the Policy Planning Staff from Kissinger's retirement as Secretary of State. To a remarkable degree, containment has been a product, not so much of what the Russians have done, or what has happened elsewhere in the world, but of internal forces operating within the United States.[18]

But the whole tenor of the Gaddis's argument is that internal pressures somehow thwarted a rational international policy, that they represented a distortion of a policy that was fundamentally directed towards an external reality. This becomes clear in the chapter of his book on détente where he notes what he sees as an inconsistency between the behaviour of Nixon and Kissinger towards communist states and their behaviour towards social movements. He seems bemused by the fact that Nixon and Kissinger could tolerate China and the Soviet Union but could not tolerate 'independent Marxism'. They could not allow a victory for Hanoi and hence invaded Cambodia and prolonged the Vietnam war for four years. They could not tolerate the Allende government in Chile, nor the Eurocommunists in Western Europe.[19]

Kennan, in fact, expresses a similar bewilderment:

The greatest mystery of my own role in Washington in those years, as I see it today, was why so much attention was paid in certain instances, as in the case of the telegram of February 1946 from Moscow, and the X-article, to what I had to say and so little in others. The only answer could be that Washington's reactions were deeply subjective, influenced more by domestic political moods and institutional position.[20]

The puzzle is resolved if we interpret the East–West conflict in a different light. The post-revisionists see the East–West conflict as a traditional great power conflict of interest, in which irrational behaviour is sometimes induced by domestic pressures. The orthodox historians see American behaviour as a rational response, a great power response, to Soviet behaviour which stems from the internal nature of the Soviet Union. The revisionists, on the other hand, by and large see Soviet behaviour as a more or less rational response to American behaviour which has to be explained in terms of the inner nature of the American system. The different positions can be expressed schematically, thus:

		Soviet Union reacting to:	
		External conflict	Internal conflict
US reacting to:	External conflict	Post-revisionists	Orthodox
	Internal conflict	Revisionists	

If we were to interpret the East–West conflict in a way that could be fitted into the fourth box, as an *imaginary* conflict which conceals parallel but largely separate internal conflicts, then the paradox of Nixon and Kissinger's behaviour is explained. On this interpretation, cold war and détente, conflict and cooperation, are different ways of managing internal conflicts. Kissinger and Nixon *needed* détente precisely in order to manage domestic, that is intra-West, conflicts at less cost.

Differing assumptions about the East–West conflict

These different stories about the origins of the cold war stem from different world views. Inherited language and theory combined with political predispositions define the contours of what is considered appropriate to investigate. Both the orthodox and post-revisionist historians are realists. They see the world largely through a politico-military lens. The orthodox historians are perhaps more idealist. They put more emphasis on democracy and see the totalitarian nature of the Soviet system as an obstacle to global democracy. The post-revisionists are willing to take economic factors into account in so far as they explain divergences from a rational realistic approach, but they do sometimes seem nervous of any argument that might appear to smack of socio-economic determinism, and this sometimes results in unrealism.

The revisionists, on the other hand, emerge from a Marxian tradition; they see the world through a socio-economic lense. This is perhaps why their analyses do not seem able to take into account the nature of the Soviet system.

These mindsets inherited from the past imply a certain blindness about aspects of the post-war period. Certain events, phenomena or developments were ignored or bypassed by all these schools of thought. The orthodox and post-revisionist historians often seem unaware of the deep-rooted internal conflicts within the West and in the Third World. Kennan himself is remarkably distant and even dismissive about the Third World.[21] The revisionist historians, on the other hand, often appear to be apologizing for what happened in Eastern Europe, with the exception of a few Trotskyist accounts.[22]

Indeed, on the whole, reading this literature one is struck by an extraordinary callousness towards the fate of the East European peoples. The orthodox historians and polemicists weep crocodile tears for the peoples of Eastern Europe. They loudly proclaim the injustices of Stalinism. And yet it was Western governments who halted Western credits and imposed trade embargoes in 1947. The East European countries were much poorer than the West European countries and their war devastation was proportionately greater. What is more, it has been calculated that the Soviet Union extracted from these countries – in the form of war reparations, profits from joint stock companies and unfair pricing procedures – an amount which totalled around 14 billion dollars, approximately the same as was spent on Marshall Aid.[23] The post-revisionists, on the other hand, consider that the fate of Eastern Europe is secondary to the concern with great-power stability.

Part of the explanation is the cold war itself. Any well-meaning liberal or socialist who tried to tell the truth about Eastern Europe found himself or herself in the same dilemma as George Kennan in 1945. Kennan, who had lived mostly abroad for many years, expressed in his long telegram a genuine outrage about Stalinism. But that genuine outrage merely fed domestic anti-communism in the United States, and domestic anti-communism is a phenomenon distinct from serious criticism of the Soviet Union. For a long time, the Western situation has been such that any critical statement about Eastern Europe and the Soviet Union was used as a justification or legitimation for the structures of the imaginary war. And yet, such is the ingenuity of the cold war formula that the failure to be critical, to tell the truth about the East, discredited and marginalized the left.

A similar, perhaps worse, situation pertained in the East, where the threat from imperialism explained repression within. Anyone brave enough to challenge the Western threat hypothesis used to risk the charge of being an agent of imperialism. At the same time, criticism of the West was a kind of collusion with oppression.

The alternative was myopia, assisted by the division of Europe itself. The reduction in trade, the restrictions on travel and so on gave rise to real ignorance about events on the other side of the East–West divide. The actual behaviour of the socialist states did not, in fact, impinge in tangible ways on Western society (and vice versa).

The 'other side' became a blank sheet on which to sketch the mirror image of one's own preoccupations. Views about what was happening, on the other hand, tended to be a reflection of domestic political positions rather than descriptions of what was actually happening. And these views inevitably influenced the thinking of historians.

In a sense the imaginary war was, and is even today, so effective because it drew on deeply rooted modes of thought. Realism, Marxism and Idealism grew out of the separation of the economic and the political and the civil and the military which accompanied the rise of capitalism and the states system. They provided the language in which different political positions were expressed. While all three modes of thought, but especially Marxism and Idealism, had something to offer an analysis of the post-war system, all missed certain novel aspects of the post-war system which required a new language to be understood. Or, put another way, all three modes of thought gave rise to stories about the cold war that, in effect, upheld the cold war. They gave rise to good–bad stories which reflected and indeed served to maintain domestic differences. Even though this was far from what was intended, by the revisionists at least, the stories were used to conceal alternative interpretations which might have helped to undermine the cold war. This point is developed in the next two chapters.

Notes

1 'The ability to get to the verge without getting into the war is the necessary art. If you cannot master it, you inevitably get into a war. If you try to run away from it, if you are scared to go to the brink, you are lost.' Quoted in John Lewis Gaddis, *Strategies of Containment: A Critical Appraisal of Postwar Amerian Security Policy* (Oxford University Press, 1982), p. 151. All the same, according to Khrushchev, Dulles 'knew how far he could push us, and he never pushed us too far ... When Dulles died, I told my friends that although he had been a man who had lived and breathed hatred of communism and who despised progress, he never stepped over the brink which he was always talking about in his speeches; and for that reason alone we should lament his passing.' *Khrushchev Remembers* (André Deutsch, 1971), p. 398.

2 See, particularly, D. F. Fleming, *The Cold War and its Origins*,

1917–1960 (2 vols, Doubleday, 1961); and André Fontaine, *History of the Cold War from the October Revolution to the Korean War, 1917–1950*, tr. D. D. Page (Secker and Warburg, 1968).

3 According to Fleming:

> Within the limits of the exhaustion and chaos which lay around them, the Reds waged the first total war. They had to do so in order to survive. In the fires of this grim testing time, they also hammered out the machinery of the totalitarian state – organised terror by the secret police, the planned use of all national resources, nationalisation of all industry, class war in the villages in order to feed the starving cities (which later ended in the forced collectivisation of the land) by a monolithic, highly disciplined Party controlling all activity, military or civil, and a powerful army, taught and schooled with every means at command. (*Cold War*, p. 32)

4 See, for example, Fontaine, *History*; Hugh Thomas, *Armed Truce: Beginnings of Cold War, 1945–6* (Hamish Hamilton, 1986); Alan S. Milward, *Reconstruction of Western Europe, 1945–51* (Methuen, 1984).

5 See, for example, Isaac Deutscher, *The Great Contest: Russia and the West* (Oxford University Press, 1960), for a classic statement of the socialist version of the cold war; or Raymond Aron, *War and Industrial Society*, Auguste Comte Memorial Lecture, 3 (Oxford University Press, 1958), and Alistair Buchan, *War in Modern Society* (C. A. Watts, 1966), for more orthodox accounts of the cold war.

6 For useful surveys, including surveys of surveys, see Barton Bernstein, 'Les États Unis et les origines de la guerre froide', *Revue de l'Histoire de la Deuxième Guerre Mondiale*, 3, July 1976 (Presses Universitaires de France); and Stuart Morn's 'The Russians are coming', *Times Higher Education Supplement*, 28 July 1978.

7 See Herbert Feis, *Churchill, Roosevelt, Stalin: The War They Waged and the Peace They Sought* (Princeton University Press, 1957); *Between War and Peace: The Potsdam Conference* (Princeton University Press, 1957); and *Japan Subdued: The Atomic Bomb and the End of the World II* (Princeton University Press, 1957). More recent orthodox accounts include Lynn Etheridge Davis, *The Cold War Begins: Soviet–American Conflict over Eastern Europe* (Princeton University Press, 1974); and Vojtech Mastny, *Russia's Road to the Cold War: Diplomacy, Warfare and the Politics of Communism, 1941–45* (Columbia University Press, 1979).

8 The classic statement of the revisionist thesis is William Appleman Williams, *The Tragedy of American Diplomacy* (World Publishing, 1959). Williams's ideas were taken up and developed in Gar Alper-

owitz, *Atomic Diplomacy: Hiroshima and Potsdam, the Use of the Atomic Bomb and the Confrontation with Soviet Power* (updated and expanded edn, Penguin, 1985); Joyce and Gabriel Kolko, *The Limits of Power: The World and United States Foreign Policy, 1945–54* (Harper and Row, 1972); Waler Lafeber, *America, Russia and the Cold War, 1945–71* (John Wiley, 1972); and, more recently, Richard Barnet, *The Alliance* (Simon and Schuster, 1984).

 9 John Lewis Gaddis uses the term in 'The emerging post-revisionist synthesis on the origins of the cold war', *Diplomatic History*, 8, Summer 1983.

10 These include John Lewis Gaddis, *The United States and the Origins of the Cold War, 1941–47* (Columbia University Press, 1972); Ernest R. May, *'Lessons' of the Past* (Oxford University Press, 1973); Daniel Yergin, *Shattered Peace: The Origins of the Cold War and the National Security State* (Houghton Mifflin, 1978).

11 See, for example, Zbigniew Brzezinski, *Totalitarian Dictatorship and Autocracy* (Harvard University Press, 1956). The mood of that period is well described in 'Russia and the cold war', chapter 5 of George Kennan's *Memoirs 1950–63* (Little, Brown, 1972). According to Gaddis, *Strategies*, Dulles was very fond of quoting Stalin's book, *Problems of Leninism*, which he regarded as equivalent to Hitler's *Mein Kampf*.

12 Quoted in Mastny, *Russia's Road*, p. 283; see also Edward Mark, 'American policy towards Eastern Europe and the origins of the cold war, 1941–46: an alternative interpretation', *Journal of American History*, 68, September 1981.

13 John Lewis Gaddis, 'The long peace', *International Security*, 10:4, Spring 1986, p. 142.

14 Yergin, *Shattered Peace*.

15 Actually Roosevelt seems to have been rather uncomfortable with the spheres of influence approach and was pushing for at least the appearance of self-determination at Yalta. He did not approve of the famous percentages deal suggested in Moscow in October 1944 and described in Churchill's memoirs, in which Stalin and Churchill tried to agree on how to apportion influence in Eastern Europe and the Balkans. Mastny provides a fascinating account of the whole story, which can now be pieced together from newly available documents at the UK Public Record Office. (The story as originally recorded only appears in an early draft of the minutes of the meeting preserved among the papers of the British embassy in Moscow: the story was deleted in the final minutes. However, the 'notorious' slip of paper in which the percentages were recorded by Stalin can be found in the prime minister's file in the Public

Record Office.) The following day, it seems, Molotov and Eden haggled over their percentages; they could not agree about respective interests in Hungary, which seems to indicate how serious the Russians were about spheres of influence. Subsequently, Churchill seems to have been rather embarrassed by the affair. In a memo composed the day after the meeting, Churchill argued 'elaborately, but tortuously, that the figures were to serve merely as a rough guide about the extent of the respective interests, that they showed how much these really coincided, and that in any case they applied for the period of the war only.' Mastny, *Russia's Road*, p. 209.

16 Walter Lippmann strongly criticized George Kennan's X article in a series of *New York Times* articles which were subsequently published as a book, *The Cold War* (Harper & Row, 1972). In an anguished letter to Lippmann, which was never actually sent, Kennan claimed that he had been misunderstood: 'The Russians don't want to invade. It is not in their tradition. They tried it once in Finland and got their fingers burned. They don't want war of any kind. Above all, they don't want the open responsibility that official invasion brings with it. They prefer to do the job politically, with stooge forces. Note well: When I say politically, that does not mean without violence. But it means that the violence is nominally *domestic*, not *international* violence. It is, if you will, a police violence ... not a military violence.' George Kennan, *Memoirs 1925–50* (Hutchinson, 1968), p. 361.

17 Although technically it was the Russians that refused Marshall Aid, it seems that the Americans always intended that the programme would be offered in such a way that the Russians, and their satellites, should be seen to have refused, so Kennan suggests in his memoirs. Recent studies of the British role suggest that it was Bevin, the British foreign secretary, who was determined that the Russians should be excluded. Bidault, the French foreign secretary, also wanted to exclude the Russians but was nervous about doing so because of French public opinion. See William C. Cromwell, 'The Marshall Plan, Britain and the cold war', *Review of International Studies*, 8, 1982, p. 233–49. This is why the Americans did not make use of the United Nations body, the Economic Commission for Europe (ECE), and instead established a separate body for administering Marshall Aid, the Organisation for European Economic Cooperation (OEEC), which later became the Organisation for Economic Cooperation and Development (OECD), which included all the advanced industrial countries. My father, Nicholas Kaldor, joined the ECE in 1947, and I remember him telling me that when he accepted the job, he and Gunnar Myrdal, the first director of ECE, expected that they

would be drawing up an economic recovery plan for all of Europe, based on American credits.

18 Gaddis, *Strategies*, p. 357.
19 Ibid., chs 9 and 10.
20 Kennan, *Memoirs 1925–50*, p. 403.
21 See, for example, George Kennan, *The Cloud of Danger: Some Current Problems of American Foreign Policy* (Hutchinson, 1978).
22 See, for example, Chris Harman, *Bureaucracy and the Revolution in Eastern Europe* (Pluto, 1974).
23 See Paul Marer, 'Intrabloc economic relations and prospects', in David Holloway and Jane M. O. Sharpe, eds, *The Warsaw Pact; Alliance in Transition?* (Macmillan, 1984).

4

Stalinism and East Central Europe

After 1917, the Soviet Union spawned a new system in which the separation between authoritative and material reproduction, between the political and the economic, no longer applied. The Soviet Union integrated authoritative and material reproduction and even, during the Stalinist era, human reproduction. (It ruthlessly excluded natural reproduction so that, today, the ecological crisis in Eastern Europe is probably worse than anywhere in the world.) It was a new system, as Fernando Claudin points out, 'new not only to history, but to the theoretical predictions of Marxism'.[1]

The system was developed in Russia and the other nations under Russian domination that make up the Soviet Union. After the Second World War, it was extended to the so-called People's Democracies of Eastern Europe, to China, North Korea, and later Vietnam and Cuba. Rudi Bahro, the East German writer, points out that had it not been for China and Eastern Europe, the Russian experience might have been regarded as an accident of history. As it was, the Soviet experience became the norm of socialism, the archetypal example. Consequently, it also represented the defeat and tragedy of the socialist idea.[2]

To understand the reproduction of international relations between the socialist states in Europe requires some understanding of the Soviet system. For it was this system that was imposed on Eastern Europe in the years 1947–52. It is, of course, not possible to offer a full analysis of the Soviet society. The following is an attempt to point out certain elements of such an analysis, based on the works of mainly East European writers.[3]

The Soviet system

The first point (generally stressed by the analysts of the Soviet system) is the backwardness of the Russian empire at the time of the Bolshevik takeover. This backwardness is not merely a matter of economic underdevelopment, a point which is also stressed by official Soviet ideologies – the miserable poverty of the mass of the population. It is social; it has to do with the nature of the social formation which characterized Russia up to the time of the Bolshevik revolution. This social formation has been variously described as 'semi-Asiatic' or as 'Eastern absolutism'. The term 'Asiatic mode of production', taken from Marx and Engels, refers to a social forma-tion characterized by a state which is highly centralized in order to carry out certain essential social projects such as irrigation, flood control or making war, based on dependent forms of labour. In the case of Russia, the social project was war – waves of invasions having served the same purposee as floods or drought in other Asiatic societies. Generally, in these societies, the state is dominated by a priestly caste whose rule is legitimized by a set of religious or secular (in the case of Confucianism) beliefs. The Russian system is said to be semi-Asiatic because it combined the characteristics of an Asiatic mode of production with European feudalism. The term 'Eastern absolutism' was coined by Perry Anderson in his book *Lineages of the Absolutist State*.[4] The term emphasizes the European character of the Eastern absolutist states (Russia, Prussia and Habsburg) and their mutual development as part of a European states system after the crisis of feudalism in the late fifteenth century.[5]

The point on which these various analyses concur is the divergence in the historical development of Eastern Europe somewhere between the thirteenth and sixteenth centuries. At a time when serfdom was disappearing in the West, the so-called second serfdom was intro-duced in the East. In particular in Russia hereditary, that is, private, nobility was replaced by a prebendal form of property, that is to say, non-inheritable estates granted to military commanders or their officials in exchange for services to the state. The (temporary) landholders could not sell or transfer the land or even make changes in the mode of cultivation. The consequence was a highly centralized society in which even the Orthodox church was integrated into the state and the situation of the peasantry was close to that of slave labour. The rule of the tsars was ensured by a combination of brutal coercion carried out by a vast military and police apparatus, and a mystical, semi-religious, chauvinistic tradition, which involved the deification of the tsars. The practice, for example, of forced labour camps to carry out certain projects long preceded the Bolshevik revolution.[6] Even after the abolition of serfdom in 1867, the situation of the peasants did not improve. The industry which developed in the late nineteenth and early twentieth centuries was largely war-related.

Some East European writers argue that the current division of Europe corresponds not so much to the disposition of Russian and American troops at the end of the Second World War as to the dividing line between Eastern and Western absolutism in the seventeenth and eighteenth centuries. However, such writers concede that the historical development of East Central Europe was distinct from that of Russia.[7] The Austro-Hungarian empire was a mixture of Western and Eastern systems in which the imperial state was much weaker than in the Russian and Prussian empires; there was greater national and cultural autonomy. The *Junker* militarism of East Prussia and Brandenburg was combined with West German capitalism in the middle of the nineteenth century.

These arguments are fascinating and undoubtedly do explain certain historical predispositions which help us to understand the emergence of Stalinism. But they should not be over-emphasized. There can be a kind of fatalism in these historical explanations. They seem to suggest that democracy is not possible in societies with highly centralized traditions. Milan Kundera, for example, wants to exclude Russia from Europe because Russian history is not compatible with European cultural traditions, which are essentially bound up with the idea of the individual.[8] There are always alternative ways of interpreting the past. In the light of the present, it is easy to identify a unidimensional set of causes. But it is also possible to locate other traditions, the tradition of Soviets and workers' councils in Russia and East Central Europe, for example, which offer the possibility of a different kind of present.[9]

The second element in any analysis of the Soviet system is the heritage of socialist ideas. Schumpeter, in his famous essay on social

democracy,[10] argued that neither Leninism nor Fabianism were
Marxist philosophies. Marx was concerned with the development of
the working class as a whole. In putting the emphasis on a vanguard
party of intellectuals, Lenin, according to Schumpeter, had 'irrevocably broken away from classical Marxism'. On the other hand, the
Fabians, who put specific proposals to the state for social legislation,
were not Marxist either. Only German social democracy, which
created a mass working-class party and yet – despite the social
legislation of Bismarck and his successors – found itself in a
permanent state of antagonism, was truly Marxist. The British
situation allowed too much consensus, too much access to government. Russia lacked a large working class, and political activity could
only be undertaken by small bands of highly committed intellectuals
ready to brave the political underground. Already, in his debate with
Bakunin, Marx had criticized the Russian revolutionary tradition,
accusing Bakuninists of regarding themselves as 'the privileged
representatives of the idea of revolution', of setting themselves up as
'a general staff'.[11]

And yet both Fabianism and Leninism *did* draw on Marxist ideas.
Most importantly, they shared the Marxist concept of class based on
property relations, and regarded the abolition of private property as
an essential precondition for socialism. In the case of Russia there
was rather little private property and, as Lenin wrote later, that was
the easiest part of the revolution. Both Fabianism and Leninism,
moreover, were committed to raising the living standards of the mass
of the populations and, for the Fabians, this probably took prece-
dence over the abolition of private property. The fact that they
addressed themselves to the state and saw themselves as agents of the
working class has to be understood partly in terms of the failure of
Marxism to offer an analysis of the state or of class relations, defined
in terms of domination and authority. (This is not strictly true, of
course. Marx (and Engels) saw the state as a form of compulsion
which reflected class exploitation. Once exploitation had been
abolished and communism attained, the state was expected to
'wither away'. In the transitional period, Marx and Engels did
envisage a role for the state and indeed the demands in the
Communist Manifesto were addressed to the state. Moreover, in
Marx's more political writings, especially the *Eighteenth Brumaire*

and *The Civil War in France*, he describes brilliantly the way the particular character of the state machinery reflects a particular class composition in society. The same general point is made by Engels, particularly in 'The force theory' in *Anti-Dühring*. Nevertheless, the presumption of the state either as a dependent variable or as lying outside the theoretical schema is what emerges from these somewhat brief references to the state.)

That Fabians and Leninists saw themselves as privileged members of the working class, as disinterested intellectuals able to act on behalf of the working class, can also be explained by the fact, often stressed by disillusioned communist writers, that Marxism and socialism were really doctrines for intellectuals. Because they offered such powerful and appealing methods of analysing society, they had a particular attraction for intellectuals.

Konrad and Szelényi describe the socialist system as a rational redistributive system, in contrast to a traditional redistributive system. The difference between a rational redistributive system and a traditional redistributive system is economic growth. The traditional redistributive systems, the Asiatic or semi-Asiatic modes of production, were only concerned with simple reproduction, with extracting sufficient resources to reproduce the state machinery and the irrigation or flood control systems or whatever. The rational redistributive system requires a perpetual increase in the surplus available to the state for redistribution. This involves the rationalization of the bureaucracy, the execution of economic laws, and so on.

The element of rationality does have its roots in socialist ideas, and was a notion shared by Fabians and Leninists. The Fabians were somewhat more liberal. In their vision of socialism, a parliamentary state governed by Fabians and elected by the working class would carry out rational projects to further the development of the working class. They also emphasized municipal socialism and cooperatives as alternatives to private property. The Leninists, on the other hand, thought it was enough for the vanguard party to achieve power to carry out these plans. Lenin's ideas are made rather clear in *The State and Revolution*. He did think that it would be necessary 'to smash the old bureaucratic machine'. But he also thought it would be necessary immediately to construct a new one. He likened his vision of the socialist system to the operation of the postal service:

To organise the *whole* national economy on the lines of the postal service, so that the technicians, foremen, bookkeepers, as well as *all* officials, shall receive salaries no higher than 'a workman's wage', all under the control and leadership of the armed proletariat – this is our immediate aim. It is such a state standing on such an economic foundation that we need.[12]

Lenin was sceptical about parliamentarianism, which he viewed as capitalist democracy, citing Marx's comment that parliament offers the oppressed the opportunity every few years 'to decide which particular representatives of the oppressing classes shall represent and repress them in parliament!' He makes it clear that there can be no freedom until oppression is eliminated and, therefore, the state ceases to exist.[13]

While Fabianism and Leninism differed on the form of the state (and this is of course very important) they shared a similar concept of the state's economic function under socialism, which can be traced back to Marx. This was precisely the butt of Bakunin's criticism of Marx. He argued that Marx wanted to establish: 'a single state bank concentrating in its hands all commercial, industrial, agricultural and even scientific production, and to divide the mass of the people into two armies, one industrial and the other agricultural, under the direct command of state engineers, who will form a new privileged scientific-political class'.[14]

A rational redistributive system began to emerge in Russia in the last years of the tsars under pressure from Western capitalism.[15] And this pressure continued to be an important aspect of rational redistribution, especially during the period of war communism and during the 1930s and 1940s. But the decisive change with the Bolshevik revolution was the notion of economic growth, in order both to raise living standards and to compete with the West. This was an essential component of the state's ideology and legitimacy.[16] No wonder the celebrated Fabians, Beatrice and Sidney Webb, were so impressed when they visited the Soviet Union in the 1930s.

The third element in any analysis of the Soviet system is the specific character of Stalinism. For it was Stalinism that was exported to Eastern Europe in the late 1940s. The emergence of Stalinism in the Soviet Union in the early 1930s amounted to a second revolution, although there were intimations of the Stalinist system during the period of war communism. Stalinism had certain distinct features which marked it out from the period of the New Economic Policy (NEP) which preceded it and the post-Stalinist system which followed. Under the NEP, agriculture was in the hands of the private peasants; a new class of kulaks was created by the expropriation of the tsarist landed estates. Small private enterprises also continued to function. The party apparatus, characterized by relative internal democracy, controlled the state machinery, and intellectuals enjoyed a certain degree of cultural autonomy and pluralism. Under Stalinism, agriculture was forcibly collectivized, increasing the surplus extracted from the land as well as the available workforce so as to undertake a rapid programme of industrialization and military build-up under the directive of the five-year plans (first introduced in 1928). A single individual, Stalin, with the backing of the secret police, controlled the machinery of state in place of the purged party apparatus.[17] The terror, combined with a draconian labour code, served to discipline workers, peasants and intellectuals. In place of Leninism, a semi-mystical Stalinist ideology emerged which combined Marxism, Russian chauvinism and the personality cult.

In a famous lecture given in Belgrade in June 1957, one year after Gomulka's accession to power in Poland, Oskar Lange, a leading Polish reform economist, described the Stalinist system as a '*sui generis* war economy'. By this he meant a system comparable to the organization of capitalist economies in wartime. 'In capitalist countries, similar methods, viz. concentration of all resources in order to avoid leakages of resources to everything that was considered non-essential, i.e. everything not connected with the prosecution of war, were used during war-time.'[18] Lange was of the view that 'methods of the war economy' were 'necessary in a revolutionary period of transition'. All the same, he was at pains to point out that these methods were not intrinsically socialist. For example, compulsory deliveries of agricultural products 'were first introduced by the occupation army of Kaiser Wilhelm the Second, whom I do not think anybody regards as a champion of Socialism'.[19]

The analogy of the war economy can be taken further. It was not just that methods of the war economy were used. It was also that the Stalinist system was geared for war and only really functioned efficiently in wartime. The first two five-year plans, up to the outbreak of the Second World War, involved the creation of gigantic 'American style' factories which produced or could be converted to produce armaments. Mass production, as Yakovlev, the aircraft designer makes clear, was introduced not for consumption, as in the United States, but for war.[20] (There were also other reasons for emphasizing large-scale production, to train large numbers of unskilled peasants, to reap economies of scale in raw materials and the sheer size of the Soviet Union.)

The form of regulation in such a system was the administrative directive. Given the powerlessness of the consumer, administrative directives were determined by the subjective preferences of those who issued the directives. During the 1930s, Stalin took a personal interest in armaments production, studying the experiences of other countries, sending notes and telephoning the designers of various types of armaments. All the same, the outbreak of war demonstrated 'all sorts of fallacies and miscalculations'. In the first few months of the war, much of the armaments industry was destroyed or captured and many of the weapons proved inferior to their German counterparts. However, the Stalinist system proved capable of extraordinary feats during wartime. Industry had to be evacuated to the eastern part of the USSR and the final output of armaments proved comparable in numbers and equality to the American effort, despite the enormous costs.[21] Table 4.1 gives some indication of the scale of the effort.

Table 4.1 National income, industrial and agricultural output (1940 = 100)

	1941	1942	1943	1944
National income	92	66	74	88
Gross industrial output	98	77	90	104
Armaments	140	186	224	251
Fuel	94	53	59	75
Gross agricultural output	62	38	37	54

Source: Alec Nove, *An Economic History of the USSR*, 3rd edn (Penguin, 1984).

By 1942, armaments accounted for 52 per cent of national income, according to Alec Nove the 'highest ever reached anywhere'.[22] The

Soviet Union produced 489,000 guns, 136,800 planes and 102,500 tanks and self-propelled guns during the war. In comparison, imports from Britain and the United States were negligible. Lend-lease supplies of machine tools, locomotives, non-ferrous metals, etc., were undoubtedly important in overcoming bottlenecks. Nevertheless, the Soviet wartime achievement was primarily indigenous.

The development of a war economy seems to have been inextricably bound up with a pervasive sense of paranoia and insecurity that characterized the Stalinist period. Before Stalin, of course, the Bolsheviks were concerned to protect socialism from the onslaught of Western capitalism. This was especially important after the acceptance of the socialism-in-one-country thesis in the mid-1920s. It was not only concern about possible Western military intervention as in the civil war, but also the need to protect socialism in an economic sense. Industrialization was necessary not merely to pay for the means to defend the country against external threats but also so that socialism could win the ideological competition with capitalism (a point that was later to become part of the ideological armoury of the imaginary war).

Under Stalinism, however, there was an increasing preoccupation with military insecurity, both real and imagined, and this seems to have been linked to the scale of domestic repression. On the one hand, fear of war and defeat in war genuinely constituted fear for the survival of the regime, especially after the rise of Hitler. It was after all the strength of German militarism against the tsarist forces in the First World War that had created the occasion for the Bolshevik revolution.[23]

On the other hand, the external threat can be viewed as an outward expression of Stalin's own paranoia, which must be explained primarily in terms of the times, the chaos, frustration and the enormous obstacles experienced in constructing the Stalinist system.[24] Deutscher talks about the 'vicious circle' of terror that was set in motion by domestic repression. The more that people are arrested, tortured, deported to Siberia, executed, the more fears grow that these crimes will be revealed, that plots and conspiracies will develop, and the more arrests, deportations, executions, etc., are required to conceal the truth and forestall conspiracy, real or imagined.[25] This escalatory sense of insecurity was both internal and external (victims of repression were invariably agents of imperialism), and to some extent reproduced the historical Russian experience of insecurity.[26]

Most Soviet scholars, both right and left, argue that Stalinism was a necessary consequence of the Bolshevik revolution, which had to raise living standards if it was to succeed in a hostile international environment.[27] No other method could have transformed a backward agrarian society into the second strongest military and industrial power. Stephen Cohen suggests,[28] interestingly, that this was not so, that collectivization resulted in a big reduction in food production and hence the available surplus. (Some five million peasants starved to death in the famine of 1933 which was the consequence of collectivization.) The purge of technical experts and military officers greatly reduced the efficiency of industry and the army and resulted in the early defeats at the beginning of the war. (Stalin's personal interest was a substitute for expertise.) He argues that Bukharin's ideas and the NEP offered the possibility of a more humane, though not democratic, form of socialism in the Soviet Union. The question arises, of course, as to whether a Bukharinist system could have withstood the test of war, or whether it would have converged towards a Stalinist model.

Whether or not Cohen is right, and it would be nice as well as sad to think he is, it *was* the Stalinist system that inherited the Bolshevik revolution and has left its indelible imprint on subsequent history. The post-Stalinist system reverted to a more collective style of leadership, with genuine debate inside the Central Committee; it established, more or less, party control of the police; it liberalized agriculture, to a greater or lesser degree; and it tolerated greater autonomy in private life and in the natural sciences. Nevertheless, the residue of Stalinism runs extremely deep, as Khrushchev discovered and Gorbachev is discovering. Although millions were purged, millions more either benefited or were implicated in some way and it was the latter who, on the whole, survived. Moreover, Stalinism does seem to have struck a populist emotional chord among the millions of newly created intellectuals and workers at least in Russia. It did, after all, raise standards of living, even though most people remained extremely poor. It did massively raise the rate of literacy, and expand educational opportunities and the prospect of upward mobility. And, above all, it did justify the enormous sacrifices and losses that almost every Russian family experienced. One has only to see the grandeur of the Stalinist 'wedding cake' architecture, the subterranean palaces of the Moscow metro (built, like the pyramids, with slave labour) and the socialist realist murals of worker, peasant and poetic idylls to realize the power of Stalinist culture. And finally, of course, the de-Stalinization process, drawing attention as it does to the massive problems of inefficiency, waste, drunkenness, etc., serves to renew memories, perhaps selective, of a period of achievement, discipline and efficiency. De-Stalinization is, as it were, a personal reproach to all those who were implicated in Stalinism through crime, belief or sacrifice.

The Stalinist system and what might be described as the Bukharinist system can be represented as two alternative models of authoritative reproduction. Under the Bukharinist system there is some separation of material and authoritative reproduction. Agriculture is regulated by market means. Industry is under the control of the state and regulated by market means, involving a wage relationship, but nevertheless also involving extra-economic forms of compulsion such as physical coercion and ideological incentive (the construction of socialism). Under this model, the primary aim of economic growth is to maintain the ideological incentive, to demonstrate that socialism is being constructed and to provide some kind of collective return for individual effort that involves some increase in living standards.

Under the Stalinist system, both agriculture and industry are regulated by authoritative means and the main forms of regulation are physical or 'administrative' – the dreaded labour code. Failure to measure up to Stakhanovite productivity goals risks arrest or deportation. According to this model, the main purpose of economic growth is the expansion of the military and police apparatuses that carry out the coercive measures. Basic necessities are provided to reproduce soldiers and workers. The spiralling sense of insecurity, to which Western dynamism contributes, ever expands these reproductive requirements.

The initial cold war period

The Stalinist system was imposed on East Central Europe following the creation of the Cominform in 1947. Ostensibly, it was a reaction to the Truman doctrine and the Marshall Plan. Claudin argues that between the dissolution of the Comintern in 1943 and the creation of the Cominform in 1947, Stalin's main aim was cooperation with the Western powers. To this end, Stalin was willing to rein in the Italian and French communist parties so that they became accomplices in the reconstruction of the discredited West European bourgeois elites, and to tolerate coalition governments in East Central Europe. As cooperation became more difficult, he adopted a more antagonistic posture both with respect to the satellites and to the behaviour of Western communist parties.[29] It was at the first Cominform meeting that Zhdanov, Stalin's spokesman on ideological matters, formulated the 'two camp doctrine', the theory of an inevitable struggle between imperialism and anti-imperialism.

Undoubtedly, Western hostility was a factor in explaining what happened after the creation of the Cominform. But whether or not it was fuelled by fears of capitalist encirclement, sooner or later insecurity about the newly formed buffer zone in East Central Europe was likely to grow. Apart from the Bohemia–Silesia industrial triangle and the manufacturing nuclei in Warsaw, Budapest and Bucharest, most of East Central Europe had constituted an agricultural hinterland for Germany, and to a much lesser extent for Austria and Italy. Trade with Western Europe had amounted to nearly 70 per cent of the total trade of East Central Europe in 1938, and largely consisted of the exchange of German industrial products for raw materials and food. Trade had been disrupted by the war but, by 1947, it was beginning to be restored. Moreover, the Americans were offering economic assistance in small amounts in return for 'good' political behaviour. Hungary, for example, received American credits after the election victory of the bourgeois Smallholders party.[30]

It is not unreasonable to suppose that Stalin was afraid that growing links with the West could lure the satellites out of control – not necessarily into the Western camp but towards some form of autonomy which might offer an alternative model to Stalinism and, indeed, reveal the truth about past Soviet political crimes committed in these areas. Kennan argued as early as 1944 that cover-up, especially concerning the murder of Polish officers at Katyn and the deportation to Soviet camps of millions of Poles, was the main reason why the Soviet Union could never accept a non-communist government in Poland.[31] It may be that Stalin had as much reason to refuse participation in the Marshall Plan as the Americans had in excluding him.

If these were indeed Stalin's fears, they were amply confirmed by the split with Yugoslavia in 1948. In fact, the Yugoslavs were not supported by Western credits; they faced Western trade embargoes at the time. The Yugoslav leadership was able to mobilize mass support for Tito's position by telling the truth – by publishing the exchange of letters between Stalin and Tito and revealing the content of Soviet–Yugoslav differences, which included the behaviour of the Red Army in Yugoslavia (in contrast to that of the British military mission!), the role of Soviet secret operatives in Yugoslavia, the communist takeovers in the satellite countries in the winter of 1947–8, the exploitative joint stock companies and unfair terms of trade, the handover of Trieste (which Slovene partisans had liberated) to Italy, etc., etc. As Claudin puts it: 'For men who professed the Stalinist religion, it was not easy, even with all sources of information available at the time, suddenly to shift to secular Marxism.'[32]

Subsequently, the show trials throughout East Central Europe, reminiscent of the Soviet trials of 1937–8 (although the Czech trials came later), and the purge of the 'home' communists (those who had spent the war years fighting in the resistance in their own countries) were clearly directed against the Titoist heresy. At the first of the show trials, against Laszlo Rajk, the Hungarian Foreign Minister and former resistance leader, the prosecutor said: 'This trial is not strictly speaking the trial of Laszlo Rajk and his accomplices ... It is clear that in condemning Laszlo Rajk and his band of conspirators the Hungarian People's Tribunal also politically condemns those traitors of Yugoslavia, the criminal band of Tito, Kardelj and Djilas. It is in this that the international importance of this trial lies.'[33]

By eliminating the indigenous communist elements, and by implicating the remainder of the communist apparatus in the Stalinist

political crime, Stalin laid the basis for the reproduction of the
relationship between the Soviet Union and East Central Europe in
subsequent years. 'One of the main reasons for the Soviet army's
intervention in Hungary [in 1956], as of that which took place in
Czechoslovakia twelve years later ...' claims Claudin, 'was to
prevent the uncovering of political crimes in the People's
Democracies.'[34] What held the communists together, says Šimečka,
was 'above all, an awareness of sharing "the original sin"'.[35]

The spread of terror, the construction of a Stalinist political elite,
was, of course, bound up with the imposition of the Stalinist
economic system. The Second World War represented the apex, the
decisive experience of the Stalinist system. The onset of the cold war
was a way of reproducing that experience, of exporting the know-
how of the Soviet Union in the way it was best equipped to handle. It
provided the basis for rapid reconstruction through 'warlike'
pressures.[36] Without Western aid and trade, the Stalinist war economy was the obvious choice for Eastern Europe.

During this period, the Stalinist system was imposed on East
Central Europe almost down to the last detail. Plans for autarkic and
self-sufficient industrial development were drawn up, with considerable emphasis on steel and heavy industry and, after Korea, the
production of armaments. (In the years 1951–5, for example, it has
been estimated that some 11 per cent of all industrial development in
Poland was for military purposes.)[37] Agriculture was forcibly collectivized. Autonomous private life, such as cafés or non-political
clubs, was strictly curtailed.[38] Soviet army regulations were imposed
on East Central European armed forces 'down to the most trivial
details' and Soviet officers were put in positions of command and
'insisted on privileges and rights ... which could only be regarded as
humiliating'.[39] In Poland, a Soviet marshal, Konstantin Rokosovsky,
was appointed Minister of Defence in 1949. Personality cults were
introduced in all East European countries in which local leaders
basked in Stalin's reflected light.[40]

By the time Stalin died, the economies of Eastern Europe were
irrevocably sundered from the West. By 1953, the proportion of
trade with Western Europe had fallen to 14.4 per cent. This was
not simply because of the autarky and the insulation of the
Stalinist years. It was also the consequence of Western hostility. The

coordinating committee, CoCom, was established by the US in 1949, to coordinate strategic embargoes on the East by Western countries. The CoCom list of goods to be embargoed was introduced in 1949 and, from that date until 1954, it covered approximately 50 per cent of goods normally traded with the East. There were also separate restrictions in US trade legislation.

After Stalin's death

After Stalin's death came the first 'thaw', as it was termed by the Russian writer Ilya Ehrenburg. It affected all three pillars of the Stalinist system. It involved a moderation of East–West hostility, and a loosening of control both between the Soviet Union and the so-called People's Democracies, and within East European countries – in effect, a modification of relations between and within socialist states. Fejto describes reform at that time as 'therapy' – a kind of attempt to cure the sickness (the psychological and moral degradation) of oppression: 'Thus after integration, came diversification and self-determination; after the terror, a gradual relaxation, even if with temporary pauses and setbacks; after the great trials, the great rehabilitations; after unquestioning obedience, resistance; after isolation, the opening of doors. And all this in cycles of ebb and flow, freezing and thaw.'[41]

The relaxation after Stalin's death involved:

- an end of the siege mentality of 1948–53, a new emphasis on the principles of peaceful coexistence, a readiness to open channels of communication and even trade with West;
- a readiness to tolerate polycentrism among socialist countries. Particularly important in this respect was Khrushchev's visit to Yugoslavia in 1955.[42] According to the New Course, East European communist parties would adopt domestic policies to suit domestic conditions;
- a series of domestic reforms which included relaxation of the terror, party control over the police, a slowdown in economic growth especially investment, reallocation of resources to agriculture and to consumption goods (including the partial conversion of the armament industry towards the production of consumer durables), liberalization of agriculture (including a halt or diminution of collectivization and

less discrimination against private farmers, especially the abolition or reduction of compulsory deliveries), and greater tolerance towards private enterprise (artisans, cafés and restaurants, small-scale industry, private housing). Joint stock companies were dismantled and reparations came to an end.

These changes were to affect different countries differently – a pattern that was to be repeated in subsequent periods of relaxation. The cold war had an homogenizing effect on socialist countries; détente brought out the differences in each country. Hungary and Poland, in this period, witnessed the emergence of revisionism among intellectuals, a commitment to a decentralized, democratic, internationalist form of socialism. The club movement spread rapidly in both countries; thousands listened to Marxist philosophers such as György Lukács in Hungary or Leszek Kolakowski in Poland. The revisionists gained control of the party in both countries and these movements were to lead to the events of October 1956, the revolution in Hungary and the Polish compromise which allowed Gomulka to retain power. Although the reforms in Poland were eventually whittled down, so that the Polish system reverted to conservatism in the 1960s, Gomulka's victory meant that agriculture remained in private hands, there was always more space for intellectuals, and the experience of workers' councils (such an important feature in Hungary and Poland in 1956) was to inform subsequent movements. In the GDR and Czechoslovakia, Albania and Romania, de-Stalinization was much more limited – indeed the Stalinist regimes established in those countries were fearful of the warm wind blowing from Moscow.

The Soviet invasion of Hungary in 1956 brought into being what Fejto describes as a 'Holy Alliance' of East European, Soviet and Chinese Stalinists against revisionists and national communism. The 1957 Moscow conference of communist parties reaffirmed the unity of the socialist camp under Soviet leadership. The conference even marked a return to the two-camp strategy of 1948–53. Mao said that communists should not be intimidated by nuclear blackmail. China was a large country with 600 million people. Even if 300 million people died in a nuclear war, 300 million would be left to rebuild socialism. The Yugoslavs could not sign the final declaration and

Soviet–Yugoslav relations rapidly deteriorated. The most 'spectacular victory', as Fetjo puts it, for the Holy Alliance was the execution of Imre Nagy and three of his friends on 17 June 1958. 'The Peking press rejoiced; Prague, Sofia, and Tirana also expressed satisfaction. Poland bowed its head. Hungary, overwhelmed by the loss of some of her best sons, was stupified, humiliated and impotent.'[43]

Subsequently, liberalization was renewed, but more cautiously within the framework of consolidation of the socialist bloc, through the activation of multinational institutions like the Warsaw Pact and Comecon. This was the period of the emerging Sino–Soviet split, expressed as an ideological dispute about 'peaceful coexistence' versus 'anti-imperialist struggle'. Albania sided with China as a way of preserving its autonomy, and Romania steered a middle course. Romania was able, in 1963, to defeat proposals to transform Comecon into a supranational planning authority, fearful that this would lead to a division of labour between northern industrial socialist economies and southern agricultural economies.

The second half of the 1950s was a period of rapid economic growth, probably both because of the reforms, especially in agriculture, and because of the delayed effects of the investment drive of the Stalinist period. (If the statistics are to be believed, these were the highest growth rates ever achieved by any country, capitalist or socialist, in history). Khrushchev was confident that socialism would eventually win the competition with capitalism. However, in the early 1960s, growth began to slow down, especially the growth of real wages.

From the mid-1960s, there was a new wave of reforms which affected all the East European countries. It was initiated by Kosygin's reforms in 1965 (although the GDR's New Economic System was introduced earlier in 1963). The reforms of the 1960s went much further than the reforms of the 1950s, especially in Hungary and Yugoslavia. Indeed these two countries could no longer be described as command or centralized economies: the reforms introduced important elements of market regulation. However, with the exception of Czechoslovakia and Yugoslavia, the reforms were largely confined to the economic sphere and efforts were made to reduce the political fall-out from reform. The Hungarians stressed that the New Economic Mechanism introduced on 1 January 1968 was merely

concerned with raising the level of economic efficiency. Indeed
several commentators suggest that political leaders in Eastern Europe
explicitly envisaged that increased consumption could be a sort of
substitute for political rights – a way of keeping the population
quiescent.[44] Of course, economic reform did necessitate a certain
degree of political liberalization – an open debate about economic
policy, for example, a greater tolerance and involvement of intellectuals.

In Yugoslavia, the economic reform was the consequence of a
political struggle which resulted in the defeat of the neo-Stalinists and
the removal of Rankovic, Tito's Beria, the creator and chief of the
Yugoslav secret police. The events of 1966–7 have sometimes been
described as the second Yugoslav revolution.[45]

In Czechoslovakia, economic reform was explicitly linked to
political reform. Political reform was seen as essential to overcome
the obstacles to economic reform and, likewise, economic reform
was seen as the basis for political reform, for movement towards a
pluralistic system. The Prague Spring was watched with alarm in
Poland (then in the throes of a new anti-Semitic purge), the GDR and
the Soviet Union. The bloc intervention, by five members of the
Warsaw Pact, marked the beginning of a new period of 'normalization', which was to affect the whole of Eastern Europe.

Szelényi, in a recent article, describes the mood among East
European intellectuals during the 1960s.[46] It was an expectant
mood, a time when intellectuals believed that the irrationalities of
Stalinism would give way to expert intellectual advice. It was the
time when Lukács coined the phrase: 'Even the worst socialism is
better than the best capitalism.' A book called *Civilisation at the
Crossroads* by Radovan Richta was popular at the time (it seems to
have been an Eastern equivalent of Anthony Crosland's *The Future
of Socialism*, which had expressed the Atlanticist consensus a few
years earlier). It was, says Szelényi, 'a forceful apologia for the
scientific-technological revolution and a call for a new world order in
which neither greedy capitalists nor incompetent bureaucrats can
prevent competent and unselfish experts from doing their job and
running society'.[47]

The consolidation of the Eastern bloc

During the Stalinist period, relations between the Soviet Union and the East Central European countries were strictly bilateral. In the period immediately after Stalin's death, Khrushchev seems to have envisaged a more consensual relationship among the socialist countries; this was implied by his use of the term proletarian internationalism.[48] After the intervention in Hungary in 1956, the Soviet Union (together with the new East European elites) developed various multilateral forms of coordination and control.

Comecon, the Council for Mutual Economic Assistance or CMEA, was founded in 1947 as a reaction to the establishment of OEEC (the agency responsible for Marshall Aid). Because of the statist nature of central plans, relations between centrally planned economies are even today mainly bilateral; multilateral negotiations are rather cumbersome. However, in the late 1950s Comecon did begin to play a more active role. This involved greater planning of trade, the exchange of raw materials and food for Comecon manufactured products, and bloc-wide infrastructure projects such as electricity grids and oil pipelines.

The Warsaw Pact was created in 1955. It had been widely interpreted as a diplomatic manoeuvre in response to the rearmament of West Germany. The Soviet Union offered to disband the Warsaw Pact if the West would disband Nato. Between 1955 and 1958, East European armies were reduced (reportedly by some 2.5 million) and, after 1956, the Hungarian army was virtually disbanded. Soviet officers returned to the Soviet Union or left the armed forces.

From the early 1960s, East European armies were increasingly integrated in a Warsaw Pact command system, with its headquarters housed in the Soviet Ministry of Defence. At that time, a new Soviet military doctrine was formulated, which was published in Sokolovsky's *Military Strategy* in 1962, and which explicitly called for the incorporation of East European armies in joint theatre actions under Soviet command.[49] During this period, joint exercises were initiated and Christopher Jones has, rather convincingly, argued that these exercises became a key mechanism for exercising political control, requiring a united command system, standardization of weaponry, elaboration of common doctrine, an integrated system of political administration, and officer training. He suggests that joint exercises are rehearsals for intervention, as in fact happened in Czechoslovakia in 1968.[50]

But it can be argued that even though the Warsaw Pact represented a form of direct military control, as evidenced in 1968 or later in the manoeuvres on Poland's borders in 1981, it also represented a form of psychological control. What the Warsaw Pact achieved was the reproduction of the imaginary war within a bloc-wide framework. Fear of the enemy which legitimized the imposition of Stalinism in the late 1940s was concretized in joint preparations for war. The Warsaw Pact constituted a common conception about the nature of the East–West conflict, a shared vision of a future war, which helped to weld together the political (and military) outlook of Warsaw Pact establishments.

The Warsaw Pact was never as effective as a discourse as Nato. Much more important in holding the East together were interparty relations, dominated by the Communist Party of the Soviet Union. Party control within individual countries, through party committees at workplaces, schools, barracks, etc., the parallel party bureaucracy, and the nomenklatura system (through which the party controls key appointments) was linked to a network of consultation, exchange and negotiation between the East European parties, the training of bloc personnel in the Soviet Union, joint discussions about ideology, frequent meetings of party secretaries, as well as connections between the security apparatuses and joint intelligence gathering. Interparty relations constituted ideological, physical, and indeed economic, forms of coercion. The military interventions, the real wars, of 1956 and 1968 could be said to have represented a failure or a breakdown in the functioning of party mechanisms as well as in the indirect forms of control represented by the imaginary war.

Coercion and instability

When advocates of the 'long peace' argue that it has brought stability, they are really referring only to a handful of Western capitalist advanced industrial societies. In contrast to Western Europe, East Central Europe was *not* stable. Or rather, periods of apparent stability were deceptive; they were really periods of suppressed instability. East Central Europe, in fact, experienced both war and brutal repression. Stalinism was not able to draw strength from any cultural tradition in Central European history as it may have done in Russia. What is more, it was imposed by an outside occupying power. Any relaxation of military or police coercion resulted in social and political upheaval, and this produced, in turn, a renewal of coercive measures for fear that the upheaval might challenge the Soviet regime itself, either because it would contribute to military insecurity, or because it might offer a more attractive model of socialism, or because it might result in the revelation of past political crimes. But the very *instability* of East Central Europe was the reason for reproducing the military and police apparatus, for continued preparations for war, and for real wars.

Notes

1 Fernando Claudin, *The Communist Movement: From Comintern to Cominform* (Penguin, 1975), p. 599.
2 As Bahro puts it, the socialist idea became 'the fate of the revolutionaries who bore it into Russia. Its perversion into a new ideology of domination, into the catechism of a modern state church, reached its logical culmination in the annihilation of the old Bolshevik vanguard by Stalin's power apparatus. The historical course of the Soviet Union was a subjective intellectual and moral tragedy for all Communists who can be taken seriously at the intellectual level.' *The Alternative in Eastern Europe* (New Left Books, 1978), p. 21.
3 See, particularly, ibid.; George Konrad and Ivan Szelényi, *Intellectuals on the Road to Class Power* (Harvester, 1979); Ferenc Fehér, Agnes Heller and György Markus, *Dictatorship Over Needs: An Analysis of Soviet Societies* (Basil Blackwell, 1983).
4 Perry Anderson, *Lineages of the Absolutist State* (New Left Books, 1974).
5 Bahro uses the term 'semi-Asiatic'. The use of this term emphasizes the similarity with other Asiatic modes of production, China, India, Egypt, etc., and hence explains the appeal of the Soviet system for Third World countries. The Russian system was semi-Asiatic in the sense that it also

inherited European feudalism. However, the term Asiatic does seem to conceal important differences among the Asian empires. The Moghul empire, for example, was much more decentralized and pluralistic than the Chinese empire. For Konrad and Szelényi, in *Intellectuals*, the emphasis on Asiatic as opposed to European forms of development, which they describe as traditional redistributive systems, arises from the influence on the East of Turkish and Tartar waves of expansion. This resulted in the adoption, at least by Russia, of some of the organizational forms of the Tartar military empire. Anderson puts more emphasis on the Western influence as a result of Swedish expansion.

6 'Ivan the Terrible, for example, who finally broke the power of the Tartar khans and had himself crowned Tsar of All Russia, decimated and plundered the hereditary aristocracy and organised a part of the service nobility into a modern political police; with the surplus products collected by the State he established foundries, arsenals and shipyards, and manned them not with wage workers but with serfs and forced labour.' Konrad and Szelényi, *Intellectuals*, p. 93.

7 Jenö Szücs, 'Three historical regions of Europe', in John Keane, ed., *Civil Society and the State* (Verso, 1988).

8 Milan Kundera, 'The tragedy of Central Europe', *New York Review of Books*, xxxi:7, 26 April, 1984.

9 This point is made by Istvan Rev, 'Local autonomy or centralism – when was the original sin committed?', *International Journal of Urban and Regional Research*, 8:1, March 1984.

10 Schumpeter, *Capitalism, Socialism and Democracy* (George Allen and Unwin, 1943).

11 Quoted in Claudin, *Communist Movement*, p. 627.

12 V. I. Lenin, *The State and Revolution* (1918), 2nd edn (Foreign Languages Press, 1970), p. 59, author's emphasis.

13 See *State and Revolution*:

And the dictatorship of the proletariat, i.e. the organisation of the vanguard of the oppressed as the ruling class for the purpose of suppressing the oppressors, cannot result merely in an expansion of democracy. *Simultaneously* with an immense expansion of democracy, which *for the first time* becomes democracy for the poor, democracy for the people, and not democracy for the money bags, the dictatorship of the proletariat imposes a series of restrictions on the freedom of the oppressors, the exploiters, the capitalists. We must suppress them in order to free humanity from wage slavery, their resistance must be crushed by force; it is clear, where there is violence there is no freedom and no democracy. (p. 105, author's emphasis)

14 Quoted in Bahro, *Alternative*, p. 41.

15 Konrad and Szelényi say that those bureaucrats who survived the

Bolshevik revolution 'found themselves in the comical situation of Monsieur Jourdain, who discovered to his astonishment that he had been speaking prose all his life. However much they loathed the Reds, the bureaucrats who had run the war economy could not help realising, once the storm had passed, that they had been thinking all along in terms of an expanded rational redistribution.' *Intellectuals*, p. 101.

16 'Just think of the picture the old socialists painted,' writes Bahro, 'the dynamic of social and economic development, and the effort of all in solidarity for the common good! That same "great beginning" which Lenin so enthusiastically described when the workers on the Moscow–Kazan railway started their first revolutionary *subbotnik* [weekend work]. This was precisely the ultimate foundation for our confidence in the superiority of the socialist mode of production, our obstinate persistence in the conviction that we would "catch up with and overtake" capitalism in a relatively short period.' *Alternative*, p. 203.

17 Party congresses took place much less frequently. Five years elapsed between the 17th Party Congress and the 18th Party Congress and 13 years were to elapse between the 18th and the 19th. Of the 1,966 delegates to the 17th Party Congress in 1934, 1,108 were expelled from the Party, arrested or worse. Of the 139 members and alternates elected to the central committee in 1934, 98 were to be executed. In 1937–8, at the height of the terror, one-third of party members were purged. See Adam B. Ulam, *A History of Soviet Russia* (Praeger, 1976).

18 Oskar Lange, 'Role of planning in socialistic economy', lecture delivered on 19 November 1957 at the Institute for International Politics and Economics in Belgrade, in Oskar Lange, ed., *Problems of Political Economy of Socialism* (Peoples Publishing House, New Delhi, 1962), p. 18.

19 Ibid., p. 19

20 See Alexander Yakovlev, *The Aim of a Lifetime: The Story of Alexander Yakovlev, Designer of the YAK fighter plane* (Progress Publishers, Moscow, 1972).

21 Yakovlev says: 'If it were not a Socialist country but pre-revolutionary Russia, it would collapse, like Poland, France and other bourgeois countries in Europe.' Ibid., p. 144.

22 Alec Nove, *An Economic History of the USSR*, 3rd edn (Penguin, 1984), p. 274.

23 Isaac Deutscher imagines a conversation between Stalin and the ghost of the last tsar:

'Your end is approaching,' the phantom whispers. 'Exploiting the chaos of war, you destroyed my throne. Now the chaos of another war is going to engulf you.'

'You dethroned monarchs, you really learn nothing,' the living man replies. 'Surely you were defeated not by the war itself, but by the Bolshevik Party. To be sure, we used the conditions created by war to our advantage but . . .'

'Are you quite sure,' the ghost interrupts, 'that no opposition is going to use a new war for its advantage? Remember the terrible turmoil in Petersburg when the news came that the Germans had captured Riga? What if the Germans appear in Riga again, or in Kiev, in the Caucasus or at the gates of Moscow?

'I am telling you, you had the formidable Bolshevik Party against you, while I have exiled Trotsky and crushed all my other opponents.'

The Phantom roars with laughter. 'In 1914–17 did I not keep you in Siberia and were not Lenin and Trotsky in exile . . .' (Isaac Deutscher, *Stalin* (1949) (Penguin, 1982), p. 373)

24 Moshe Lewin argues that the terror was a product of the frustrations and ineptitude of the government. He says that the 1930s were a period of 'spontaneity and drift', that the government was unable in practice to impose control and direct society. The 'authorities complained that people did not go where asked, found ways of doing things their own way, exploited any loophole to play or outplay the system, and helped themselves through networks of friends, acquaintances, briberies and adventurous risks.' Moshe Lewin, *The Gorbachev Phenomenon: A Historical Interpretation* (Radius, 1988), p. 27.

25 Towards the end of his life, Stalin's immediate entourage was filled with plots and counterplots and his suspicions correspondingly grew. 'He would look at you,' Khrushchev recalls, 'and say: "Why are your eyes so shifty today?" or "Why are you turning today and avoiding looking me directly in the eyes?".' Quoted in Deutscher, *Stalin*, p. 596.

26 This was a point made by George Kennan in the 'long telegram'. He argued that the sense of military insecurity 'had, indeed, little to do with conditions outside of Russia: that it arises mainly from basic inner-Russian necessities which existed before recent war and exist today':

At the bottom of the Kremlin's neurotic view of world affairs is traditional and instinctive Russian sense of insecurity. Originally this was insecurity of a peaceful agricultural people trying to live on vast exposed plain in neighbour-hood of fierce nomadic people. To this was added, as Russia came into contact with economically advanced West, fear of more competent, more powerful, more highly organised societies in that area. But this latter type of insecurity was one which afflicted rather Russian rulers than Russian people; for Russian rulers have invariably sensed that their rule was relatively archaic in form, fragile and artificial in its psychological foundation, unable to stand comparison with political systems of Western countries. For this reason they have always feared foreign penetration, feared direct contact between western world and their own, feared what would happen if Russians learned truth about world without or if foreigners learned truth about world within. And they have learned to seek security only in patient but deadly struggle for total destruction of rival power, never in compacts and comprises with it. ('Telegraphic message of February 22 1946', reproduced in George Kennan, *Memoirs 1925–50* (Hutchinson, 1968), pp. 549–50.

27 Even Trotsky argued that the despotism of the state was a result of 'the iron necessity to give birth to and support a privileged minority so long as it is impossible to guarantee genuine equality'. Leon Trotsky, *Revolution Betrayed: What is the Soviet Union and Where is it Going?* (Faber, 1937), p. 55.

28 Stephen Cohen, *Rethinking the Soviet Experience* (Oxford University Press, 1985).

29 The French and Italian communists vehemently criticized the Yugoslavs at the first Cominform meeting, presumably with the implicit backing of Stalin and his ideologue Zhdanov. For an account of the meeting, see Claudin, *Communist Movement*, pp. 381–5.

30 For a full account, see Joyce and Gabriel Kolko, *The Limits of Power* (Harper and Row, 1972), ch. 70.

31 Kennan recalls a discussion with the councillor of the Polish embassy in Washington in 1944:

I came away from this discussion with the strong feeling that while Stalin's hostile actions towards the government-in-exile were no doubt partly attributable simply to Russia's improved military and political position, they were not fully explicable except in terms of an acute embarrassment, on the Soviet side, over excesses perpetrated by the Soviet police authorities against the Poles in 1939 and 1940, and a resulting determination that there should be in Poland in the postwar period no government that would have either the inclination or the ability to probe uncomfortably into the past and to make a public issue of these actions of the Soviet authorities ... What was bothering Stalin was not, as many people tended to assume, just the desire to have a 'friendly government' on the other side of the Polish frontier. What was bothering him was the need for collaboration of any future Polish political authority in repressing evidences and memories of actions by Soviet police authorities in the period 1939–41, for which no adequate and respectable excuse could be found. It was clear that a Polish authority that could be depended on to give such collaboration could never be other than a Communist one under Soviet control. (*Memoirs 1925–50*, p. 203)

32 A meeting of communists in Belgrade decided to send Stalin the following telegram: 'We believe sincerely in you. We believe that you will do all in your power to silence this unjust accusation against our Party and Central Committee.' Claudin, *Communist Movement*, p. 506.

33 Quoted in ibid., p. 517.

34 Ibid.

35 Milan Šimečka, 'From class obsessions to dialogue: détente and the changing political culture of Eastern Europe', in Mary Kaldor, Gerard Holden and Richard Falk, eds, *The New Détente* (Verso, 1989).

36 Thad P. Alton, 'East European GNPs: origins of products, final uses, rates of growth and international comparisons', in *East European Economies: Slow Growth in the 1980s*, vol. 1: *Economic Policy and Performance*, Joint Economic Committee, 90th Congress, 1st Session (Washington DC, 1985).

37 Michael Kaser, *Comecon: Integration Problems of the Planned Economies* (Oxford University Press, 1967):

Industrialisation on the Soviet model was embodied in the objectives of a socialist society, and because the Soviet authorities sought only to introduce their established pattern, any attempt at national adaptation was repressed . . . In Poland, for example, the techniques used to draw up the Three-Year Plan, based upon a harmonious growth of consumption and investment, were replaced in 1949 by the much cruder Soviet procedure, which yielded a Six-Year Plan comprising a concentration of industrial resources on capital goods, on the one hand, and on agricultural targets which were no more than fantasy, on the other. (p. 18)

38 Istvan Rev, 'The anti-ecological nature of centralisation', in Mary Kaldor, Gerard Holden and Richard Falk, eds, *New Détente*.

39 Malcolm Mackintosh, 'The Warsaw treaty organisation: a history', in David Holloway and Jane M. O. Sharpe, eds, *The Warsaw Pact: Alliance in Transition?* (Macmillan, 1984), p. 142.

40 According to Gomulka, the post-1956 Polish leader:

The cult of personality is a certain system which prevailed in the Soviet Union and which was grafted on to probably all Communist Parties . . . The essence of the system consisted in the fact that an individual hierarchic ladder of cults was created . . . In the bloc of socialist states it was Stalin who stood at the top of this hierarchic ladder of cults. All those who stood on lower rungs of the ladder bowed their heads before him . . . The first secretaries of the Central Committee of the Parties of the various countries who sat on the second rung of the ladder of the cult of personality, in turn, donned the robes of infallibility and wisdom. But their cult radiated only on the territory of the countries where they stood at the top of the national cult ladder. This cult could be called only a reflected brilliance, a borrowed light. It shone as the moon does. (Quoted in Karen Dawisha, *Eastern Europe: Gorbachev and Reform* (Cambridge University Press, 1988), p. 71)

41 François Fejto, *A History of the People's Democracies* (1969) (Penguin, 1977), p. 25.

42 The joint Yugoslav–Soviet declaration affirmed:

> Faithfulness to the principles of mutual respect and non-intervention in internal affairs for whatever reason, economic, political, or ideological, because matters of internal organisation, of different social systems, *and different forms of socialist development* remain solely the concern of each country individually.
>
> Acknowledgement of the principle that military blocs heighten international tension, sap the mutual confidence of nations and increase the danger of war. (Quoted in ibid, p. 53, emphasis added)

Some writers suggest that Soviet–Yugoslav reconciliation might have arrested the evolution of Yugoslav socialism towards some sort of social democracy. The conflict between the Yugoslav leadership and Milovan Djilas erupted at this time.

43 Fejto, *History of the People's Democracies*, p. 143.
44 Sarah Terry talks about 'an implied social contract between regime and society whereby the leaderships committed themselves to rising levels of well-being in exchange for the political acquiescence of their populations'. 'The implications of economic and political succession', in *East European Economies: Slow Growth*, vol. 1: *Economic Policy and Performance*, p. 903.
45 Fejto, *History of the People's Democracies*.
46 Ivan Szelényi, 'The prospects and limits of the East European new class project: an auto-critical reflection on the intellectuals and the road to class power', *Politics and Society*, 15:2, 1986–7.
47 Ibid., p. 112.
48 See Margot Light, *The Soviet Theory of International Relations* (Harvester, 1988), ch. 6.
49 *Military Strategy: Soviet Doctrines and Concepts* (Pall Mall, 1963). According to Marshal Iakubovsky in the *Soviet Military Encyclopaedia*:

> One of the most important directions of socialist military cooperation is the coordination of efforts in the further development of military theory and in the working out of a unity of views on the character and methods of waging war on the basis of Marxist-Leninist ideology.
>
> For these purposes business-like contacts have been established among military-scientific institutions; theoretical conferences are regularly conducted and there is a joint working out of military-historical studies. (Quoted in Christopher D. Jones, *Soviet Influence in Eastern Europe: Political Autonomy and the Warsaw Pact* (Praeger, 1981), p. 151)

50 Jones, *Soviet Influence*. Jones also argues that the aim of Warsaw Pact integration is to prevent independent defence policies capable of resisting Soviet intervention. He argues that the development of territorial defence postures in Yugoslavia, Romania and Albania was the basis for

the relative political autonomy of these countries. He cites proposals drawn up by the Gottwald Military Academy in Czechoslovakia for alternative territorially based defence during the Prague Spring as a major reason for the Soviet military intervention. This interpretation has the merit of emphasizing the internal functions of the Warsaw Pact. But it ignores the ideological role of the Warsaw Pact, as defender against external threat, and it neglects broader non-military political resistance. In Yugoslavia, the Soviet Union faced the prospect of military *and* political resistance to Soviet intervention on a broad scale. Romania and Albania were neither militarily nor strategically significant. They were of marginal use in a military defence against a Western threat, real or imagined. They did not offer an alternative model of socialism; on the contrary, they reverted to very disagreeable forms of Stalinism. For an excellent analysis of different interpretations of the Warsaw Pact, see Gerard Holden, *The Warsaw Pact: Soviet Security and Bloc Politics* (UNU/Basil Blackwell, 1989), especially ch. 2.

5

The Making of Atlanticism

If the orthodox historians offer insights into the functioning of the socialist states system, it is the revisionist historians who provide the most convincing clues to an analysis of Atlanticism. The different stories about Western behaviour told by orthodox and revisionist historians can partly be explained in terms of different levels of analysis. The orthodox historians focus on reasons, on why politicians decided to take a particular course of action, and they make use of memoirs, letters, diplomatic archives. The revisionists put more emphasis on causes, underlying socio-economic factors that give rise to a particular set of choices, and they make use of statistics, official documents, etc.

Politicians may have many reasons for the policies they adopt; they may be concerned about the next election or their personal relationship with other world leaders or even, perish the thought, economic self-interest. But whether or not their policies succeed or are followed in a consistent way by subsequent political leaders does depend on causes, on the social, political and economic framework within which they are situated. The 1940s were a period of experiment. The cold war began to settle down into its characteristic pattern in the 1950s. It did so because the cold war, as a political formula, seemed capable of mobilizing a consensus in both the United States and Western Europe (at least the northern part) and thereby reproduced itself through the electoral process and the ties of the alliance.

This does not mean that the reasons are irrelevant. For one thing, reasons are rarely unrelated to causes. The thinking of politicians is shaped by their own social experience, by the public response to their ideas and proposals, or by institutional bias within government, and all these, in turn, will tend to result from or reflect more general social and economic, domestic and international trends.

But more importantly, any particular policy direction is the product of the interaction between reasons and causes, between the subjective and the objective, the particular and the general. The causes, the objective conditions within which politicians operate, define the contours of what is possible. Politicians who step outside these contours are, sooner or later, defeated. Or put another way, policies have to satisfy certain social or economic requirements. Those that fail do not last long. There may, however, be many different ways of succeeding or of keeping within the contours of the possible. And these, in turn, may shape the social and economic requirements, the contours of action, in the future.

In order to understand the success of Atlanticism in the post-war period, it is necessary to describe both the specific economic conjuncture at the end of the Second World War and the participants in the process of creating Atlanticism.

The rise of Fordism

The United States, in the early part of the twentieth century, pioneered a new pattern of industrial development, often known as Fordism, which displaced the craft-based heavy industry pattern of industrial development, associated with railways and steam engines, that characterized the late nineteenth century. Fordism, pioneered by Henry Ford, involved the introduction of mass production techniques using semi-skilled operatives, the spread of relatively cheap manufactured consumer durables, especially automobiles, and the intensive use of energy, especially oil. It arose from the specific cultural, geographical and social context of early twentieth-century America: space, abundance of raw materials, an expanding labour force, relative egalitarianism, opportunity for initiative.

During the first three decades of the twentieth century, the United States achieved spectacular rates of economic growth. By 1929, the United States accounted for over 40 per cent of world manufactured output. The US produced over 2.9 million motor vehicles, compared with 211,000 in France, 182,000 in Britain and 117,000 in Germany. However, the depression of the 1930s affected the United States more severely than any other country. In 1938, the US accounted for less than 30 per cent of world manufactured output. The experience of the depression was to shape profoundly the outlook of politicians in the post-war period.

The depression can be explained in terms of a disjuncture between the pattern of industrial development and the political institutions. Economic change had outrun political change. This was expressed in a disjuncture between production and consumption, both domestically within the United States and internationally. Domestically, the United States faced what Rostow has called a 'double structural adjustment'.[1] On the one hand, there was reduced purchasing power by farmers and from foreign markets on account of the fall in the prices of food and raw materials in the late 1920s, and this was exacerbated by the collapse of the 1920s personal credit boom and growing protectionism in the 1930s. On the other hand, there was greatly increased productive capacity as a result of the introduction of Fordist methods of work organization, especially in the new leading sectors, automobiles, chemicals and electricity.

Internationally, the problem was that although the centre of economic gravity had shifted to the United States, this was not reflected in international economic relations, shaped by the distribution of political power before 1914. Kindleberger has argued that the depression was caused by the absence of a hegemonic power capable of guaranteeing a liberal international economy; Britain was no longer able to carry out this role and the United States was unwilling.[2] Indeed, during the 1930s Britain was able to use the privileged role of sterling and a system of imperial preference to protect the British economy from the worst effects of the depression.

The Second World War temporarily resolved the problem with a huge expansion of demand as a result of the domestic war effort and of the lend-lease programme. The American government can be said to have chanced on a solution to pre-war problems during the war and this may be why post-war institutions drew so heavily on the experience of the Second World War. After the war, pent-up consumer demand ensured the full employment of capacity, at least for a couple of years. Europe, of course, was devastated. Whereas US gross national product increased by 65 per cent in the ten years 1938 to 1948, the combined gross national product of the main West European countries *declined* by 13 per cent. And this figure conceals wide differences between countries. In 1948, GNP of the Western zones of Germany was less than half what it had been in 1938 (see Table 5.1).

Table 5.1   GNP of Western Europe and the United States at constant prices, 1938–50

	1938	1948	1950
Belgium	100	115	124
France	100	45	64
West Germany	100	45	64
Italy	100	92	104
Netherlands	100	114	127
Norway	100	122	131
Sweden	100	133	148
Switzerland	100	125	131
UK	100	106	114
Western Europe	100	87	102
United States	100	165	179

Source: Herman van der Wee, *Prosperity and Upheaval, 1945–1980* (Pelican, 1987), p. 30.

At the end of the war, lend-lease was abruptly terminated and the United Nations programme for relief and rehabilitation was phased out. All the West European countries desperately needed American assistance to buy equipment, food, etc. necessary for reconstruction. Britain, in particular, had run down gold and dollar reserves during the war and had liquidated a large proportion of its overseas investment and so was forced to request a loan from the United States after the termination of lend-lease. The 'dollar shortage' in Europe, and indeed in the rest of the world, was to persist well into the 1950s. By the late 1940s, it was clear to many economists that a dose of government spending both at home and abroad (in order to stimulate foreign markets) was needed in order to overcome the over-capacity of the American economy. This was achieved by cold war policies.

The revisionist historians explain the cold war primarily in terms of the expansionist tendencies of the capitalist economic system, arising from the inherent tendency to excess capacity. This does not mean that the politicians were necessarily expansionist, concerned to expand power or markets. The politicians had the task of managing these tendencies. They may not have been aware that this was what they were doing, although many of them do seem to have had some grasp of the economic problems they faced. The point was that whatever the reason for adopting a particular policy, only those policies which resolved the economic problem were capable of succeeding.

It was certainly not the only way post-war economic problems could have been solved. Domestic demand in the United States could also have been boosted by social spending, as many New Dealers such as Leon Keyserling, chairman of the Council of Economic Advisers, would have preferred. And regulation of the international economy might have been undertaken by a supranational authority, as Keynes suggested with his international clearing union proposal in 1943, with aid channelled through the United Nations system. Such an approach might have prevented many, but not all, of the dire economic troubles we face today.

If there is a gap in the revisionist argument, it is the explanation of why the cold war prevailed and not the Keynesian or Rooseveltian alternative. Orthodox, and post-revisionist, historians would say that the answer is the Soviet threat – 'a new awareness of the global balance of power and the effect recent developments in the technology of warfare might have on it'.[3] But the question is, why did Western leaders take an alarmist view of the Soviet threat, given the exhaustion and devastation experienced by the Soviet Union, as a result of the war, and why did they fix on a military response? It is true that the Soviet Union enjoyed a substantial conventional preponderance in Central Europe. But these forces were mainly garrison forces, there to keep order in Eastern Europe or else because they had not yet been demobilized.[4] Dulles said on several occasions that he did not expect a Soviet invasion and nor did other 'responsible leaders'. All the evidence, including that provided by orthodox historians, suggests that the Soviet Union did not intend to expand beyond the occupation zone established during the Second World War.[5] The same view of Soviet intentions prevailed in Europe, which was after all much closer to the East–West border. Even after a Soviet military build-up in the early 1950s, American officials expressed concerns that there were in Europe 'officials who acted or prepared to act as though the Soviet menace were actually on the wane'.[6]

There were, of course, powerful communist parties in France, Italy and Greece which were pro-Soviet. But that does not explain the militarization of the cold war. Why did the military conception of national security come to predominate in American and, later, European thinking? Why was the perception of the Soviet Union as an external threat to prevail over other perceptions of the international situation?

US politics

Alan Wolfe suggests that the answer is to be found in the domestic political complexion of the United States immediately after the war. He argues that anti-communist ideology combined with rising military spending was the only way American political leaders could persuade Congress and the American public to support a global role. Indeed, he argues that there was a gap between public rhetoric and private assessment that continued right up to the Reagan presidency.[7]

Wolfe argues, first of all, that anti-communism allowed for a bipartisan consensus among Democrats and Republicans. The first two years after the war were marked by a conservative backlash. The Republicans did well in the 1946 congressional elections and were able to reverse some of the policies of the New Deal era. (Most strikingly, the 1946 Taft–Hartley Act reversed hard-won rights to industrial action.) Truman was not expected to win the 1948 election. During this period, American foreign policy was marked by withdrawal – massive demobilization and the termination of wartime aid programmes. The tough negotiations on the British loan – the insistence that Britain reintroduce sterling convertibility and abandon imperial preferences – illustrate the mood. Anti-communism was a way of winning the Republicans over to globalism and Wolfe points out that the term 'national security' had a clear link with the New Deal's conception of 'social security': 'The Cold War and the New Deal existed within the same language of discourse; both demanded action by government and both required planning. Intellectuals needed to come to Washington to organize both crusades. Both were responses to dire emergency – economic chaos in the one, international chaos in the other.'[8]

The need to create a bipartisan consensus was in part the consequence of the political structure of the US, which was better at expressing special interests than generating a unified approach to policy. The problem as Wolfe puts it was how to 'lodge a twentieth century empire within an eighteenth century polity'.[9] On the one hand, military spending did mobilize the support of special interests – Congressmen with military bases in their districts, the aircraft industry lobby, etc. (Although most historians of the period including revisionists dismiss the importance of a military-industrial complex prior to 1950, my own view is that the aircraft industry, faced with the prospect of collapse after the war, did in fact play a key role in the decision to double aircraft appropriations in 1948, and there were further increases in the following year.)[10] On the other hand, in US history, war had provided, in Alan Wolfe's words, 'a sufficient state of emergency to make governance possible. For all postwar presidents who aspired to activism, a permanent state of war – which is, domestically, what the Cold War promised – was perhaps the only way to justify an agenda emphasizing policy coordination and planning in a political system organized for brokerage and patronage.'[11]

What Wolfe does not explain, and it needs explaining, is why American political leaders were able to play on anti-communism. It may be that public rhetoric differed from private assessment, and there is a good deal of evidence to show that the Soviet threat was exaggerated over the years for domestic political purposes.[12] Nevertheless, anti-communism seems to have appealed to something deep in the American psyche. Although political leaders may not have shared the public emotionalism that was displayed in the aftermath of the McMahon Act of 1946 (which was passed to keep the atomic bomb a secret) and during the McCarthy period, leaders like Truman, Dulles and Eisenhower do seem to have had a fairly crude view of communism (blanketing together all forms of totalitarianism) and were certainly unwilling to tolerate communists in government.[13] (Stalin also had a crude view of capitalism; his failure to distinguish Nazism from democracy explains his pre-war flirtation with Hitler as well as the ease with which the wartime alliance was transformed into the cold war.)

Anti-communism as a form of 'mass hysteria', to use George Kennan's words, which it was to become in the early 1950s, was certainly quite distinct from, say, the anti-communism of many Europeans who were familiar with communist parties and the nature of Stalinism. It seems to have had little to do, in fact, with any rational assessment of the Soviet Union – indeed, as Kennan pointed out, it 'blinded people to the real nature of our national problems'.[14] William Graf has drawn a distinction between rational and irrational anti-communism, or regressive and progressive anti-communism.[15] American anti-communism was irrational and regressive. The American Communist party was tiny, although it did have some positions of influence within the trade unions at the end of the war. Yet anti-communism seems to have contributed, not to the defence of democracy, but to intolerance and repression. Kennan, shocked by the treatment of many honest and reputable foreign service officers, comments on the way in which McCarthyism involved:

a rousing anti-intellectualism, a mistrust of thought, a suspicion of education, a suspicion of the effect of foreign contacts and foreign influences on the individual personality, a demand for conformity within the framework of provincial chauvinism ... It seemed to me that I sensed, in these tendencies, a primitivism and an underlying brutality that threatened not just freedom of thought in the political sense but the cultural progress of the country generally.[16]

Anti-communism seems to have touched some deep sense of insecurity among Americans. One can only speculate about its causes. Was it to do with the fact that so many Americans had come to the United States to escape religious persecution in Europe and were subconsciously fearful, even perhaps after several generations, that the Atlantic Ocean would no longer protect them from their past? Was it to do with the insecurity of immigrants in a new country and lack of rootedness? Or with the sheer size of the United States, the difficulty of establishing an identity in such a large country.

Whatever the sources of American anti-communism, it is worth noting that it was, in some way, bound up with the atomic bomb. The decision to keep the bomb a secret, expressed in the McMahon Act of 1946, seems to have triggered the first post-war wave of anti-communism, the search for spies and traitors who might reveal the secret. The detonation of a Soviet bomb and the launch of Sputnik in 1957 seems to have had a similar effect. Robert Jay Lifton talks about the 'mythological combination of secrecy and security'.[17] American presidents were preoccupied with the 'psychological balance of power' (Eisenhower) as well as fear of humiliation (Kennedy). The acquisition of countless nuclear weapons in the 1950s was supposed to augment this 'psychological balance of power'. It seems almost obvious in retrospect that the psychological balance of power was directed at Americans' own sense of insecurity and that fear of humiliation was humiliation in the eyes of fellow Americans.

Kennan argues that the American government did not create anti-communism. But successive administrations failed to control or stop the phenomenon. It was, therefore, to leave 'a lasting impact on American political life. For two decades in to the future there would not be a President who would not stand in a certain terror of the anti-Communist right wing of the political spectrum and would not temper his actions with a view to placating it and averting its possible hostility'.[18] The point could be put a little differently. Successive American leaders made use of anti-communism to justify their global policies and, in so doing, unleashed an ideology that was to provide a foundation for the cold war. They appealed to some primeval instincts, as weak politicians have often done, which may have been better left buried.

Except in West Germany, anti-communism never reached the same proportions in Europe – although it was strongest in those countries where a communist threat was least. It is the anti-communism it confronted as well as distance that partly explain the left's apologia for the Soviet system – it seemed the only way to counter anti-communism. And indeed, precisely because the Soviet system was walled up behind the protective bricks of the cold war, there was no reason why the left's view of what was happening in the East should have been any more or less realistic than the view of the irrational right.

Anti-communist rhetoric was to be a hallmark of the Eisenhower administration which came to power on 1 January 1953. However, Eisenhower was a fiscal conservative and never accepted the Keynesian ideas that inspired NSC-68, the document that advocated a military build-up shortly before the outbreak of the Korean war. His 'new look' strategy which emphasized the role of nuclear weapons and the US willingness to counter any threat with nuclear retaliation was viewed as a way of reducing the American conventional military commitment to Europe and the cost of America's military capabilities. Throughout the 1950s, unemployment in the United States remained high.

West European politics

European domestic politics were also very important in explaining the cold war, for rather different reasons.

If the domestic American political scene shifted to the right in the aftermath of the Second World War, the opposite happened in Europe. From around 1943 to 1947, Europe was in the grip of what might be described as a transcontinental revolutionary mood. West European establishments had, during the wartime period, been utterly discredited by appeasement or collaboration. The overwhelming victory of the Labour party in Britain in 1945 was the first public intimation of what was happening. The pattern of left-wing victories was to be repeated all over Western Europe, and most post-war governments consisted of centre–left coalitions in which left-leaning Christian parties joined with Socialist and Communist parties. (Indeed, American distrust of socialism was certainly one factor in the unwillingness to grant the loan to Britain in 1945.) And in these first two years, most governments introduced policies of nationalization, welfare and planning.

New phenomena in the post-war period were the Christian Democrat parties in Germany, Italy, the Netherlands, Belgium and France (under the name Mouvement Républicaine Populaire – MRP). These were to replace the establishment parties of the pre-war period and, even today, include a range of political opinion.

The nature of the left parties varied in different parts of Europe. In historical terms, the north–south divide is perhaps as important as the east–west divide. The southern European countries were largely agrarian, Catholic, ancient market economies with rather weak states (of course the Orthodox church is important in Greece). France and Italy cross the north–south divide, which is an important factor in their internal political life, especially in Italy. All the southern European countries had large communist parties. (These were, of course, suppressed in fascist Spain and Portugal.) In Greece, Italy and France, the communist parties had played a central role in the resistance and, consequently, gained enormously in popularity. It was determination to hold on to what they had gained in the resistance that led to the civil war in Greece. That this did not happen in France and Italy, where the resistance liberated large parts of the country, may have been due to Stalin's anxiety to cooperate with the British and Americans. In the French elections of October 1945, the Communist party won 26.2 per cent of the vote, and in November 1946 this vote increased to 28.2 per cent. In Italy, the Communists won 19 per cent of the vote in 1946. In these countries, also, the Socialist parties tended to be more Marxist and intellectual than the worker parties of the north.

The onset of the cold war effectively brought about the disenfranchisement of Communists and of left-wing Socialists, like the Nenni Socialists in Italy, who opposed the cold war. The Communists were manoeuvred out of the French and Italian cabinets in early 1947 and, at least in the Italian case, this *was* the direct result of American pressure.[19] Communist-led strikes in France and Italy in the autumn of 1947 were brutally repressed. The onset of the cold war also split the trade union movements in France and Italy along East–West lines.

Although France and Italy participated in all the initiatives which led up to the formation of Nato, there was, presumably as a result of domestic pressure, somewhat greater circumspection about an overt anti-Soviet position. Bidault, the French foreign minister, was anxious during the Marshall Plan negotiations not to be seen to be excluding the Soviet Union. Subsequently, it was France that took the initiatives for the establishment of the European Coal and Steel Community, which was to be the forerunner of the European Community. The Americans supported this initiative both because it was a way of integrating the Western zones of Germany into the West European economy and because it was a way of unifying the European market and contributing to economic liberalization. All the same, and this was in the minds of the instigators – Schuman, who replaced Bidault as foreign minister, and Jean Monnet – the construction of a Franco-German relationship and the economic integration of the 'lands of Charlemagne' (as De Gaulle had expressed it during the war) did constitute a continental counterweight to the United States within the Atlantic alliance. This was to become important during the 1970s and 1980s.

In north-western Europe – Scandinavia, Britain and the Benelux countries – the dominant forces of the left were Social Democratic or Labour parties. Especially in Britain and the Benelux countries, these parties were labourist and Fabian. By labourist, I mean that they represented the industrial working classes and were primarily interested in getting a better deal for workers. In so far as they adopted intellectual socialist ideas, these tended to be Fabian – aimed at practical policies to be implemented by a socialist parliamentary majority.[20] Although there had been in all these parties pacifist international wings strongly dominated by the liberalism of an earlier era – and this was undoubtedly responsible for example, for Labour's commitment to the independence of India – in general, these parties were not much interested in foreign policy, which made them susceptible to the advice of permanent officials. What is more, among the leadership of these parties there was a strongly nationalistic bent – they were, after all, furthering the interests of a national working class – and this inclined them towards the preservation of empires, especially in Britain and the Netherlands. Ernest Bevin, Labour's foreign secretary and perhaps the single most influential person in the evolution of the cold war in the late 1940s, had proposed in 1938, in an article in his union journal, the creation of a European Commonwealth that would pool colonial territories. That 'would give us greater security than we get trying to maintain the old balance of power'.[21]

It was determination to retain Britain's great-power status that lay behind the decision to acquire the atomic bomb.[22] Likewise, in the case of Greece and Turkey, Bevin's concern was strategic rather than political. Like Churchill, he considered it vital that the Near East be part of the British sphere of influence in order to control access to the British empire. It must be remembered that, even in its impoverished post-war state, Britain was still, at that time in 1946, the second largest industrial power and its empire was still intact.

These Social Democratic and Labour parties of north-west Europe were also strongly anti-communist, mainly as a result of their experience with communist parties and their commitment to democracy. Their anti-communism can perhaps be described as rational, although undoubtedly Bevin tended to exaggerate, perhaps for the benefit of the Americans. By all accounts, Bevin tended to treat the Soviet Union as a breakaway communist trade union.[23] These parties, and more especially the British Labour party, played a central role in drawing the United States into global and European politics. First, the British issued an ultimatum about Greece and Turkey which led to the Truman doctrine. Then they contributed to the proposals for Marshall Aid. Then Bevin negotiated the Brussels treaty between Britain, France, Italy and the Benelux countries, which was to be the forerunner of Nato. Bevin regarded himself as the creator of Nato. The first ten days of April 1947, when the treaty was signed, were, according to his biographer, the greatest in his life, the climax of his political career.[24]

Bevin and others in north-west Europe played this cold war role primarily out of economic necessity – the need to reproduce the American generosity of the Second World War; partly out of vestiges of pre-war nationalism – the hope that the US would help these countries to retain their empires; and partly for fear that, without the US, the political spectrum would shift leftwards and no harmonious domestic political consensus would be possible. The harsh winter of 1947 compounded the economic problems inherited from the war. Unemployment in Britain rose to 15 per cent and the trade deficit grew. In effect the government was forced to suspend economic aid to Greece and Turkey. The British government also decided to refer the Palestinian problem to the United Nations and to hand over power in the Indian subcontinent not later than June 1948.[25] In addition, Bevin played a key role in bringing about the division of Germany. The British could not afford to subsidize their zone, and were fearful that subsidies might end up a way of financing reparations from the Eastern zone. Therefore they put forward the Bevin plan for the recovery of West Germany within Western Europe. Bevin personally wrote to Marshall to intercede when it looked as though the Americans might come to some agreement with the Soviet Union.[26]

Bevin described the Brussels treaty as a 'spiritual federation',[27] a political coming together of non-communist governments in Western Europe. An additional factor in the Brussels treaty, especially for France and the Benelux countries, was the fear of a resurgent Germany. Later, the pressure for an American military commitment to Europe was viewed as the main way to secure an economic commitment, to persuade the Americans and especially Congress that the United States needed to spend money in Europe. This view is confirmed by Paul Nitze, who was Kennan's successor at the State Department's policy planning unit: 'It is untrue that we thought the Russians were about to attack ... our prime concern had remained the economic situation in Europe.'[28]

Bevin succeeded in creating the conditions for the reproduction of the Anglo-American alliance during the Second World War – the economic assistance, the cohesion, the domestic planning and coordination. The impulse for militarization arose out of the specific political complexion of the United States. The arguments were contained in the well-known document, NSC-68, prepared in the spring of 1950. Then came the Korean war, which apparently confirmed the hypothesis of an external Soviet threat.

The consolidation of the alliance did betoken a shift to the right and the victory of 'warfare' over 'welfare' – at least during the 1950s. In particular, this shift provided more political space for European nationalism, at any rate in Britain and France. It was Britain and France that blocked the Atlanticist proposal for a European Defence Community which would contain the rearmament of Germany. Britain stayed outside the EDC. The proposal was finally defeated in the French National Assembly, to the jubilant singing of the *Marseillaise* by both Gaullists and Communists. Nevertheless, an integrated command structure was established during this period, primarily in order to integrate German armed forces.

During the 1950s, there was disagreement between the United States and its West European partners both about imperialism (policies towards Indo-China, the Middle East and Africa) and about nuclear weapons. Both Britain and France continued to develop independent nuclear forces and the German defence minister Franz Josef Strauss even began to advocate nuclear weapons for Germany.

For Britain, the Anglo-French intervention in Egypt to retake control of the Suez Canal was one of the last major imperialist adventures. In France, it was followed by the advent of Gaullism and the eventual withdrawal of France from the integrated command structure.

The German political situation was in a category all of its own – distinct both from southern Europe and the north-western democracies. In the aftermath of the war, the predominant mood by most accounts was 'bewilderment, shock and apathy'.[29] If there was a political orientation, it was towards democratic socialism. The anti-fascist movement (antifa) that sprang up at the Liberation and occupied factories and estates was democratic socialist – it was banned by all four occupying powers. Subsequently, pre-1933 parties and unions were licensed by the occupying powers. In municipal and *Länder* elections that were held in the Western zones in the years after the war, it was clear that the Social Democrats commanded a majority of votes and would have continued to do so in a unified Germany.

The Social Democratic party (SPD) was like the other social democratic parties in that it was a mass working-class party and not a vanguard party. But it shared with communist parties and with southern socialist parties a Marxist intellectual tradition. Its leader, Kurt Schumacher, had lost an arm in the First World War, had spent ten years in a Nazi prison camp, and subsequently lost a leg from ill-health. He was deeply committed to unification. He was anti-communist, in a progressive sense, believing that the creation of West Germany effectively meant that those 20 million Germans living in the Eastern half were having to pay for the crimes of all Germany both through reparations and through submission to totalitarian rule. He referred to Adenauer as the 'Chancellor of the Allies'. The Christian Democrats (CDU; and their Bavarian wing, the Christian Socialists, the CSU) won the 1949 Federal elections, after the Basic Law was promulgated, by a hair's breadth. It is fascinating to speculate what might have happened had Schumacher won that election. Would he have fallen into line? Or would West Germany have become ungovernable?

In any case, the SPD was unable to win power until after it abandoned hopes for reunification, and abandoned radical domestic social and economic programmes, which it did at the Bad Godesberg convention of 1959. What primarily remained of the distinctive character of German social democracy was the preoccupation with German–German relations and, therefore, the East–West question. West Germany during the 1950s was characterized by orthodox, free market economic policies and by a particularly virulent form of anti-communism. Many former Nazis were restored to positions of power in industry, the military, and even in the CDU itself. Adenauer's state secretary at the Chancellery and closest confidant was Dr Hans Globke, who had been instrumental in drafting Hitler's infamous Nuremberg race laws. Political bans even affected non-political organizations like the Union of Persons Persecuted by the Nazis (in which, it is true, communists played a key role). Graf suggests that anti-communism in West Germany was partly the consequence of the German tradition – the Second Reich had discriminated against Social Democrats, anti-social democratic measures had included censorship, persecution, bans and *Berufsverbot*, the practice of refusing to allow Social Democrats or anyone of dubious political background to be a public servant – and the anti-communism of the Nazis. It was also a way of evading the Nazi past. 'Anti-communism', says Graf, 'for West Germans, provided a point of common cause with Western victors and hence, even at this late date, a means of avoiding being called to account for their complicity.'[30] It was also a way of forging the new German state. *Alleinvertretungsanspruch* was the claim of the Western state to represent the German 'essence' – literally, the claim to represent oneself. '"Germany" is thus defined as the area where the traditional social order remains with its values, norms and modes of behaviour, while "the Zone" is where foreign powers rule through local agents.'[31]

The 1950s and 1960s are sometimes described as the 'golden age' of capitalist accumulation.[32] In Western Europe, unprecedented rates of economic growth were achieved. Fordist methods of work organization were introduced, wages rose, as did private consumption.

The abolition of the European Payments Union (created in 1950 to protect European currencies) created a vast dollar zone and ushered in a period of Atlantic interdependence.

By the 1960s, a new political consensus had been established between the United States and Western Europe. The return of the Democrats in the US marked the explicit adoption of Keynesian ideas. And, in Western Europe, the Labour party returned to power in the UK, the German SPD entered a coalition government, as did the Italian Socialists. These parties had become Atlanticist, technocratic, confident about the ability of rational managers to harness capitalism to the goals of mass prosperity and stability. This period has been called the 'meridian of Atlanticism'.[33]

The reproduction of Atlanticism

The argument can be recapped. Atlanticism, as it were, inherited the European states system. What came into being during the cold war period was a concert of advanced capitalist nations, much along the lines that prominent American conservatives like John Foster Dulles or Herbert Hoover had envisaged in the 1920s.[34] It was designed to avoid war. By integrating the armed forces of advanced capitalist countries through Nato, and bilateral treaties with Japan and ANZUS (Australia, New Zealand, United States), the concert ensured that conflicts among these countries would be managed without resort to force. And, like the concerts of Metternich and Bismarck which preceded it, it was above all designed to maintain order in the advanced capitalist world and in the dependent territories. It was a global states system, dominated by America, from which the socialist states were excluded and excluded themselves.

This global concert was fashioned by a political process of trial and error that began as early as 1914. That it succeeded where Wilsonianism or isolationism failed is due to the fact that it was compatible with, and indeed helped to shape, the worldwide diffusion of a Fordist pattern of industrial development that emerged in the United States in the early part of the twentieth century; consequently it injected a new lease of life into capitalist economic expansion, which in turn reinforced the legitimacy of the new international political arrangements.

There were certain specific features of the global concert, and of Atlanticism in particular, that gave rise to this new compatibility or synthesis between the prevailing pattern of industrial development and the institutional framework, between allocative and authoritative relationships.

First of all, just as Stalinism in the period 1947–53 created a new East European elite whose survival depended on the relationship with the Soviet Union, so the cold war forged a new Atlanticist elite in the West whose very existence seemed bound up with the Atlantic relationship. In Western Europe, this involved the restoration of parts of the pre-war establishments, the legitimation of social democracy, the marginalization of the nationalistic right wing and the exclusion from the political process of large parts of society which had played a key role in the resistance to Fascism. In the United States, Atlanticism meant a compromise between the New Dealers and the anti-communist right in the Republican party, between those with global interests and those with local or special interests.

It is worth noting that a conscious effort was made to construct this new Atlanticist identity, with generous financial help from the CIA. Magazines like *Encounter, Socialist Commentary, Tempo Presente*, conferences like the Bilderberg conferences and the Congress for Cultural Freedom, as well as scholarships to study in the United States, created an Atlanticist network which could be said to have paralleled, in a looser, less disciplined way, the interparty networks of the East.

The Atlanticists shared a common political outlook. The process of creating and institutionalizing the Atlantic alliance could be said to have reconciled the divergent views that characterized Europe and America in 1945. The *sine qua non* of Atlanticism was acceptance of the notion of the imaginary war, a common interest in combating the Soviet threat. In particular, this was represented by a belief in the US 'nuclear umbrella' (a wonderfully anodyne term). Consequently, divergence and convergence of views within the Atlanticist consensus were expressed in debates about nuclear strategy (these are described in chapter 11 below).

The common Atlanticist political outlook involved a commitment to parliamentarianism and a form of managed capitalism which combined a liberal international economy with state interventionism at home. Atlanticists shared the view that within a system of private enterprise, involving the free flow internationally of goods and capital (although not labour), a democratically elected state should intervene to encourage growth, maintain full employment and control inflation.

Secondly, Atlanticism underpinned post-war international economic arrangements.[35] Despite the hopes of Keynes and Harry Dexter White (later subject to McCarthyite persecution) for a supranational authority able to issue a truly international currency, as proposed at Bretton Woods in 1944, what actually came into effect was a dollar system. The US was able to lubricate the international economy via the provision of military and economic assistance and the stationing of troops overseas; and through these instruments the US was able, at the same time, to insist on the reduction of barriers to trade and capital mobility and to deal with problems arising from rapid global expansion.

In fact, the liberalism of the international economy, established through US-backed institutions like GATT, IMF, the World Bank or OECD (then OEEC), favoured the products of Fordism. The advanced capitalist countries continued to maintain protectionist policies against agricultural products, tropical foodstuffs, minerals, as well as non-tariff barriers against semi-processed products which were the main exports of the Third World countries. In addition, protectionism on older manufactures – iron and steel, textiles and clothing – were higher than the norm.

During the 1950s, the Europeans did retain a certain level of protectionism against US products, although the establishment of institutions like the European Payments Union, the European Coal and Steel Community (the Schuman Plan), and later in 1958 the European Economic Community, broke down national barriers to trade. Western Europe's economic recovery was internally generated in the sense that domestic demand provided the primary stimulus for investment. The growth of the internal market and continued protectionism encouraged the expansion of US capital investment in Western Europe during this period and this was an important method by which American products and processes were transferred to Europe.[36]

Thirdly, Atlanticism influenced the domestic, social and technological institutions that were required for industrial restructuring. Both American and Western European governments favoured increased state intervention in the post-war period. But there were differences in the form of state intervention. The US put more emphasis on military spending as an economic regulator. The Europeans put more emphasis on welfare, nationalization and planning. Both forms of state intervention sustained demand and encouraged private consumption – an essential prerequisite for the diffusion of Fordism.[37]

Although these differences were to be maintained throughout the post-war period and, indeed, to increase during the 1970s, the formation of Nato was important in bringing the priorities of Western European governments closer to those of the United States. It was not only that military spending was favoured over welfare spending. (A dramatic moment was the decision of a British Labour government in 1952 to introduce charges for prescriptions in order to pay for rearmament.) It was also the case that the integration of armed forces and the joint determination of security requirements within Nato also influenced technological choices – a preference for nuclear energy and oil instead of coal, and for roads and airfields instead of railways. Security questions were, in fact, effectively removed from national political discourse, at least in Europe, so that large areas of policy affecting the budget, manpower, technology, etc. were no longer subject to public scrutiny (if they ever were). They were determined collectively, by a small Atlanticist policy-making elite, in Brussels and in Washington, rather than by legislatures in national capitals.

In social terms, Atlanticism could be said to have been associated with the depoliticization of consumers and workers. A culture of private consumerism spread from the United States to Western Europe. And, especially after the split of the international trade union movement in 1949, engineered by CIA-financed American trade unions, especially the American Federation of Labour, the American brand of trade unionism was extended to Europe. European trade unions became increasingly economistic; that is to say, they confined their demands to pay and conditions.[38] (This was not always the case; in Germany, the tradition of demands for workers' control and the immediate post-war experience of workers' councils led to some important codetermination agreements – *Mitbestimmung.*)

Finally, Atlanticism also involved what might be described as a spheres-of-influence policy among the advanced Western countries. Initially, several European countries hoped that they would be able to hang on to their colonies. In fact, the Americans encouraged a process of decolonization but took over many of the ties of economic and military dependence formerly held by the colonial powers. The US replaced Japan, France and Holland in the Far East; and France and Britain in the Near East. European hegemony in Africa was tolerated and the US maintained and strengthened its sphere of influence in Latin America. At that time, Soviet capacity to provide economic and military assistance was rather limited. So the spheres-of-influence policy minimized the possibilities for Third World countries of playing off international rivalries. This argument is consistent with the view of Noam Chomsky and others[39] that the cold war was directed against radical forces in the Third World who had no way of improving the terms under which they participated in the global states system, except through turning to the Soviet Union.

These four features of Atlanticism explain why the cold war succeeded, not why it began. They explain how cold war policies generated a combination of popular consent for and vested institutional interest in their continuation. There were, of course, other policies that might also have suceeded and perhaps succeeded better. That the cold war formula was adopted has to be explained in terms of the need to reconcile deepseated political differences both within the United States and between the United States and Western Europe.

The 1960s was the period when the correct formula seemed to have been found, when it seemed possible to relax the confrontation and the brinkmanship. And yet at the very moment when optimism about Atlanticism seemed greatest, the consensus was rudely shaken by the Vietnam war and the student revolt. What happened in 1968 and 1969, at least in Europe, and especially in France, Italy and Germany, was both a resurgence of the past and an intimation of the future. The students of 1968 were the first post-war generation, the children of those who collaborated or resisted. In part, they were protesting against the restoration of those who were implicated in Nazi crimes. In Germany, outrage against the participation of Social Democrats in a coalition government headed by an ex-Nazi, Kiesinger, was one element. The students linked failure to deal with Nazism to the failure to question involvement in Vietnam. And, in part, they were protesting on behalf of those who had been excluded by the post-war consensus. 'Who is Danny Cohn Bendit?' the French students cried. 'He is a German, a Jew and a Marxist.'

But 1968 was also a reaction to mass consumption society, to the economism of social democracy and post-war trade unionism – measuring the advance of socialism in the levels of wages and minding their own political business – and to the transformation of intellectuals into technocrats to manage growth without foreseeable end. And, in this, the students and workers of 1968 anticipated the social movements of the 1970s and 1980s.

Notes

1 See W. W. Rostow, *The World Economy: History and Prospect* (University of Texas Press, 1978), ch. 15.
2 See Charles Kindleberger, *The World in Depression* (Allen Lane, 1978). Kindleberger's argument has been taken up by a series of writers concerned about the decline of the American empire and the importance of hegemonic stability. See especially: Robert Gilpin, *War and Change in World Politics* (Cambridge University Press, 1982); Robert Keohane, *After Hegemony: Cooperation and Discord in the World Political Economy* (Princeton University Press, 1984); Paul Kennedy, *The Rise and Fall of the Great Powers: Economic Change and Military Conflict 1500 to 2000* (Unwin Hyman, 1988).
3 John Lewis Gaddis, 'The emerging post-revisionist synthesis on the origins of the cold war', *Diplomatic History*, 8, Summer 1983, p. 173.
4 A 1946 naval intelligence report argued that 'maintenance of large occupational forces in Eastern Europe is dictated to a certain extent by the necessity of "farming out" millions of men for whom living and accommodations cannot be spared in the USSR.' Quoted in Joyce and Gabriel Kolko, *The Limits of Power* (Harper and Row, 1972), p. 33. The change in perceptions of Soviet military power in the late 1940s is discussed further in chapter 11 below.
5 See for example Vojtech Mastny, *Russia's Road to the Cold War*

(Columbia University Press, 1979). William Taubman, *Stalin's American Policy: From Entente to Détente to Cold War* (W. W. Norton, 1982), argues that Marshall Aid was the turning point in Stalin's attitude. Previously, Stalin had favoured détente.

6 Quoted in Kees van der Pijl, *The Making of an Atlantic Ruling Class* (Verso, 1984), p. 182.

7 See Alan Wolfe, 'American domestic politics and the alliance', in Mary Kaldor and Richard Falk, eds, *Dealignment* (UNU/Basil Blackwell, 1987); also Alan Wolfe, 'The irony of anti-communism: ideology and interest in postwar American foreign policy', in *Socialist Register 1984* (Merlin Press, 1984).

8 Wolfe, 'American domestic politics', p. 69.

9 Ibid.

10 See Mary Kaldor, *The Baroque Arsenal* (André Deutsch, 1982).

11 Wolfe, 'American domestic politics', p. 69.

12 At the time of the Truman doctrine, Clark Clifford described it as 'the opening gun in a campaign to bring people to [the] realization that the war isn't over by any means'. And a US information officer who was expected to present the doctrine said that 'the only way we can sell the public our new policy is by emphasising the necessity of holding the line.' Quoted in John Lewis Gaddis, *The United States and the Origins of the Cold War 1941–47* (Columbia University Press, 1972), p. 351.

13 An encounter between Senator Vandenberg and Maurice Thorez, leader of the French Communist party, illustrates something of the naïveté of American anti-communism. According to the French chief of protocol, at a dinner in Paris in May 1946: 'Senator Vandenberg, who sat next to me, could not take his eyes off Maurice Thorez' beaming face. "How can such a healthy man be a Communist?" he kept repeating.' Quoted in Alfred Grosser, *The Western Alliance: European–American Relations since 1945* (Macmillan, 1980), p. 56.

14 George Kennan, *Memoirs 1950–63* (Little, Brown, 1972), p. 222.

15 William Graf, 'Anti-communism in the Federal Republic of Germany', in *Socialist Register 1984*.

16 Kennan, *Memoirs 1950–63* pp. 223–4.

17 Robert Jay Lifton and Richard Falk, *Indefensible Weapons: The Political and Psychological Case against Nuclearism* (Basic Books, 1982), p. 27.

18 Kennan, *Memoirs 1950–63*, p. 228.

19 In May 1947, General Marshall made it clear through a diplomatic note from the US ambassador that the condition for aid to Italy was the expulsion of Socialists and Communists from the government. Within

days the prime minister, De Gasperi, had dissolved the government and subsequently established a centre-right government. See Alan A. Platt and Robert Leonardi, 'American foreign policy and the postwar Italian left', *Political Science Quarterly*, Summer 1978. Subsequently, in the 1948 elections, CIA propaganda efforts contributed to the defeat of the Communists. For a description, see Richard Barnet, *The Alliance* (Simon and Schuster, 1982), p. 140. Kennan proposed outlawing the Italian Communist party (PCI) and inviting civil war 'which would give us grounds for reoccupation [of] Foggia fields or any other facilities we might wish'. This would result in 'much violence' but 'I think it would be preferable to a bloodless election victory ... which would give the Communists the entire peninsula at one coup.' Quoted in Barnet, *The Alliance*, p. 139.

20 Clement Attlee, Labour prime minister, epitomized this attitude. 'The British labour movement', he said,

'has never consisted of a body of theorists or of revolutionaries who were so absorbed in Utopian dreams that they were unwilling to deal with the actualities of everyday life. From the first, British Socialists have taken their share whenever possible in the responsibility of the Government. The British system of local government has proved to be an excellent training ground. Long before there were more than a handful of Labour members in Parliament, Socialists had won their way on to local councils and were influencing administrations. By showing what could be done in a small sphere they were able to convert many sceptical workers who would only believe what they saw in being.' (Quoted in John Saville, 'Ernest Bevin and the cold war, 1945–50', in *Socialist Register 1984*, p. 71).

21 Quoted in Saville, 'Ernest Bevin', p. 74.
22 Bevin arrived late at the cabinet subcommittee that was to decide upon the atomic bomb. The committee consisted of Stafford Cripps, Hugh Dalton and Attlee. Bevin had fallen asleep after a good lunch. Cripps and Dalton were against acquiring the bomb – they thought it was too expensive. Bevin said: 'We've got to have this ... I don't mind for myself but I don't want any other Foreign Secretary of this country to be talked at or by a Secretary of State in the United States as I have just had in my discussion with Mr Byrnes. We have got to have this thing over here whatever it costs ... We've got to have the bloody Union Jack flying on top of it.' Ibid., p. 89. Attlee agreed with him.
23 After the Russians' refusal to reduce their demand for 10 billion dollars in reparations from Germany in November 1947, Bevin said to Molotov:

You cannot look on me as an enemy of Russia. Why, when our Government was trying to stamp out your Revolution, who was it that stopped it? It was I, Ernest Bevin. I called out the transport workers and they refused to load the ships. I wanted you to have your own revolution in your own way and without interference. Now I am speaking as a friend. You are playing a very dangerous game. And I can't make out why. You don't really believe that any American wants to go to war with you – or, at least, no responsible American. We most certainly don't want to. But you are playing with fire, Mr Molotov ... If war comes between you and America in the East, then we may be able to remain neutral. But if war comes between you and America in the West, then we shall be on America's side. Make no mistake about that. That would be the end of Russia and your revolution. (Quoted in Daniel Yergin, *Shattered Peace* (Houghton Mifflin, 1978), pp. 331–2)

24 Alan Bullock, *Ernest Bevin: Foreign Secretary, 1945–51* (Heinemann, 1983).
25 See David Reynolds, 'The origins of the cold war: the European dimension', *Historical Journal*, 28:2, 1985, pp. 497–515.
26 According to Anne Deighton:

The British threatened that they could simply not afford even to contemplate the granting of current reparations yet. They argued that such an arrangement would be clumsy and unworkable and would retard the recovery of Germany and with it Europe and Britain too. The Americans would be left with enormous financial burdens. They would be feeding the German cow in the West while it was being milked in the East. Liberated Europe's problems, the British argued, began and ended with Germany. If Germany could recover economically, so would the rest of Europe. If Germany played hostage to the needs of the Soviet economy, it would fester and become a cesspool, attractive only to the ideas of communism. ('The "frozen front": the Labour government, the division of Germany and the origins of the cold war, 1945–7', *International Affairs*, 63:3, Summer 1987, p. 460)

27 Robin Edmonds, *Setting the Mould: The United States and Britain, 1945–1950* (Clarendon Press, 1986).
28 Paul Nitze, 'NSC 68 and the Soviet threat', *International Security*, Spring 1980.
29 Graf, 'Anti-communism'; see also Barnet, *The Alliance*, ch. 1.
30 Graf, 'Anti-communism', p. 169.
31 Ibid.
32 Angus Maddison, *Phases of Economic Growth* (Oxford University Press, 1982).
33 Van der Pijl, *Atlantic Ruling Class*. He quotes poll data to show that West European leaders' acceptance of the US reached its peak in 1961.
34 William Appleman Williams, *The Tragedy of American Diplomacy* (World Publishing, 1959), describes how this concept came into being

after the defeat of Wilson over the League of Nations. Such a concept would accept the 'open door' policy and stand firm against the Soviet Union and revolutionary powers. Economic expansion was regarded as the 'antidote to Bolshevism'.

35 This argument is developed in my book, *The Disintegrating West* (Allen Lane, 1978). See also Fred L. Block, *The Origins of International Economic Disorder* (University of California Press, 1977).

36 In fact, the Marshall Plan included specific technological projects, like continuous wide-strip mills for the steel industry, crucial for reducing the cost of sheet steel for automobiles and consumer durables. Later the European Coal and Steel Community (Schuman Plan) broke the cartels which prevented the installation of new steel technologies. A former president of the Studebaker car company, Hoffman, told a group of US Senators that the Schuman Plan facilitated the diffusion of Fordism:

> Heretofore, the price has been too high and wages too low for people to buy the products of the steel industry here. We take a ton of steel and put it in an automobile, and you know how very few people can afford to buy an automobile in Europe. So, if you start this process, raising wages and lowering prices, you can get that great expanding market in Europe and that will take care of this increased production. Henry Ford introduced us to this principle and when he did so, he started a revolution that we are still benefiting by, and I think that the Schuman Plan may have that result in Europe. (Quoted in van der Pijl, *Atlantic Ruling Class*, p. 150)

37 David Calleo offers a very interesting analysis of the fiscal differences between the United States and Western Europe. In Western Europe, government spending and government receipts were consistently higher as a share of GNP. Moreover, defence spending as a share of government spending was much higher in the United States than in Western Europe. He argues that, as compared with the United States, the European middle classes are beneficiaries of the welfare state; welfare is not just a 'charity for the poor' as in the United States. Moreover, in the United States there is a much higher proportion of direct to indirect taxes so that the burden of taxation falls mainly on the American middle classes. Hence the American middle classes prefer tax exemptions to increased spending on welfare. See *Beyond American Hegemony: The Future of the Atlantic Alliance* (Wheatsheaf, 1987).

38 This process is well described by van der Pijl, *Atlantic Ruling Class*. He argues that: 'Welding together the reformist trade unions in the North Atlantic area, and isolating the communist or class-conscious socialist elements, were the most conspicuous achievements of the Marshall offensive with respect to the European working class ... through the

purging and reorganisation of the trade-union movement, an important step had been taken towards the restructuration of Western European labour relations to match the American pattern . . .' (pp. 155–6).

39 See, for example, Noam Chomsky, 'The United States: from Greece to El Salvador', in Noam Chomsky, John Gittings and Jonathan Steele, *Super Powers in Collision: The New Cold War of the 1980s*, 2nd edn (Penguin, 1984).

6

Was there an East–West Conflict?

Obviously, in one sense, there was an East–West conflict. During the cold war period, both sides built up military forces for use against each other. Both sides adopted the language of conflict, hurling hostile abuse across the East–West divide. And at certain moments in the cold war period, in the two Berlin crises or the Cuba missile crisis, there were real fears that actual war might break out.

Historians of the cold war, whether orthodox, revisionist or post-revisionist, presuppose a fundamental conflict of interest which underlay the paraphernalia of cold war. The revisionists presuppose a fundamental conflict between capitalism and socialism along Marxist lines – a class conflict between the owners of capital and those employed by capital. Capitalism cannot tolerate socialism because it involves the abolition of private property, a far-reaching redistribution of power and wealth and the closure of markets. As one group of left-wing authors put it: 'The two blocs represent the distorted image, on the international plane, of domestic antagonism between the classes.'[1]

The orthodox historians are idealists. They presuppose a fundamental conflict between freedom and totalitarianism. Totalitarianism cannot tolerate freedom – it would reveal too much. Hence its existence, whether communist or Fascist, poses a permanent threat to democracy. The post-revisionists, products of a later era, presuppose a traditional great power conflict, within a realist framework.

How do these characterizations of the East–West conflict stand up to an analysis of the nature of Stalinism and Atlanticism?

Capitalism versus socialism

There was indeed, in the early post-war period, a conflict between capitalism and socialism within the West. But it is difficult to argue that this domestic conflict was a reflection of or part of an external conflict with the Soviet Union. It is true that there were powerful communist parties in southern Europe which were pro-Soviet. However, they were also mass parties. And it is likely, as in Yugoslavia, that political strength and obedience to Stalin would have become incompatible. Indeed, that is what happened. Already by 1947, workers were restless about the rather moderate cooperative role played by party leaders in the post-war coalitions. Subsequently, the decline of the French party and the rise of the Italian party can, in part, be ascribed to their differing relationships with the Soviet Union and, by the same token, to their domestic situation.

The evolution of the cold war gave rise to an Atlanticist compromise between capitalism and social democracy or, more specifically Fordism and Fabianism, in the West. This compromise was expressed in a new composition of West European and American elites, new structures of government – the welfare and warfare states, a liberal/capitalist international economy, the integration of national military power into new multinational structures, and a spheres-of-influence policy *vis à vis* the Third World. The cold war stimulated and justified the process of compromise and, at the same time, marginalized and discredited those who could not accept its terms.

There were many people in Europe who would have preferred alternatives: more independent nationalist postures, for example, or more internationalist cooperative postures. Only a tiny minority would have actually chosen to join the Soviet-dominated states system. On the contrary, the imposition of Stalinism on East Central Europe displayed a particularly nasty model of socialism – an object lesson for those who might otherwise have aspired to socialist ideas. The very existence of a Soviet-dominated states system squeezed the political space available for a distinctively non-Soviet socialist approach. Migone points out that the experiences of Chile and Czechoslovakia are the extreme illustration of this point.[2]

In what sense, indeed, can it be said that Stalinism was more 'socialist' than Atlanticism? If socialism merely means statism, then it is true that the Soviet Union was more socialist. Atlanticism also introduced an important element of statism into the functioning of Western societies. But if socialism means the social, political and economic advance of the working class, it is not self-evident that Stalinism was more socialist than Atlanticism. The Soviet system did eliminate unemployment and provide basic material benefits for the poorest people. (Even today, however, there are, for example, children working in the cotton fields of Uzbekistan.) On the other hand, Atlanticism greatly improved the material conditions of working people, especially in Europe, with the introduction of universal welfare benefits, and it also increased the power of trade unions, at least in the economic sphere. It is true that Stalinism was more egalitarian in a material sense. It eliminated extreme concentrations of material wealth, although the nomenklatura had special material privileges like holiday homes or special shops. But Stalinism was politically very inegalitarian, involving extreme concentrations of political power.

The Soviet system did eliminate the capitalist class, which was actually very small at the time of the Bolshevik revolution, and also the landowning class. Power was effectively handed over to the party and later to Stalin. The orthodox Soviet argument is that the party and later the person of Stalin represented the working class. It is true that the party included many working people; Stalin himself came from very humble origins. In the Soviet Union, and later in Eastern Europe, workers were often favoured over intellectuals. All the same, this argument neglects the reproduction of state power. It is not the origin of state power that is relevant but how it is reproduced. Party power depended on physical coercion and the police; indeed, it was peasants and workers even more than intellectuals who suffered as a result of collectivization and of labour discipline. Power was not reproduced through a process of obtaining consent, or even participation, from workers.

In Western Europe, working-class parties also came to power; Ernest Bevin, after all, was a true representative of the working class. This did not mean, however, that the working classes were 'in power'. Workers did have more say, although not enough, in the reproduction of power, both through the electoral process and through institutions like trade unions or socialist parties, than they had enjoyed in the past.

In other words, to typify Stalinism as socialist or Atlanticism as capitalist is, in itself, misleading.

The situation was different in the Third World which, during the cold war period, remained predominantly within the Western sphere of influence. While many Third World countries, after decolonization, were statist, large parts of the population experienced miserable poverty. China and the Soviet Union were, in effect, Third World countries and perhaps it is more appropriate to compare the Soviet system with the various social systems that characterized Third World countries within the Western sphere of influence. The contrast between the conditions of Chinese peasants and Indian peasants was often noted by observers in the 1950s and 1960s. The Soviet and Chinese models offered a method of overcoming poverty and backwardness quickly. However, stagnation and the failure of agriculture in the 1970s and 1980s combined with the success of the capitalist NICs (Newly Industrializing Countries) in the Far East has muted the appeal of the Soviet model for movements in the Third World. Even so, Third World nationalist movements were not, on the whole, pro-Soviet. They accepted Soviet military and economic assistance either to balance Western aid and sustain a non-aligned position or because they had no alternative.

The West could and did intervene militarily against radical Third World regimes or liberation movements – Guatemala, Iran, Lebanon, Chile, Philippines: the list is long. These conflicts were presented as part of the East–West conflict but, in fact, they were West–South conflicts. While many of America's opponents in the Third World described themselves as socialist and even received aid from the Soviet Union, they operated within the Western-dominated states system. The West did not have the same interest in intervention *within* the Soviet states system. The very existence of the Soviet Union, the example of Soviet domination of East Central Europe, enabled Western leaders to legitimize their interventions in the Third World in terms of a global struggle between good and evil.

Freedom versus totalitarianism

Just as there was a conflict between capitalism and socialism *within* the West, so there was a conflict between freedom and totalitarianism *within* the East. In this respect, there was an asymmetry between East and West, for Western democracy undoubtedly exercised a greater pull for people living in Eastern Europe than the Soviet socialism exerted on people living in the West. The construction of the Berlin Wall in 1961 is a vivid expression of this fact. (Some two million people, out of a population of 18 million, left East Germany for the West between 1949 and 1956.)

Nevertheless, the main challenge to Stalinism during this period came from alternative models of socialism, from the revisionists and 'home' communists like Gomulka, Imre Nagy, and later Dubcek. It was Titoism, after all, that triggered the Stalinist purges in the late 1940s. The notion of an ideological conflict between capitalism and socialism did, during this period, have some ideological appeal and this was because socialist ideas still had some popular resonance.

If the typology of Stalinism as socialism and Atlanticism as capitalism is misleading, the typology of Stalinism as totalitarianism and Atlanticism as democracy is perhaps too simple. Stalinism was totalitarian both in the sense that it allowed no independent spaces in society and in the sense used by Hannah Arendt that totalitarianism requires everyone to become accomplices in the system.[3] Post-Stalinism did allow some independent spaces and even in some cases a degree of depoliticization – hence, Kadar's famous phrase that all who are not against us are with us.

Clearly, Atlanticism was and is democratic, at least for the most part. Regular elections were and are held; citizens have been free to organize and criticize. This was not true, of course, during the cold war period in Portugal, Spain, Greece and Turkey and is not true, even today, in Turkey. There are also certain respects in which democracy in the sense of political participation has been curtailed within the Atlantic region. To some extent, this arises from the Fabian (or New Deal) tradition: the paternalism of state intervention, the emphasis on economic rather than political demands from trade unions, the concern with the material condition of the consumer.

Moreover, the democratic process varies in different countries, depending on the electoral system, the balance between national and local government, the style of the opposition, the role of the media, etc. In particular, one important aspect of Atlanticism, the imaginary war, has constituted a limitation on the proper functioning of the democratic process.

First of all, in a formal sense, the permanent state of pretend war justifies an infringement of certain rights which is normally only warranted in wartime.[4] In particular, 'national security' has become a legitimation for secrecy, shielding areas of public concern from scrutiny. Decisions about defence that have profound importance for the future have often been taken by a handful of people without any public discussion; such decisions include the decision to go ahead with the British and French nuclear weapons programmes, and decisions about the construction of Amerian bases and the deployment of American forces in West European countries. In addition, *Berufsverbot*, civil defence preparations, espionage, the suspension of trade union rights at sensitive military installations, the role of security forces like the CIA in domestic surveillance, all constitute examples of wartime practices to which we have become accustomed.

Secondly, the ideology of imaginary war did become what might be called a totalitarian ideology, in Arendt's sense, in the sense that all who participated in power became accomplices in the fantasy of an East–West confrontation. Belief in a Soviet threat and the need for military preparedness, especially the notion that nuclear weapons provided 'protection', anti-communism, and the need for Western unity, all became conditions for participation in power structures, or even for important positions in civil society. In the 1950s, these conditions were made brutally clear through McCarthyism, especially in the United States and West Germany. Later, what East Europeans call self-censorship, a kind of self-reproducing accomplice system, ensured that those who rejected the assumption of East–West conflict were excluded and, indeed, identified with the 'other'. To be against nuclear weapons was to be pro-Soviet in the zero-sum game of imaginary war. Or to criticize Western democracy was to fail to recognize the evils of the Soviet system. (And, of course, some critics of Atlanticism fell into the trap by apologizing for the Soviet Union as a way of mitigating anti-communism.)

In addition, there were many countries in the Third World that experienced dictatorships or military governments. These were not totalitarian because non-industrial countries lack the technology for total surveillance. But such regimes often engaged in brutal forms of physical repression – executions, murder, torture. Such countries could not be described as Atlanticist, of course, but they were part of a global states system dominated by the West, and they were generally supported by the West. In other words, there was and is a conflict about democracy in *both* East and West, but these are, first and foremost, *internal* conflicts.

Great power rivalry

The notion of a great power conflict, which underlies the realist version of the East–West conflict, implies that great powers expand where they can or else must defend themselves from the expansion of others. The mere existence of military capabilities is sufficient for potentially aggressive intentions to be presupposed, and therefore to argue that they must be offset or 'balanced' by equivalent military capabilities. This assertion is essentially an act of faith; this is how great powers behave.

Put this way, there is not much to refute. But the assumption of inherently expansionist great power behaviour is deeply pessimistic. It means that we can never envisage any alternative to war or containment as a way of regulating relations between states. On the other hand, if we try to differentiate great power behaviour according to specific requirements for authoritative reproduction, it might be possible to identify modes of behaviour which are more amenable to peaceful, democratic forms of international regulation.

The historical roots of realism can be traced to an earlier period in which economic expansion was tied to land and in which there was no clear distinction between economic and political forms of reproduction. The territorial expansion of the feudal lord or king, or one of the great slave-based empires, was a requirement of authoritative reproduction – the source of legitimacy, a necessity for survival. With the universalization of commodity relations – occurring under both capitalism and modern socialism (via the collectivization of agriculture) – that is, with the introduction of exchange relations, that argument no longer applies. Consequently, the impulse for territorial expansion is no longer an assumption of state behaviour but rather has to be explained.

It can be argued that neither the Soviet Union nor the United States had any interest in territorial expansion in the post-war period. American capitalism was certainly expansionist but overseas expansion could be better regulated through a flexible global states system than through the expansion of the American nation state. There were interventions in the Third World to manage the global states system, but the existence of an alternative suzerain states system was part of the mechanism of management.

Stalin, it seems, did toy with the idea of incorporating East Central European states into the Soviet Union. The Soviet system required external sources of technology and trade and these were acquired initially from the newly created suzerain states in the East. But they could also be acquired through trade, which presupposed acceptance of the capitalist system. The term 'peaceful coexistence' began to be used extensively after the acceptance of socialism in one country and, even during the Stalinist period, it remained a principle of Soviet foreign policy.[5]

The reproduction of the Soviet system was based on defensive paranoia and an obsession with security. It is always possible to conceive of a situation in which fear of attack could result in preemptive expansion; all the same, the evidence suggests a determination on the part of Stalin and others to avoid war with the West.

Official versions of the East–West conflict were not actually ideological although they were presented in ideological terms. On both sides official spokespeople seemed to conceive of the conflict in great power terms – realism dressed up as Marxism or Idealism. When Zhdanov presented his two camp doctrine at the first Cominform meeting of 1947, he was careful not to mention the struggle for socialism within capitalist countries. Hence the main aim of the anti-imperialist camp was 'to fight against the expansion of imperialism and the threat of new wars, the strengthening of democracy [that is, Stalinism] and the elimination of the traces of fascism'.[6] In practice the Soviet Union never allowed support for revolutionary

movements in the Third World to jeopardize the security of the
Soviet state. Likewise, the American statements about the defence of
freedom were always a way of talking about the defence of America
and, perhaps to a lesser extent, Western Europe. In practice, the US
was rather unwilling to take steps to support efforts to achieve
democracy in Eastern Europe, as, for example, in its negative
response to requests for economic assistance in the months leading
up to the Czech coup of 1948; despite the rhetoric of rollback in the
early 1950s, it became clear after the Hungarian revolution of 1956
that the United States would not step over Dulles's brink. Pro-
American dictatorships in the Third World or in Turkey, say, were
and are counted as 'free' because they are pro-American.

Just as Bismarck and Cavour sustained conservative governments
in the late nineteenth century by using the radical emancipatory
language of the nationalism of the early nineteenth century, so the
West used the language of Wilsonian idealism – democracy, self-
determination, collective security – and the East used the language of
Marxism to conceal the construction of new edifices of power and
hierarchy.

Atlanticism and Stalinism

There were, of course, elements of conflict in the East–West relationship. The West undoubtedly represented an appealing alternative
to Stalinism, even though the main challenge to Stalinism and
post-Stalinism during the cold war period came from revisionist
communists. Likewise, the Soviet and Chinese model offered an
alternative for the poorest peoples of the Third World, as well as a
source of alternative military and economic assistance, at least after
1955; all the same, the nationalist movements that challenged
Atlantic colonialism and neo-colonialism were not, on the whole,
Stalinist and did not plan to emulate the Soviet model. On both sides,
there was a military build-up in the 1950s and this undoubtedly gave
rise to perceptions of aggressive intention.

These elements of conflict were, however, outweighed by the
complementarity of the two systems – both needed the other in order
to regulate domestic and interstate relations *within* both systems. In

East Central Europe, the perception of a Western threat, the notion of a perpetual struggle between imperialism and socialism, created the kind of war situation necessary for the reproduction of Stalinism. In part, the imposition of Stalinism can be explained in economic terms; the economic situation of East Central Europe was far worse than the situation in Western Europe – Stalinist methods were the most obvious known methods for rapid reconstruction, in the absence of Western aid. But the fact that the Soviet Union could not accept the conditions attached to Western aid (they were, of course, proposed in the expectation that the Soviet Union would refuse) has to be explained in political terms: greater autonomy for East Central European countries would lead to unacceptable revelations. The cold war in Eastern Europe created a new elite of accomplices whose loyalty to the Soviet Union was reinforced through various party, security and military networks and who guided the establishment of pseudo-war economies on the Soviet model.

Within the Atlantic system, the existence of a Soviet military threat and the belief in an epic struggle between the forces of freedom and the forces of communism served to legitimize a continuing American economic commitment to war-devastated Western Europe. It took the form of an anti-Soviet military commitment because this was the only way that West European socialists could reassure Americans about their credentials to receive assistance and it was the only way the Democratic leadership in the United States could persuade a conservative Congress not to retreat into isolationism. The cold war reproduced the Anglo-Saxon alliance of the Second World War and extended it to Western Europe; it welded together a new Atlanticist elite which could preside over an economically interdependent Atlantic community.

The complementarity of Atlanticism and Stalinism was implicitly accepted during the spheres-of-influence approach, which lasted until 1947, and during détente, which succeeded the cold war period. The unwillingness of the British and Amerians to support resistance movements in the Soviet 'sphere of operations' during the Second World War[7] and Stalin's lack of support for the Greek communists anticipated the agreements on mutual non-interference and the Sonnenfeldt doctrine which characterized the détente period.

Both cold war and détente were, in fact, ways of waging imaginary war. Both were predicated on the internal cohesion of the blocs and on substantial military preparations. Détente was supposed to be a bit less dangerous and perhaps less costly. However, and this is the subject of the next part of this book, this approach was inherently unstable. It lacked the psychological discipline of confrontation. In the cold war period, the complementarity of systems meant the existence of an 'other', a danger, a fear, an unpalatable alternative which explained the need for domestic regulation. In other words, the fact that the world was characterized by two different systems did not mean that the systems were incompatible or in conflict. On the contrary, their very existence was mutually reinforcing.

The cold war period could be said to have resulted in an homogenization of systems. Stalinism was imposed on East Central Europe. The American model of capitalism, the Fordist pattern of industrial development, was spread to other advanced industrialized countries through political compromise, trade and investment and military integration. This process of homogenization enhanced the complementarity of the two systems by excluding other alternatives.

The East–West conflict can thus be described as an idea or, more accurately, as an ideology, an imaginary war. It was an idea that was institutionalized in the formation of new elites and in military and industrial structures during the 1950s and 1960s. It was an idea which persisted in the West because it was accompanied by stability and prosperity, and in the East because too many people were criminally implicated. It was an idea which drew heavily on the experience of the Second World War.[8]

Finally, the success of the idea was bound up with the discovery of nuclear weapons, the ability of human beings to inflict enormous destructive damage and the psychological difficulty of coming to terms with this fact. This was particularly relevant in the West where American strength was seen to reside in nuclear weapons and where the implications were publicly discussed. Political leaders had virtually become gods, able to determine the future of mankind. Everything was to be tolerated, their ideas had to be respected, to avoid the greater disaster. In a sense, perhaps, the cold war can be described as a gigantic confidence trick.

Two final comments. First, if this description of the cold war seems to be too schematic, to be imposing order on a complicated anarchic world, this in itself is a product of the cold war idea. Both Marxism and Idealism are rooted in progressive thought, in the assumptions of the Enlightenment that human beings can discover 'solutions' to social and natural problems. The cold war was presented as a conflict of solutions to a complicated set of problems – democracy versus socialism.

Secondly, and relatedly, it is a description of the cold war which also sounds strangely archaic. Yes, there was a conflict between capitalism and socialism in the West, but there were many varieties of social organization that could be fitted within these categories. And somehow these are categories which do not seem applicable to explain the difficulties, the contradictions, the issues of the present day. Indeed, the very compromise that Atlanticism brought about gave rise to new conflicts which seem to be outside these categories, at least as traditionally defined – the nature of democracy, gender, the environment. The notion of a conflict between democracy and totalitarianism within the West as well as the East seems more relevant. But even so, there were very few states that by the end of the 1960s could still be described as totalitarian – Albania, perhaps, or Romania. There were varieties of authoritarianism and varieties of democracy and if we are to confront seriously the issue of democracy we need new methods of categorizing forms of authoritative reproduction that avoid a blanketing together of all democracies and all authoritarian systems.

To trace a route out of the orderly maze of the cold war is to encounter the mess and confusions of our everyday experience. Categories of thought drawn from history gave the cold war its peculiar order. Those categories seem less and less relevant. And yet without new categories and new schemes, it is difficult to make sufficient sense of our experience to guide social and political action.

Notes

1 Philip Armstrong, Andrew Glyn and John Harrison, *Capitalism since World War II* (Fontana, 1984), p. 44.

2 Giangiacomo Migone, 'The decline of the bipolar system, or a second look at the history of the cold war', in Mary Kaldor, Gerard Holden and Richard Falk, eds, *The New Détente* (UNU/Verso, 1989).

3 Hannah Arendt, *The Burden of our Time* (Secker and Warburg, 1951).
4 For a development of this argument, see Richard Falk, 'Nuclear weapons
   and the death of democracy' and 'Nuclear weapons and the renewal of
   democracy', in *The Promise of World Order* (Wheatsheaf, 1989).
5 See Margot Light, *The Soviet Theory of International Relations* (Wheatsheaf, 1988).
6 Quoted in Fernando Claudin, *The Communist Movement* (Penguin,
   1975), p. 468.
7 For a description of British and American behaviour during the Warsaw
   uprising and in Slovenia, see Vojtech Mastny, *Russia's Road to the Cold
   War* (Columbia University Press, 1979).
8 Even today, the memory of the Second World War is the reference point
   for imaginary war. Western leaders constantly refer to the dangers of
   appeasement and the lessons of Pearl Harbor. Soviet leaders refer to the
   sacrifices of the Second World War and the need to avoid any repetition
   of that experience – a joint government–party declaration on the fortieth
   anniversary of the Second World War is typical:

   The war forced on the Soviet Union the loss of twenty million of its sons and
   daughters. No family remained unsinged by the flames of war. Our pain and
   sorrow will never subside; the grief of soldiers' widows, mothers and orphans is
   inconsolable. The harsh and instructive lessons of the war cannot be forgotten . . .
   The historic Yalta and Potsdam Agreements [dividing Europe] . . . have been
   dependably serving Europeans' security interests and deterring militaristic and
   revivalist ambitions for forty years. (Quoted in Karen Dawisha, *Eastern Europe*
   (Cambridge University Press, 1988), p. 18)

PART III
Détente and New Cold War

7

Differing Conceptions of Détente

'Détente' means relaxation. The term 'détente' came into use during the 1960s. It was used by President Kennedy in 1963, by De Gaulle when he made his overtures to the Soviet Union in the mid-1960s and in the 1967 Harmel report, a Nato document which emphasized the dual policy of détente and deterrence. Détente is both a mode of the East–West relationship and a way of describing particular periods in the history of the East–West conflict. In a sense, both détente and cold war have always been present in the East–West relationship; they are often described as different ways of managing the relationship.

Those who analyse the East–West conflict generally identify cycles of détente and cold war. There are wide variations in the periodization of such cycles; the dates chosen tend to reflect different explanatory approaches.[1] The period after Stalin's death and after the end of the Korean war is often considered to be a détente period. It is certainly true that high-level East–West contacts were resumed during this period, with US–Soviet summits in 1955 and 1959. In both East and West, military spending as a share of gross national product declined. In the East, the Soviet leaders began to emphasize 'peaceful coexistence' and initiated the New Course, a policy of toleration towards experiment in socialist countries and, in 1955, Khrushchev was reconciled with Tito. (This tolerance, however, reached its limits in Hungary in 1956.) There was also a considerable domestic loosening; past errors and crimes were admitted and many victims of Stalinism were rehabilitated.

All the same, it was also a period of intense ideological competition. Dulles, the US Secretary of State, used Stalin's book, *Problems of Leninism*, as a guide to communism, drawing an analogy to *Mein Kampf*. Khrushchev made it clear that 'peaceful coexistence' referred to governments and not to ideologies.[2] It was during this period that he used the famous phrase 'We will bury the enemies of the Revolution.' Moreover, both sides put considerable emphasis on nuclear weapons. The US accumulated large numbers and varieties of nuclear weapons during the 1950s and considered their use in Korea, Indo-China, and Quemoy and Matsu. Khrushchev boasted, often inaccurately, about the capabilities of Soviet rockets.[3]

This part of the book covers the period that lasted from the late 1960s, after the Prague Spring and the student revolt, to the middle of the 1980s, up to Gorbachev's accession to power. Already, after the Cuban missile crisis in 1962, serious negotiations with the Soviet Union had been initiated first by Kennedy and later by De Gaulle and Willy Brandt when he became West German chancellor. The Partial Test Ban treaty, the treaty banning weapons in outer space and the agreement to establish a hotline (a permanently open telephone line between the US President and the Soviet leader) were reached in 1963. US–Soviet détente was interrupted by the Vietnam war as well as by the Soviet invasion of Czechoslovakia (described by Michel Debré as 'an accident on the road to détente'). However, during this period, the French and subsequently the West Germans began to pursue an independent détente policy. Brandt's Ostpolitik led to the *de facto* recognition of two German states and the settlement of post-war territorial disputes in Europe.

The early 1970s, after the end of the Vietnam war and with a series of US–Soviet summits, the SALT (Strategic Arms Limitation Talks) I agreement and the expansion of East–West economic relations, are generally considered to be the heyday of détente. The period culminated in the Helsinki Final Act of 1975, signed by all European states plus the United States and Canada. The Helsinki Final Act confirmed the territorial status quo in Europe and at the same time offered the possibility of changing the social and political status quo through its commitment to human rights, both individual and socio-economic.

From the mid-1970s, the US–Soviet relationship deteriorated, although détente in Europe persisted. The Soviet invasion of Afghanistan, which closely followed the Nato decision to deploy cruise and Pershing missiles in Europe, is generally considered to mark the beginning of a new cold war.

This part of the book is about the rise and fall of détente after 1968. The aim is to answer two questions. First, why was it found necessary to initiate a détente policy? Was this just chance or was it because the cold war formula was no longer working as well as previously? Secondly, why did détente fail? Why did the cold war bounce back?

The cold war was able to reproduce itself up to the mid-1960s because it produced conditions of stability and consensus in the West, and because it rationalized coercion in the East. Did this change in the late sixties? And, if so, why?

The debate about détente and new cold war

There is no established historiography of détente comparable to the scholarly debate about the origins of the cold war described in chapter 3. But détente has given rise to a voluminous literature, most of it popular and political. It is possible to categorize various arguments about the content of détente and the reasons for its failure and to show how these relate to differing assumptions about the nature of the East–West conflict.

First of all, there is what might be described as the anti-détente view, which derives from the orthodox version of the East–West conflict as an irreconcilable clash between freedom and totalitarianism. This view was expressed in a rash of articles, pamphlets and books put out by conservative groups in the United States in the late 1970s. These groups included, for example, the Committee on the Present Danger (named after a similar committee established in 1950) and the Coalition for Peace through Strength, consisting of 175 Senators and Congressmen, and 89 special interest groups such as the Reserve Officers Association, the American Federation of Small Businesses or Americans for a Safe Israel.

The basic argument was that détente was a sign of weakness, an expression of lack of American resolve. The decline in American military spending in the early 1970s had allowed the Soviet Union to catch up and even overtake the United States militarily. A CIA report in 1976 which revised its estimate of Soviet military spending upwards (even though the CIA itself was at pains to point out that this was merely a change in the method of calculation rather than in actual military spending) and the so-called Team B report commissioned by President Ford seemed to provide evidence for this proposition. Likewise, the withdrawal of the United States from Vietnam was thought to have encouraged the Soviet Union to play a more active role in the Third World and this was linked to a series of successful revolutions in the Third World during the 1970s, especially in the Middle East and Africa – Brzezinski's 'arc of crisis' (Brzezinski was President Carter's National Security Adviser). The Carter doctrine of 1980, enunciated after the Soviet invasion of Afghanistan, was explicitly designed for the containment of a southwards push by the Soviet Union towards the Persian Gulf.[4]

An interesting variant of the orthodox argument emerged in opposition circles in Eastern Europe during the same period, and may have partly prompted the Carter administration's preoccupation with human rights. This was the view that détente was a way in which the West assented to Soviet domination of Eastern Europe and continued oppression in socialist countries. When Kissinger and Nixon went to Moscow in 1972, several Jewish activists were arrested and detained without charges for the duration of their visit, yet neither Nixon nor Kissinger nor any of their entourage took up the issue. In 1975, remarks made by Helmut Sonnenfeldt to a conference of US ambassadors to Eastern Europe about the 'organic' relationship between Eastern Europe and the Soviet Union were widely interpreted (or misinterpreted according to Sonnenfeldt himself) as a kind of 'spheres of influence' or 'condominium' approach. As Milan Šimečka, a member of the human rights group in Czechoslavakia, Charter 77, has written:

I doubt very much that the seventies can be regarded as a period of détente at all . . . I remember how all those disarmament talks in the seventies – and even Helsinki itself – looked very dubious dealing to us, like a party at the expense of the East European countries, something we paid for in the shape of imprisonment, decline and stagnation.[5]

Šimečka goes on to say that this

was not entirely true, of course, and as it turned out, what seemed no more than agreements on paper about human rights were, amazingly enough, to prove instrumental in achieving certain improvements . . . If nothing else, by confirming the outcome of World War II, Helsinki served to rid the Soviet Union of its old obsessions about external threats and this subsequently had a positive effect on its attitude to détente.[6]

In other words, détente did, in the event, provide space for domestic change in socialist countries, by removing the immediacy of the imaginary war, through the provisions about human rights in the Helsinki declaration and as a result of East–West contacts. On this interpretation, it was Soviet concern to insulate Eastern Europe and the Soviet Union from the ideological risks of détente that was, at least in part, responsible for the failure of détente.

The antithesis of the anti-détente view is the view that derives from a revisionist version of the East–West conflict, the notion of an intersystemic conflict between capitalism and socialism. Unlike orthodox analyses, revisionist accounts of the East–West conflict can envisage a demilitarization of the conflict. This, in a sense, is what is meant by 'peaceful coexistence'. Orthodox analyses of the 'great contest' cannot disentangle the military element of the relationship because totalitarianism is bound up with militarism. However, the conflict between socialism and capitalism is about ways of organizing societies and economies. Thus, it is possible to envisage the conflict being waged by non-military means. Hence, Soviet commentators argue that détente failed because political détente, the settlement of outstanding disputes in Europe and warmer relations between East and West, was not followed by 'military détente'.[7] The obstructive attitude of the United States towards arms control negotiations is seen as the obstacle to military détente. Likewise, Social Democrat thinkers like Egon Bahr, who played a central role in promoting détente in the early 1970s, put forward the concept of 'common security' as the 'military component of détente'.[8]

There is an interesting parallel between the debate about détente and new cold war and the debate about the origins of the cold war. In the debate about the first cold war, the orthodox historians focused on Soviet behaviour in the closing years of the Second World War while the revisionists were interested in American behaviour during the late 1940s. In the current debate, the orthodox polemicists focus on Soviet behaviour during the détente period, while the revisionists are more interested in American behaviour during the onset of the new cold war, in the late 1970s.

The most cogent expression of the revisionist interpretation of the onset of the new cold war is provided by Fred Halliday in *The Making of the Second Cold War*.[9] Halliday himself disclaims the term 'revisionist' and describes himself as a 'new cold war writer'. The new cold war writers are distinguished from revisionists in that they do ascribe some responsibility to the Soviet Union.[10] Halliday sees the American concern to regain military superiority *vis à vis* the Soviet Union as the primary reason for the failure of détente. This was expressed in a new round of strategic armament and in the decision to deploy cruise and Pershing missiles in Europe and to counter revolutions in the Third World. In this respect, his view mirrors the anti-détente view.

Halliday does not discount internal factors. On the contrary, he puts considerable emphasis on domestic political pressures in the United States, on rivalry among advanced capitalist countries, and on what he calls involution in socialist countries – perhaps revealingly described as 'post-capitalist'. But these internal factors are subsidiary to or ways of mediating an external conflict.[11]

Variants of the revisionist argument which have been put forward in Western peace movement circles stress these internal factors as the primary explanation for the failure of détente. Several American writers have described the rise of domestic coalitions in both the late 1940s and the late 1970s, which used the 'Soviet threat' as a way of defeating liberal policies and pursuing special interests, such as those of the defence industry.[12] Europeans have put more emphasis on the role of the cold war as a way of restoring the unity of the Atlantic bloc; the deployment of Euro missiles, for example, was explicitly viewed as a mechanism for 'recoupling' the United States and Western Europe.[13] These writers would also emphasize the importance of revolutions in the Third World, but such revolutions are treated as *internal* to a Western-dominated global system rather than as symptoms of a systemic East–West conflict.

From this point of view, the preoccupation of the United States with military superiority does not have much to do with the Soviet military build-up. Concern about the Soviet military build-up, which is often exaggerated, is rather a way of justifying the acquisition of new American weapons, either for use in the Third World, or to assert American supremacy in the Western alliance, or as a result of military-industrial pressures.

In both variants of the revisionist description of détente and new cold war, the Soviet responsibility for the failure of détente, while not denied, tends to be downplayed. The Soviet military build-up and increasingly active global role is seen as primarily reactive or defensive, even if misguided, or else as irrelevant or exaggerated for domestic Western purposes. In retrospect, the failure of the Western left or the Western peace movement or even the West European establishment to protest more vigorously about the Soviet invasion of Afghanistan is shaming. Afghanistan was seen as an American pretext to scupper the second round of talks on limiting strategic arms, SALT II; it ought not to have been allowed to disturb détente in Europe. It took place *after* the Western decision to deploy cruise and Pershing missiles, so goes the argument, when the US–Soviet relationship had already deteriorated. It was, according to one revisionist analysis, 'a decision about Afghanistan – not Pakistan, not the Gulf, not Western Europe, nor even détente'.[14]

A third interpretation of the rise and fall of détente can be derived from the view of the East–West conflict as a conflict between great powers. This is the assumption underlying the so-called post-revisionist histories of the first cold war. Some such conception of détente seems to have guided Nixon and Kissinger and is to be found in much mainstream American commentary about détente, especially the encyclopaedic study of Raymond Garthoff (even though Garthoff sharply distances himself from Kissinger).[15] Kissinger and Nixon seem to have been concerned to enhance the role of diplomacy in managing relations between the United States and the Soviet Union. The strategy of containment solely through the threat or actual use of military force had been invalidated by Vietnam. At times, they talked idealistically about creating a 'structure of peace'. At other times, they seemed to envisage détente as a non-military form of containment. Détente was defined not as 'friendship but a strategy for a relationship between adversaries'.[16] Kissinger talked in rather Pavlovian terms about 'incentives for moderation and penalties for intransigence'.[17] Kissinger was greatly influenced by his previous studies of nineteenth-century diplomacy; he had written a biography of Metternich. He was concerned about geopolitical stability and was anxious 'to purge our foreign policy of all sentimentality'.[18]

Kissinger denied that he was conducting a spheres-of-influence policy or a 'superpower condominium', yet the Basic Principles of détente signed in 1972 and some aspects of the agreement on the Prevention of Nuclear War in 1973 sound suspiciously like a sort of Metternichian concert. In the Basic Principles, the United States and the Soviet Union agreed to non-interference in internal affairs and 'to do everything in their power so that conflicts or situations will not arise which would serve to increase international tensions'.[19] In the agreement on the Prevention of Nuclear War, the United States and the Soviet Union agreed 'to act in such a manner as to prevent the development of situations capable of causing a dangerous exacerbation of their relations'.[20]

The implication of these clauses was the overriding concern with stability. This concern was desirable in so far as it reduced the risk of war but it also could be used as a way of suppressing change.

This concern with stability was also important in West European conceptions of détente and in the statements of Soviet leaders. The West Europeans were generally unwilling to follow the American lead in harshly condemning the events in Poland and Afghanistan for fear of jeopardizing détente. Likewise Soviet leaders emphasized the overwhelming common interest in avoiding war, even though concerns were expressed within leading Soviet circles about subordinating revolution to peaceful coexistence.

Those who interpret détente as a less dangerous way of managing relations between great powers tend to explain the failure of détente in terms of misperception. Détente was a difficult relationship; it was easy to relapse back into confrontational modes. Insufficient efforts were made to define a code of conduct. The Western concept of détente was different from the Soviet concept of peaceful coexistence and this was not given due recognition. Insufficient communication, especially during the years of President Carter, indecisiveness and conflicting signals from different departments of government gave rise to mutual misunderstanding. Military developments, like the deployment of SS-20s or of cruise and Pershing missiles, defined by one side as defensive and reactive modernization, were interpreted by the other side as an escalation of the arms race. The Western insistence after 1975 on human rights, seen in the West as a 'legitimate demand for the Soviet Union to behave in a civilised manner',[21] was viewed as unwarranted interference in Soviet internal affairs. Likewise, the Soviet role in Angola, Ethiopia and Afghanistan, seen in the Soviet Union as the normal behaviour of a great power and no different from the behaviour of Western countries, was seen in the West as a violation of the agreement not to exacerbate international tensions. Indeed, from the Soviet point of view, the Americans seemed to be using détente as a way of excluding Soviet participation in Third World affairs, especially in the Middle East, while they viewed détente as a way of legitimizing their own global role.

In one sense, of course, this view is correct. The leaders of the United States and the Soviet Union were seeking alternative ways of managing their relationship. As the 1970s progressed, they did increasingly react negatively to behaviour that earlier they might have tolerated. These were indeed the immediate reasons for the failure of détente.

But for the explanation to end there presupposes a subjectivity and rationality in international affairs. It presupposes that leaders, who represent nations, make and unmake policy and that relationships are the product of their ideas and philosophies and their moods at any given time. The question to ask is how these misperceptions of détente came to arise. Why was it possible to initiate a détente process and then to discard it? Why did politicians change their minds?

The answers are to be found in the arguments put forward both in opposition circles in the East and in peace movement circles in the West. The answers have to do with internal conditions in both East and West. Thus there are challenges to capitalism, or more accurately the current social system in the West, but those challenges cannot be identified with the Soviet Union. And there is a struggle for freedom in the East but it is not the same as the American championship of human rights. There is a connection between what happens in East and West, but it is not in the identification of the United States with freedom or the Soviet Union with revolution, as American and Soviet hardliners suggest. Rather it is that the actions of each government provide the other with the pretexts it needs to deal with domestic challenges.

Afghanistan, writes Dimitri Simes, was

perceived as a blessing of sorts ... After prolonged suffering, the patient known as détente had finally passed away, and there would be no need for further artificial life support treatment. In the United States, an influential school of thought clearly felt that if the Soviet 'fraternal' aggression against Afghanistan had not happened, it would have had to be invented to provide the last straw to break détente's back. And there is evidence that there was some joy among Soviet elite circles at the break as well. The world became wonderfully simple once again – us against them, good guys against bad guys.[22]

In the next two sections, I shall explore these underlying systemic factors which contributed to the changing cycles of détente and new cold war.

Notes

1 To give two examples: Alan Wolfe, in *The Rise and Fall of the Soviet Threat: Domestic Sources of the Cold War* (Institute for Policy Studies, Washington DC, 1979), divides the post-war period into three peaks (1948–52, 1957–63, 1977–80) and two valleys (1952–7, and 1963–4 and 1968–73). The peaks are characterized by alarmist reports about the nature of the Soviet threat (NSC-68, the Gaither report of 1957 and the Team B report of 1967), by new military strategies (massive retaliation, flexible response, selective nuclear options) and by increases in military spending. Wolfe is concerned to describe the rise of domestic political coalitions pressing for higher military spending. W. W. Rostow, in 'On ending the cold war', *Foreign Affairs*, Spring 1987, describes three distinct cold war cycles (1945–55, 1953–73, and 1973–87). In Rostow's view, each cycle begins with a period of unilateral disarmament by the United States which is then exploited by the Soviet Union and draws forth a belated American response.

2 In *Khrushchev Remembers* (André Deutsch, 1971), he wrote:

> We Communists, we Marxist-Leninists, believe that progress is on our side and victory will inevitably be ours. Yet the capitalists won't give an inch and still swear to fight to the bitter end. Therefore, how can we talk of peaceful coexistence with capitalist ideology? Peaceful coexistence among different systems of government is possible, but peaceful coexistence among different ideologies is not. . . . I always said that there can be no such thing as ideological peaceful coexistence. I always stressed that we would fight to the end and that we would be sure to prevail. (p. 512)

3 Khrushchev describes his trip to London in 1956 and a conversation with the Prime Minister's wife:

> During dinner Mrs Eden asked us: 'Tell me, what sort of missiles do you have? Will they fly a long way?'
> 'Yes,' I said, 'they have a very long range. They could easily reach your island and quite a bit further.' She bit her tongue. It was a little rude of me to have answered her as I had. . . . We were simply trying to remind other countries that we were powerful and deserved respect. (Ibid., p. 405)

4 For a sophisticated and relatively moderate expression of this view, see Robert Tucker, 'The purposes of American power', *Foreign Affairs*, Winter 1980–1.

5 Milan Šimečka, 'From class obsessions to dialogue: détente and the changing political culture of Eastern Europe', in Mary Kaldor, Gerard Holden and Richard Falk, eds, *The New Détente* (UNU/Verso, 1989).

6 Ibid.

7 Pavel Podlesny, 'Some lessons of the Soviet—American détente and bilateral cooperation of the 1970s,', in Kaldor, Holden and Falk, eds, *New Détente*.

8 Egon Bahr, 'Observations on the principle of common security', in Stockholm International Peace Research Institute (SIPRI), *Policies for Common Security*, (Taylor and Francis, 1985).

9 Fred Halliday, *The Making of the Second Cold War* (Verso, 1983).

10 The term 'revisionist' is used to describe new cold war writers in the sense that they subscribe to a notion of a systemic conflict between capitalism and socialism. See Fred Halliday, 'Vigilantism in international relations: Kubalka, Cruickshank and Marxist theory', *Review of International Studies*, 13, 1987.

11 'The changes in US domestic politics have played an *instigatory* role in the development of Cold War II. Those of the USSR and China have played an *enabling* role. Those of the other advanced capitalist states have played a *supportive* one, reinforcing the trends in the dominant

member of the capitalist world' (Halliday, *Making of the Second Cold War*, p. 133, emphasis in the original).

12 See Wolfe, *Rise and Fall*; Jerry W. Sanders, *Peddlars of Crisis: The Committee on the Present Danger and the Politics of Containment* (Pluto, 1983); Charles E. Nathanson, 'The social construction of the Soviet threat: a study in the politics of representation', *Alternatives*, 13:4, October 1988.

13 See Noam Chomsky, 'The United States: from Greece to El Salvador', in Noam Chomsky, John Gittings and Jonathan Steele, *Super Powers in Collision* 2nd edn (Penguin, 1984); Dan Smith and Ron Smith, 'The new cold war', *Capital and Class*, 12, Winter 1980–1; Mary Kaldor, 'The role of nuclear weapons in Western relations', in Mary Kaldor and Dan Smith, eds, *Disarming Europe* (Merlin, 1982); Hanne-Margaret Birchenback et al., 'Transatlantic crisis – a framework for an alternative West European peace policy?', in Mary Kaldor and Richard Falk, eds, *Dealignment* (UNU/Basil Blackwell, 1987).

14 Dan Smith, 'The cold war', in Dan Smith and E. P. Thompson, eds, *Prospectus for a Habitable Planet* (Penguin, 1987). Even before Afghanistan, according to Soviet commentary, the Americans had been looking for an excuse to renege on arms control negotiations. One such excuse was the Soviet brigade in Cuba revealed in the summer of 1979. In 1981, a well-known Soviet commentator Valentin Zorin said on Radio Moscow:

> And when there were no excuses they were simply fabricated. A case in point was the noise over the so-called brigade in Cuba. Today, in Washington, it is no longer even mentioned. But as soon as Poland and Afghanistan can no longer serve as excuses, the Soviet brigade in Cuba will be ushered up again or something similar will be invented. (Quoted in Raymond L. Garthoff, *Détente and Confrontation: American–Soviet Relations from Nixon to Reagan* (Brookings Institution, Washington DC, 1985), p. 840)

15 Garthoff, *Détente and Confrontation*.
16 Ibid., p. 393.
17 Ibid., p. 31.
18 Quoted in John Lewis Gaddis, *Strategies of Containment* (Oxford University Press, 1982), p. 343.
19 'Text of Basic Principles, May 29th', *Department of State Bulletin*, vol. 66, June 1972.
20 Quoted in Garthoff, *Détente and Confrontation*, p. 334.
21 Dimitri Simes, 'The death of détente', *International Security*, 5:1, 1980.
22 Ibid., p. 3.

8

Reform and 'Normalization' in Post-Stalinist Societies

The history of the Soviet Union and Eastern Europe after Stalin's death can be described as the attempt to escape the heritage of the Stalinist system – a tightly centralized war economy governed by paranoia and fear. The continued external conflict, the domination of the Soviet Union over Eastern Europe and domestic repression in so-called socialist countries were all mutually supportive pillars of the Stalinist system. It could be described as a system that was permanently in crisis. Every relaxation in any one of the three pillars ushered in a period of instability followed by renewed coercion. The problem was and is how to find a route towards stability and consensus.

Cycles of détente and cold war cannot, therefore, be separated from cycles of loosening and tightening up within the socialist bloc (generally symbolized by the Soviet–Yugoslav relationship) or from cycles of reform and 'normalization' within individual countries. These three different cycles were not always contiguous but each profoundly influenced the others.

The post-Stalinist economic system

The permanent crisis of the post-Stalinist system arises from the difficulty of sustaining a war economy in the absence of war. In the absence of war, regulation by battle is replaced by bureaucratic regulation. The East European economies were centralized in order to meet certain clearly defined targets, namely victory in war. But victory in imaginary war is very different from victory in actual war. What would constitute victory in imaginary war and how victory could be achieved has to be defined by the planners themselves. In other words, once the targets of central planning are no longer defined externally, through the actual experience of war, they have to be defined subjectively, or internally. And in this situation, strictly speaking, the centrally planned systems can no longer be described as centralized, because the planners and the political leaders are always subject to all kinds of lower level pressures. Hungarian reform economists prefer to speak of a system of 'plan bargaining' or a system of 'bureaucratic regulation'.[1] It is a vertical system, administered through vertical directives from higher to lower levels of the state apparatus, in contrast to a system of market regulation in which horizontal relationships between buyer and seller predominate. But these vertical directives are the outcome of bargaining at lower levels. Hence, Tamoás Bauer speaks of 'building up' and 'breaking down' the plan.[2]

The contradictions of the post-Stalinist system arise from the problems of managing these vertical relationships. War bestows a certain legitimacy on the political leadership; it provides a reason for discipline and hardship. The legitimacy bestowed by imaginary war is difficult to sustain. Socialism has to prove itself in the competition with capitalism; it has to show that the discipline and hardship are necessary to 'catch up and overtake capitalism'. Economic growth becomes an important element of legitimacy. Even so, the receding promised future, which always needs more time to reach, gives rise to the Big Lie, the 'as if' philosophy in which ideology is further and further removed from actual experience. To reassert central control, the leadership must resort to coercion, to the purge, which is all the more difficult to justify in the absence of war.

In the aftermath of the Second World War and the warlike conditions of the late 1940s, the East European countries were able to achieve extremely rapid rates of growth of output, especially industrial output, far exceeding growth rates achieved in the West. All the same, the system was characterized by certain inbuilt irrationalities which meant that it was very difficult to sustain these rates of growth or to translate them into material benefits for the population. These countries face recurrent and increasingly severe economic problems which I can only briefly summarize here.

First of all, systems of bureaucratic regulation generate chronic shortages – shortages of labour, shortages of raw materials, shortages of consumer goods, etc. These shortages are not absolute (in the sense that there may still exist reserves of labour or raw materials). Rather they are generated by the nature of the planning system itself. Planned economies, says Kornai, are resource-constrained, in contrast to market economies which are demand-constrained.

Resource-constrained economies tend to shortage, while demand-constrained economies tend to excess capacity (unemployment).[3] Planners relate output targets to available resources but they invariably underestimate investment requirements, even when they explicitly allow for underestimation, and this results in shortages. Actual costs of investment always tend to exceed planned costs. The main explanation for shortage, according to Kornai, is what he calls the 'soft budget constraint'. That is to say, since enterprises never face bankruptcy, and indeed possess a certain amount of bargaining power, they can always overspend. They may underestimate the costs of an investment project in order to 'hook on' to the plan or they may increase inputs in order to overcome unexpected technical problems. (There is a remarkable parallel here with the cost overrun problem in Western defence companies.)

The corollary of shortage is, of course, wastage. Because of shortage there are many unfinished investment projects. Bottlenecks result in the under-utilization of other resources: machines and workers may stand idle for want of a particular raw material.

Closely related to shortage is a second recurrent problem – inefficiency and the lack of technical progress. The only way to overcome shortage is to use resources more efficiently, to introduce resource-saving measures. Hence, the preoccupation of East European planners with the change-over from extensive growth (adding more inputs) to intensive growth (more efficient use of inputs).

Inefficiency is the direct consequence of a system of bureaucratic regulation, where resources are allocated according to political bargaining power and not to criteria of economic efficiency. Even if there were pure-minded, intelligent, uncorrupt planners, who were able to draw up and implement plans to increase human welfare without taking into account vested interest, special pleading, etc., they could never, *a priori*, know enough to determine what is efficient. The advantage of forms of regulation like the market or war is that they provide some kind of external test – profit or loss or victory or defeat in war – of how much in resources is required for what.

There are plenty of examples of the way in which output targets may fail to meet user requirements, thus resulting in waste, inefficiency or failure to satisfy need.[4] Steel output specified in tons may result in excessively heavy steel, textile output specified in yards may result in thin textiles; consumer goods specified in roubles or zlotys may result in very expensive individual goods.

In practice, of course, there is not just the inefficiency arising from lack of knowledge but also the inbuilt inefficiency of the bargaining process, in particular, the 'soft budget constraint'. It is always easier to add inputs than to save inputs. And this is especially true when there are no incentives for saving inputs but there are penalties for failing to fulfil targets. The introduction of resource-saving measures may temporarily disrupt the fulfilment of output targets.

Inefficiency implies that growth rates which are impressive on paper may not be reflected in increased satisfaction of need by either producers or consumers. Rather they may express the accretion of inappropriate outputs and the excessive use of inputs. (In fact, statistical growth rates may also have been inflated by the absorption into the socialized sector of small artisanal enterprises, which were previously not counted.)

Thus a third recurrent problem is the tendency for a perpetual imbalance between producer goods and consumer goods, or, in Marxist terms, a disproportion between department I and department II. This arises from the differential bargaining power of producers and consumers. Whereas enterprises participate in the plan bargaining process, consumers are atomized and powerless (coming into their own only during dramatic manifestations of discontent – Berlin 1953, Hungary 1956, Poland 1956, 1978, 1980, Czechoslovakia 1968).[5] The differential bargaining power is expressed by Kornai in economic terms; enterprises experience a soft budget constraint whereas households experience a hard budget constraint, that is, wages. In any competition for resources, there is an inherent tendency to favour the enterprise. For example, suppose the price is raised for a particular product which is used by both enterprises and consumers. This will reduce purchases by the consumer because there is a limit to how much the consumer can pay. But it may actually increase the amount purchased by enterprises because that particular product has become more easily available owing to the reduction in household demand. Alternatively, a reduction in consumer sales might release production capacity, making it possible to overcome bottlenecks faced by enterprises.

Because of the inherent tendency to underestimate planned costs, any drive to increase investment results in a squeeze on consumption. The only alternative, if plans are to be fulfilled, is to increase imports. Military spending cannot be squeezed because the military sector participates in the bargaining process; because the state is the consumer of military products, the armed forces also experience or at any rate used to experience a soft budget constraint (as in the West).

The argument can also be expressed in the following way. The war economy or the economy of the pseudo-war is an economy in which resources are centrally allocated and in which investment and military spending receive priority. In wartime, this is in order to increase the output of armaments and to improve the industrial base on which armaments output depends. The purpose of consumption is to reproduce soldiers and workers. In the context of imaginary war, the priority given to investment and military spending is a consequence of the structure of power relations. Industrial enterprises and the armed forces constitute part of the state apparatus and therefore have to be reproduced. This system gives rise to a permanent squeeze on consumption as well as a tendency to stagnate owing to the difficulty of managing power relations. Moreover, this is not just a consequence of domestic power relations. Because of the importance of intra-Comecon trade, especially negotiated bilateral trading relationships with the Soviet Union, the industrial structure of each individual East Central European country is tied to that of other Comecon countries. East Central European countries sell manufactured goods, especially machinery, to the Soviet Union in exchange for raw materials and energy; Soviet demands further constrain the possibilities of moving away from the industrial structure inherited from the Stalinist period.[6] The recurrent economic problems are, at one and the same time, political problems both because they are the consequence of power relationships and because they repeatedly call into question the legitimacy of those relationships.

To overcome these recurrent problems, periodic efforts were made to reform the system. The reforms varied considerably from country to country but all of them, to a lesser or greater degree, represented some kind of attempt to replace vertical relationships with horizontal relationships and to move away from the war economy.[7] Reforms tended to include:

- a devolution of decision-making, with a greater role for the market mechanism. Administrative directives were reduced and/or replaced by financial incentives; enterprises were allowed to retain more of their profits; small-scale private enterprises were permitted etc.;
- greater emphasis on agriculture and consumption and less emphasis on investment and military spending;
- a certain degree of intellectual or cultural liberalism, especially in the spheres of science and technology and economics (the reforms had to be debated).

However, the reform process is inherently contradictory since it has to be carried out by those who have most to lose both economically and politically by the reform. For that very reason, up to the advent of Gorbachev and the subsequent developments in the rest of Eastern Europe reforms tended to be fragmentary and piecemeal and in almost every case to lose momentum.[8] They were predicated on existing power relationships. Even though some countries, notably Hungary, succeeded in instituting reform better than others, attempts to take reform further, to move beyond existing power relationships were resisted, either domestically or, in the final instance, by other socialist countries, as was tragically clear in Hungary in 1956 or Czechoslovakia in 1968.

The post-Stalinist system was thus quite distinct from the Bukharinist system described in chapter 4. There was some effort to introduce market regulation, especially in agriculture, and ideological legitimacy was derived from economic growth, as well as from the imaginary struggle with the West. There was a greater degree of intellectual and cultural pluralism and some effort to return to collective decision-making within ruling parties. But all this took place within a tightly circumscribed political and economic framework inherited from the Stalinist period.

Détente or reform?

The initial moves towards détente came from the West, in the post-Khrushchev era – first from De Gaulle, then from Johnson, anxious to seek a way out of the Vietnam war, and then from Willy Brandt. There were good reasons to respond to these initiatives, if only to assuage longstanding security concerns in Europe. Even at the height of the Stalinist period, the Soviet leadership had favoured 'peaceful coexistence', that is, some mutual recognition of the territorial status quo in Europe. All the same, the Soviet leadership seems to have been hesitant. This was a period of 'normalization' following the enunciation of the Brezhnev doctrine which legitimized the intervention in Czechoslovakia. The reforms of the mid-1960s had, in every case, been curtailed. The Brezhnev politburo was ideologically conservative. After Khrushchev's fall, there seems to have been a compromise with the military which allowed a steady increase in military spending on all the services. Brezhnev saw himself as a military hero; he awarded himself military medals and advanced himself to the rank of army general and then to marshal. Doubts were expressed by allies, especially the GDR. (Indeed Ulbricht, the East German leader, had to be removed and replaced by Honecker so as to reach agreement on the status of the two Germanies.)

Two factors seem to have been important in determining a positive response. One was China. Armed clashes between China and the Soviet Union along the Ussuri river had taken place in March 1969. Brezhnev was evidently worried about a rapprochement between China and the United States.[9] The other factor, which was also important for East European leaders, was the notion of what Brezhnev called the 'foreign reserve'. By increasing imports, it was possible to initiate an old-fashioned centralized investment drive without squeezing consumption and without reducing military expenditures. Soviet commentators put considerable emphasis on the 'organic correlation' between Brezhnev's peace programme, enunciated at the 24th Congress of the CPSU held in 1971, and the ninth five-year plan which, for the first time, increased the share of consumer-oriented investments. Soviet commentators also emphasized the importance of military power as a basis for détente, echoing the Western emphasis on détente and deterrence.[10] In other words, Western credit was to provide a substitute for reform.

Interestingly, Peter Volten suggests how these concerns may have been related to the domestic political process in the Soviet Union. After Khrushchev's fall, the Soviet system reverted to collective leadership and, during the 1960s, an 'apparently successful attempt' was made 'to prevent the emergence of a dominant leader and to install genuine consensus decision-making'.[11] However, this represented a further move away from centralized control, making it extremely difficult to implement new policies or to steer the economy and society in new directions. There were divisions within the party; powerful conservatives on the central committee were able to paralyse and stifle initiatives. Hence, Brezhnev's peace programme can also be interpreted as a strategy for rising above the mire and immobilization of the collective leadership.

During the early 1970s, high growth rates were achieved in all the East European countries (see table 8.1). Real wages also rose rapidly, especially in Poland. These growth rates were, in the language of experts, import driven. Because the socialist countries could not generate sufficient exports to pay for imports, the growth of imports had to be financed with Western credit. Credit became easily available during the 1970s, both because of the accumulation of petrodollars but, more importantly, because of the 'de-politicization' of credit, which was the consequence of détente. Trade with Western Europe grew much faster than trade with the United States because the US Congress imposed all kinds of restrictions on legislation designed to relax trade – the most well known being the Jackson–Vanik amendment to the Trade Reform Act, which linked liberalization of trade with the issue of Jewish emigration.

It was hoped that the increased investment would result in increased exports. However, export capacity was limited, in part because of fixed commitments to the domestic market and to other Comecon countries. Because in some cases imports were squandered on consumption (in Poland), on ill-conceived investment projects or

Table 8.1 Average Annual Growth Rates (%) of East European Economies, 1950–85

	1951–5[a] NMP per capita	1956–60 NMP	1956–60 Average Real Wages	1961–5 NMP	1961–5 Average Real Wages	1966–70 National Income	1966–70 Average Real Wages	1971–5 NMP	1971–5 Average Real Wages	1976–80 NMP	1976–80 Average Real Wages	1981–5 NMP	1981–5 Average Real Wages
Albania	7.0	*	*	*	*	9.2	3.2[b]	6.6[c]	2.1–2.7[b]	*	*	*	*
Bulgaria	8.1	9.6	6.1	6.1	1.9	8.7	5.4	7.8	3.2	6.1	0.4	3.7	0.9
Czechoslovakia	6.9	7.0	4.6	4.6	1.2	6.9	3.5	5.7	3.5	3.7	0.7	1.8	0.4
GDR	13.0	7.1	7.4	7.4	2.5	5.2	3.7	5.4	3.7	4.1	2.7	4.5	2.0
Hungary	4.6	6.0	8.0	8.0	1.7	6.8	3.5	6.2	3.3	2.9	3.0	1.9	0.5
Poland	6.6	6.5	5.1	5.1	1.5	6.0	1.9	9.8	9.3	2.2	2.2	−0.5	−3.4
Romania	12.6	6.6	8.2	8.2	4.1	7.6	3.5	11.3	3.9	7.3	5.6	4.4	0.1
Soviet Union	11.2	9.2	*	6.6[c]	*	7.7	5.9[b]	5.7	4.6	4.3	2.4	3.6	1.4

[a] Official estimates
[b] national income per capita
[c] national income
NMP: Net Material Product
* Not Available

Sources: W. Brus, Chapters 1–4, in M. Kaser ed. *The Economic History of Eastern Europe, 1919–75, Vol III*, (Clarendon Press, 1986), for years 1950–1970; *Economic Survey of Europe*, Economic Commission for Europe, (United Nations, October, 1988) for years 1971–85; Ernest Mandel *Beyond Perestroika*, (Verso, 1989) for Soviet figures in years 1951–1970

merely used to overcome bottlenecks, it was difficult to expand export capacity. Also, East European economies had great difficulty in assimilating Western technology.[12] Western machinery imports tended to give rise to a chain of supplementary demands for spares, for appropriate inputs, etc. – driving imports up further, without increasing exports.

The situation was exacerbated by the 1973 oil crisis. Terms of trade deteriorated for all East European economies except for the Soviet Union and Poland (exporters of oil and coal). Measures taken by Western governments to counteract the rise in the price of oil resulted in a recession, which further reduced the Western market for East European exports. East European governments did not take corrective measures, preferring to 'ride out' the crisis. The second oil shock in 1979 had a similar effect, although by then corrective measures were already being taken. Whereas Western countries, especially Western Europe and Japan, began to introduce energy-saving methods after 1973, East European countries became much more energy dependent. It was much more difficult to adjust the requirements of large-scale, relatively inflexible, long-term investment projects. The volume of oil deliveries nearly doubled during the 1970s and natural gas deliveries grew tenfold. The Soviet Union was the primary supplier of energy materials; they increased from 15 per cent to 40 per cent of East European imports from the Soviet Union between 1970 and 1980. Moreover, the price of Soviet oil and gas tripled between 1975 and 1980.[13] In a viciously circular fashion, East Central European countries had to increase the volume of exports to the Soviet Union to pay for the increased cost of Soviet oil and gas. And these exports consisted of industrial products which were manufactured by the most heavily energy intensive sectors of the economy.[14]

An additional factor was growing competition from the NICs (newly industrializing countries) in Asia and Latin America (Mexico, Argentina, Brazil, Singapore, South Korea, Taiwan, Hong Kong). These countries were competing for the same patch of the OECD market, namely low-cost manufactured goods, as the East European economies. Whereas the NICs' share of the OECD market rose from 4.5 per cent to 8.1 per cent between 1970 and 1983, the share of East European countries declined from 1.5 per cent to 1.1 per cent.[15]

East European countries were also affected by the 'new protectionism', especially after 1974. In Western Europe, there has been greater use of non-tariff barriers, voluntary export restrictions and other related measures, all of which applied to East European countries. However, it is argued that because state trading organizations are more experienced at bargaining, the Comecon countries did rather better than other regions in making use of 'managed' trade.[16]

Western credit collapsed in 1982. Undoubtedly, the new cold war was a factor in the credit collapse. But the main reason was the high level of indebtedness. Estimated net convertible current debt of Comecon countries amounted to 77 billion dollars in 1982. Of this, the Soviet Union and Comecon banks accounted for 19.9 billion dollars, and Poland accounted for 25.2 billion dollars.[17] However, even before the collapse of Western credit and before the renewal of the cold war, East European countries had begun to cut back on imports from the West. (Actually, apart from the US grain embargo imposed on the Soviet Union, the new cold war did not lead to much increase in trade restrictions. The West Europeans were unwilling to curtail trade and, because of the failure to liberalize trade in the 1970s, the US had less to restrict. After the imposition of martial law in Poland in December 1981, the US did try, unsuccessfully, to gain European support for a more far-reaching policy of sanctions; the most well-publicized example was the gas pipeline incident.)[18]

The Soviet Union made a move to reduce imports in 1974, although they rose again from 1975 to 1979. The decision to cut back the growth of imports does not seem to have been just a response to the growing external imbalance, which was still manageable in relation to the overall economic size of the Soviet Union.[19] Rather there are suggestions that it had more to do with ideology – a conservative backlash within the political apparatus. One week after the US Trade Act had been signed by President Ford on 3 January 1975, it was rejected by the Soviet Union. In addition to the Jackson–Vanik amendment, the Stevenson amendment to the Export–Import Bank Bill limited to 300 million dollars the total the bank could lend the Soviet Union over the next five years without seeking further approval from Congress and banned the use of this money for the development and production of energy. Brezhnev had privately signalled his willingness to allow increased Jewish emigration; however, the issue of non-interference in internal affairs had become important within the politburo and the central committee. The economic advantages of détente seem to have been outweighed by the political costs. As Volten puts it, the Jackson–Vanik amendment 'proved to be a most effective means of strengthening opposition in Moscow and forcing Brezhnev's withdrawal'.[20]

From 1975, there was a reversion to collective leadership in foreign policy making, an increased rhetoric about socialist internationalism, a partial reversion to economic autarky and an increased emphasis on the military element in foreign policy. There seems to have been a cutback in consumption, and a squeeze on East European economies through the increased price of oil and natural gas. By 1979, the Soviet Union had restored its current account trade balance.

The growth of military spending also seems to have slowed, from 4.5 per cent annually (in constant roubles) between 1965 and 1975, to 2 per cent annually after 1976, according to CIA estimates. (This occurred at the very moment of heightened clamour in the West, especially the United States, about the Soviet military build-up.) The cutback mainly affected strategic systems. There was a continued emphasis on theatre and conventional forces, with the deployment of SS-20 missiles and the growing, albeit tiny in comparison to Nato, overseas naval role.[21]

Particularly important in the late 1970s was growing Soviet involvement in the Third World, especially in Angola, Ethiopia and Afghanistan. This was a response to a wave of revolutions which arose out of specific Third World conditions and which were, in some degree, made possible by the decline of US economic and military assistance and US interventionism after Vietnam. But Soviet involvement was also in keeping with the growing ideological mood of the late 1970s as détente policy teetered. It was part of the ideology of imaginary war that accompanied the return to autarky, the notion of a wartime atmosphere that justified austerity. Treaties of friendship and cooperation were signed with Angola, Mozambique, Ethiopia, Afghanistan, Syria and the People's Democratic Republic of Yemen. There was an increase in Soviet technical assistance and military advisers in these countries. (Cuban troops were also sent to Angola and Ethiopia.)[22]

These developments were presented as part of a shift in the 'correlation of forces' favouring the Soviet Union. Soviet leaders were criticized by conservatives in the politburo and the party for putting the goals of peaceful coexistence before the goals of proletarian internationalism. Aid for revolutionary movements in the Third World was a way of asserting the sincerity of the commitment to the struggle against US imperialism. This was particularly important after what was perceived as a setback for socialism in Egypt, the humiliation of the Egyptian repudiation of the friendship treaty with Soviet Union.

The intervention in Afghanistan took place in the context of a deteriorating East–West relationship; at every stage, the risks of a defeat for 'socialism', particularly as perceived from within the ruling elite, seemed greater than the costs of increased involvement. The intervention represented the culmination of a renewed cold war ideology *vis à vis* the Third World. Marshal Grechko spoke with pride of the Soviet 'army of internationalists'. Even so, the Soviet Union did not support all revolutionary movements in the Third World, and Soviet propaganda was at pains to point out the 'limited' nature of the intervention.[23]

Differing responses to the failure of détente

The East European countries cut back on imports in the late 1970s and were forced to impose austerity policies. Thus, in the late 1970s and early 1980s, they experienced slow rates of growth, stagnation and even in Poland, declining real wages and reductions in military spending (table 8.1). Agricultural production was particularly hard hit by the cutback in imported fertilizers, feed stocks, etc. However, the political response to this situation varied from country to country. The East European countries did not turn their backs on détente; rather their attitudes towards détente varied according to different political traditions. The Polish story is well known. The cutback in imports resulted in a fall in industrial production and a catastrophic situation in agriculture. The emergence of a new mass workers' movement, the trade union Solidarity, involved a 16-month long crisis during which the command system more or less collapsed.

The imposition of martial law in December 1981 did not resolve the economic situation despite the virtual militarization of coal mining (conscription of workers, military discipline, etc.) in order to increase exports. The Polish government veered between reform and 'normalization'. Despite repression, a flourishing opposition (Solidarity, peace and green groups, the church) continued to exist.

In Hungary, the response was to renew the reform and to intensify détente. Hungary applied for membership of the IMF and the World Bank, and the international secretary of the Hungarian Socialist Workers' party, Mátyas Szűrös, put forward the theory that small and medium powers in Europe have a special role in fostering détente and that socialist countries should not necessarily subordinate national interests to the interests of the socialist community.[24] Political, as well as economic, liberalization seems to have been viewed as a way of obtaining consent for austerity – the reversal of the 'implied social contract' of the 1970s.

The GDR also remained favourable to détente, although for quite different reasons than Hungary. The GDR was able to offset its cutback on imports from Western countries other than West Germany by an upsurge of imports from West Germany. The GDR was also able to *increase* its exports to West Germany. Thus inter-German trade increased dramatically in the early 1980s. This was possible because of special conditions pertaining to East–West trade:

- because the GDR was not considered a foreign country, GDR exports to West Germany were not subject to the normal tariffs, duties, agricultural levies, etc.;
- the GDR had access to a virtually interest-free credit facility known as the 'swing' which was originally set up in 1949 to cope with temporary imbalances in inter-German trade;
- the FRG made substantial hard currency transfers to the GDR, totalling some 3 billion DM a year. These included public fund transfers (mainly for preserving access to West Berlin, and for various services like sewage and trash disposal, postal services, etc.), private transfers (visa fees, currency exchange requirements for visitors, hard currency shop receipts, gifts) and a series of credits provided in return for freeing political prisoners.[25]

Hence, for the GDR the formula of détente as a substitute for reform, in a sense, succeeded at least until the late 1980s, because of the special relationship with West Germany. (Actually, the GDR did introduce the Kombinate reform which created a new form of industrial association but this did not involve a significant move away from the system of bureaucratic regulation.) Honecker tried to keep open channels of communication even after the deployment of cruise and Pershing missiles; and he said that the deployment of Soviet SS-12s and SS-23s in the GDR was 'no cause for celebration'.

Czechoslovakia and Bulgaria followed the Soviet line, although both introduced some domestic reforms in the early 1980s. (Czechoslovakia heavily over-invested in nuclear energy during the 1970s.) Articles criticising the small states theory as well as Honecker's proposed visit to West Germany in 1984 appeared in *Pravda* and *Rudi Pravo* (the Czechoslovak party newspaper). Romania succeeded in paying off its hard currency debt through a particularly virulent reversion to nationalistic totalitarianism, with harsh discrimination against national and cultural minorities.

These national differences in the behaviour of East Central European regimes first emerged in the 1950s 'thaw'. It is tempting to explain them in economic terms. Thus the GDR and Czechoslovakia are the most industrialized countries and perhaps for this reason the immediacy of the need for reform to increase growth and living standards was less. Albania and Romania are extremely poor, agricultural countries. Hungary and Poland are somewhere in between, partially industrialized. Yugoslavia represents a mix between the Polish and Hungarian models and the southern European socialist countries. Slovenia moved furthest towards economic and political liberalization, while Serbia displayed increasing nationalist-totalitarian tendencies. It is also the case that in Poland and Yugoslavia agriculture has remained predominantly in private hands, while in Hungary the agricultural sector has enjoyed a certain amount of autonomy. (The Hungarian reform was most successful in agriculture, which more or less adopted a system of market regulation with a relatively harmonious relationship between cooperatives and small private household plots.) In these countries also, there are large informal private sectors, which were more or less tolerated and more or less legal. (The so-called second economy is probably largest in Hungary, where it is estimated to account for 33 per cent of total active working time and to contribute as much as 20 per cent to GDP.)[26]

But this kind of economistic explanation has to be tempered by an understanding of domestic political processes. Mihály Vajda argues that these structural explanations can never 'really penetrate the essence' of these national differences. They 'disregard those differences which are embedded in history, and which affect attitudes and behaviour, first and foremost, in the relationship of people to the structure'.[27] Building on the distinctions between the three historical regions of Europe (East, West and East Central) Vajda suggests that these differences have to do with differences in the historical traditions of resistance. Because Eastern Europe, as opposed to East Central Europe, had no tradition of independent social movements, the Eastern system, as Vajda call the Soviet model, was able to come into being. In contrast, in East Central Europe, where there were such traditions, the system 'inevitably' came into 'chronic conflict with the traditional conditioning of people, expressed in their attitudes and behaviour'.[28] Czechoslovakia, for example, has the most developed democratic traditions in the region, yet it experienced one of the most conservative and repressive regimes. Vajda argues that it is precisely because of Czechoslovakia's traditions, or rather particularly the Bohemian tradition, that the destruction of autonomous culture and intellectual life was most complete. 'That is why every single person who was suspected of democratic thinking and attitudes had to be thrown on to the scrap heap.'[29] The strength of Vajda's argument is the emphasis on history and culture, as opposed to economistic mechanisms. Indeed, economic differences can be explained in historical terms – the fact that the southern European countries experienced 500 years of Turkish rule, the Western influence on Bohemia and the German states which made up the GDR, the Eastern influence on Poland and Hungary.[30] However, the weakness of such historical analyses is the implication that whatever has been, will be, thus, for example, admitting no hope for the peoples of Eastern Europe (as opposed to Central Europe), no possibility of resistance and pluralism in the Soviet Union.

Equally, or perhaps more important, there is the element of political choice. The changing character of opposition in Eastern Europe, both central and east, is very important in understanding what happened in the 1980s. Up until 1968, the main form of opposition was revisionism. Revisionism emerged out of the state apparatus and from those intellectuals who were close to the communist party. It presupposed reform from above. It arose, says Adam Michnik, from the ambiguity of the term socialism, which meant both Soviet political practice and the 'universal idea of the fraternity of the working class'.[31] It was revisionism that inspired the Polish October and Dubcek's 'socialism with a human face'. The Hungarian revolution went beyond revisionism, even though Nagy and his companions were revisionists, in its demands for a multi-party system and for withdrawal from the Warsaw Pact. Revisionism died, says Michnik, in Poland in March 1968 when the remaining revisionists were purged from the party apparatus and in Czechoslovakia in August 1968.[32] It had died earlier in Hungary in June 1958 when Nagy was executed.

Indeed throughout Eastern Europe and the Soviet Union, the intervention in Czechoslovakia was a turning point in the thinking of intellectuals. Kargalitsky says, in his book on Soviet intellectuals:

On the morning of 21 August 1968, the entire ideology of Soviet liberalism collapsed in a few minutes and all the hopes aroused by the Twentieth Congress fell to the ground. Whereas previously, liberal intellectuals had comforted themselves with the thought that, on the whole, our society had not lost its socialist character that – as Yevtushenko wrote in his *Autobiography* – the revolution was sick but not dead, the events of 1968 shattered those illusions. It was not a matter of the 'excess of Stalin' but of the system itself.[33]

Likewise, in a recent interview, Christa Wolf, the East German novelist, describes the intervention in Czechoslovakia in 1968 as an 'existential shock'.[34]

The dissident movement developed during the 1970s, especially in Poland, Hungary, Czechoslovakia and the Soviet Union. This was the period of the growth of *samizdat* publications. The dissidents saw their role as offering a moral alternative – a personal choice based on conscience and personal integrity and a way of keeping truth alive, as Havel put it in *The Power of the Powerless*.[35] The Helsinki Final Act of 1975 did provide the dissidents with an important lever with which to pressure their governments. The combination of a lessened external threat and Western concern about individual dissidents may have provided somewhat more protection.

The space opened up by the dissidents paved the way for more substantial forms of opposition. The development of Solidarity marked the rebirth of the concept of 'civil society'. Solidarity transformed the nature of opposition in Eastern Europe. It was a mass movement, not a group of (isolated) intellectuals, although, of course, it was supported by intellectuals. And it was a workers' movement in a system where the ruling elite claimed to represent the working class. Solidarity pioneered the notion of change or reform from below. The idea was that by strengthening or creating autonomous institutions, the Catholic church or independent trade unions, society could put pressure on governments. In his pathbreaking essay, 'A new evolutionism',[36] Michnik suggested that change could come about through peaceful, gradual evolution based on a series of compromises between autonomous social institutions and the state, within the limits imposed by external relationships.

Of course, civil society, in the sense that it is used here, was not an entirely new phenomenon in Eastern Europe. It already existed in the form of the Catholic church in Poland or the intellectual opposition in Hungary and had already influenced the differing evolution of East European countries. But the fact that it was conceptualized and became the inspiration for Solidarity and subsequent movements in East Central Europe emerging in the early 1980s does have something to do with détente. Michnik did not rule out the possibility of Soviet intervention. Indeed, he emphasized that the opposition in Poland had to 'learn that ... change can only come – at least in its first stages – within the framework of the "Brezhnev Doctrine"'. But he did believe that the Soviet Union was unwilling to intervene in Poland because of 'international repercussions'. Intervention in Poland, because of the scale of resistance, would have resulted in 'a war that Poland would lose on the battlefield but that the Soviet Union would lose politically'.[37] Hence, détente provided more space, although not unlimited space, for peaceful evolution. In the event, the imposition of martial law on 13 December 1981 took place in the context of a new cold war. It was an indirect intervention, in the sense that it was carried out by the Polish armed forces, after months of indirect pressure in the form of Warsaw Pact military manoeuvres on the Polish borders.

In other words, détente did provide an opportunity for domestic change, at least after 1975. Whether or not détente would lead to such change depended on internal conditions in each individual country. In particular, it depended on the extent to which autonomous groups and movements could occupy the openings afforded by détente. In Hungary, for example, an autonomous peace group, Dialogue, was allowed to exist for six months between 1982 and 1983.[38] And in the GDR the peace movement, Swords into Ploughshares, spread under the umbrella of the Protestant churches up to the deployment of cruise and Pershing missiles in October 1983.[39]

The new cold war constrained the possibilities for domestic change. In the early 1980s, the differential approaches of East European countries towards détente and towards domestic reform were constrained by the Soviet Union. There were limits to Polish and Hungarian reform in the absence of Soviet reform and limits to Hungarian and East German détente in the absence of US–Soviet détente. The Soviet Union, for example, intervened to stop Honecker's proposed visit to West Germany in 1984 and seems to have insisted on a retraction from Szűrös; peace activism in both countries was suppressed. The détente of the 1970s had foundered because it was not accompanied by domestic reform. To succeed, East–West economic cooperation would have had to have been linked to a fundamental transformation of East European systems so as to overcome the problems of shortage, inefficiency and austerity. In the early 1980s, individual national efforts at reform or at East–West détente foundered because of the constraints imposed on the socialist bloc in the context of a renewed US–Soviet confrontation.

The new cold war of the early 1980s, the retreat to confrontation, resolved none of the problems that had given rise to détente. Economic growth declined further in the early 1980s – the Brezhnev era was to become known as the period of stagnation. It was no longer possible to substitute consumption for political legitimacy. On the eve of Gorbachev's accession to power, the cycle of reform and 'normalization', detente and cold war, was exhausted. As Gorbachev put it as he embarked on the processes of perestroika and glasnost: 'There is nowhere for us to retreat.'[40]

Notes

1 See János Kornai, 'The Hungarian reform process: visions, hopes, and reality', *Journal of Economic Literature*, 24, December 1986, pp. 1687–1737.

2 Tamoás Bauer, 'Investment cycles in planned economies', *Acta Oeconomica*, 21:3, 1978, pp. 243–60.

3 János Kornai, *Contradictions and Dilemmas* (Corvina, New York, 1985).

4 Alec Nove gives plenty of examples in which output targets fail to meet user requirements:

> Steel sheet was made too heavy because the plan was in tons, and acceptance of orders from customers for thin steel threatened plan fulfilment. Road transport vehicles made useless journeys to fulfil plans in ton-kilometres. Khrushchev himself quoted the example of heavy chandeliers (plans in tons) and over-large sofas made by the furniture industry (the easiest way of fulfilling plans in roubles). (*An Economic History of the USSR*, 3rd edn (Penguin 1984), p. 357)

See also Alec Nove, *The Soviet Economic System* (Allen and Unwin, 1977).

5 For a fascinating discussion of the dual character of socialist economies involving centrally administered production and atomized consumption, Ferenc Fehér, Agnes Heller and György Markus, *Dictatorship Over Needs* (Basil Blackwell, 1983).

6 See Andras Köves, 'Problems and prospects of East–West cooperation: an East European view', in Mary Kaldor, Gerard Holden and Richard Falk, eds, *The New Détente* (UNU/Verso, 1989).

7 For a comprehensive description of the first and second waves of reform in the 1950s, see W. Brus, chapters 1–4 in M. Kaser, ed., *The Economic History of Eastern Europe, 1919–1975*, vol. 3: *Institutional Change within a Planned Economy* (Clarendon, 1986). For the Soviet reform experience, see chapter 2 of Abel Aganbegyan, *The Challenge: Economics of Perestroika* (Hutchinson, 1988).

8 In an interview with me, Imre Poszgay, the leading Hungarian reformer, likened the reform process so far to a decision to change the traffic from left to right – 'first, the bus drivers, then the taxi drivers, then everyone else'. See 'Poszgay – Hungary's man of the hour', *New Statesman*, 27 May 1988.

9 At the 1969 WTO (Warsaw Treaty Organization) summit meeting in Budapest, one participant told the *Washington Post*'s correspondent: 'Brezhnev's face was red and he did not look well. He was nervous and

impatient, his temper flared and he pounded on the table. He had only one thing on his mind – and that was China.' Quoted in Peter M. E. Volten, *Brezhnev's Peace Program: A Study of Soviet Domestic Political Process and Power* (Westview, 1982), p. 53.

10 In his speech to the 24th Congress, Brezhnev said:

> What, in fact, allows us to view the issue in this way? Primarily, the changed balance of power in the world – both socio-political and military power. Even a few years ago, the imperialists and primarily the American imperialists hoped seriously, by using the arms race, to reinforce their positions in the world arena and to simultaneously weaken the economy of the USSR and the other socialist countries, to frustrate our plans for peaceful construction. The failure of our enemies' calculations has now become completely clear. Everyone can now see that socialism is sufficiently powerful to ensure both a reliable defence and the development of its economy. (Quoted in Volten, *Brezhnev's Peace Program*, p. 64)

11 Ibid., p. 78.

12 Western contractors have cited the following reasons for poor assimilation: 'Shortages of construction workers, poor qualifications and motivation among those available, inadequate transport facilities, shortages of complementary inputs from Soviet industry (high-grade steel and electronic components, for instance) and lack of relevant manufacturing know how.' Morris Bornstein, 'West–East technology transfer: the Soviet Union', *OECD Observer*, September 1985.

13 James L. Ellis, 'Eastern Europe: changing trade patterns and perspectives', in *East European Economies: Slow Growth in the 1980s*, vol. 2: *Foreign Trade and International Finance*, Joint Economic Committee, 90th Congress, 1st Session, 28 March 1986.

14 Andras Köves, 'Some questions of energy policy in East European countries', in R. Dietz and K. Mack, eds, *Energie, Umwelt und Zusammenkeit in Europa* (Springer-Verlag, 1987).

15 Kazimierz Poznanski, 'Competition between Eastern Europe and developing countries in the Western market for manufactured goods', in *East European Economies*, see note 13.

16 George Yannopoulos, 'EC external policies and East–West trade', *Journal of Common Market Studies*, xxiv:1, September 1985.

17 *Economic Bulletin for Europe*, vol. 37, United Nations, Geneva, November 1985.

18 For an analysis of these restrictions, see Herbert Wulf, 'East–West trade as a source of tension', *Journal of Peace Research*, 19:4, 1982.

19 See George Sokolov, *The Economy of Détente: The Soviet Union and Western Capital* (Berg, 1987). Sokolov suggests that investment and

East–West cooperation compete with military spending and autarky.

20 Volten, *Brezhnev's Peace Program*, p. 115.

21 Richard Kaufman, 'Causes of the slowdown in Soviet Defense', *Survival*, 27:4, July/August 1985.

22 See Fred Halliday, *Cold War, Third World: An Essay on Soviet–American Relations* (Hutchinson/Radius, 1989).

23 According to Marshal Grechko, in 1980: 'Loyal to their international duty, Soviet servicemen, together with the servicemen of other socialist countries, went to the assistance of fraternal Czechoslovakia in 1968. At the request of Afghanistan's revolutionary government, a limited contingent of Soviet troops is now fulfilling its international duty in the Democratic Republic of Afghanistan's territory.' Quoted in Harry German, *The Brezhnev Politburo and the Decline of Détente* (Cornell University Press, 1984), p. 47.

24 Mátyas Szúrös, 'Interaction of the national and international in Hungarian policy', *New Hungarian Quarterly*, 25:93, Spring 1984.

25 According to the newspaper *Die Welt*, the going price for a political prisoner in 1983 was 50,000 DM. Between 1,000 and 1,500 prisoners were being freed annually in this way. John Garland, 'FRG–GDR economic relations', in *East European Economies: Slow Growth in the 1980s*, vol. 3: *Country Studies on Eastern Europe and Yugoslavia*, Joint Economic Committee, 90th Congress, 1st Session, Washington DC, 1986.

26 Kornai, 'The Hungarian reform process'.

27 Mihály Vajda, 'East-Central European perspectives', in John Keane, ed., *Civil Society and the State* (Verso, 1987), p. 339.

28 Ibid.

29 Ibid., p. 355.

30 See Ivan Berend and György Ranki, *The European Periphery and Industrialization, 1780–1914* (Cambridge University Press, 1982) and also Ivan Berend, 'The historical evolution of Eastern Europe as a region', *International Organisation*, 40:2, Spring 1986.

31 Adam Michnik, 'The Prague Spring ten years later', in *Letters from Prison and Other Essays* (University of California Press, 1985), p. 158.

32 Ibid.

33 Boris Kargalitsky, *The Thinking Reed: Soviet Intellectuals from 1917 to the Present* (Verso, 1988), p. 200.

34 A shortened version of the interview, entitled 'Flesh ties', was published in the *New Statesman*, 23 February 1990.

35 Vaclav Havel et al., *The Power of the Powerless: Citizens against the State in Central-Eastern Europe* (Hutchinson, 1985). This moral choice

was even expressed in a play actually performed during the Brezhnev era. One of the characters in Gelman's *We the Undersigned* says:

If a man is sensible, they get rid of him all the same. And, incidentally, that is the right thing to do. Because being good and honest is, pardon me, a pleasure for the soul! Isn't that so? It is. And if you are honest, and a chief as well, that's too much pleasure! Life is just. To one, it gives a conscience – and he's happy. To another, it gives a position – and he's happy. It's necessary that things should be right for everybody! (Quoted in Kargalitsky, *The Thinking Reed*, p. 270)

36 In Michnik, *Letters from Prison and Other Essays*.
37 Ibid., p. 144.
38 See Ferenc Köszegi, and E. P. Thompson, *The New Hungarian Peace Movement* (Merlin/European Nuclear Disarmament, 1983).
39 See John Sandford, *The Sword and the Ploughshare: Autonomous Peace Initiatives in East Germany* (Merlin/European Nuclear Disarmament, 1983).
40 Quoted in Abel Aganbegyan, *Challenge*, p. xxviii.

9

The Erosion of Atlanticism

In recent years, a good deal has been written about the relative decline of American hegemony – the increasing difficulty of financing America's global role, the impotence of American military suprema- cy, the loss of America's ideological legitimacy.[1] What has declined is not so much the American power or the American state but the American pattern of industrial development, which underlay Amer- ica's rise to political preeminence. Because American institutions shaped and were shaped by the American pattern of development, and because of the size and rigidity of the military-industrial complex, the United States has been less able to introduce or assimilate alternative patterns of industrial development than Japan, say, or some West European countries.

This is the context in which détente and new cold war have to be understood in the West. Détente offered space for social and institutional experiment, especially in Western Europe. The new cold war represented a restoration of Atlanticism; it restrained experi- ment, and reimposed a Fordist framework.

The immediate reason for détente, at least from the American point of view, was the Vietnam war. The first tentative moves towards détente had been taken earlier, during the late 1960s, by Western European governments. The Vietnam war was presented, not as the imperialist war it was, but as part of the ongoing East–West struggle. It could be described as an attempt to substanti- ate the American theory of the cold war; the notion that people living within the American sphere of influence depended on the United States, with its superior Fordist technology, to protect them from the Soviet threat. As the memory of the Second World War faded and as awareness of the destructiveness, and therefore uselessness, of nuclear weapons grew, American leaders sought ways to increase the 'credibility' of military power to sustain those perceptions of military power which would strengthen political power. Hence the theory of limited war, which led inexorably to Vietnam.

But Vietnam failed to substantiate the American version of the imaginary war. Instead the war exposed the changing political and economic situation of the United States. For those who participated in the war or watched the war on their television screens, the war undermined the belief in a struggle of good against evil. Unlike the Second World War, and even the Korean war, Vietnam generated dissent not consensus, division not unity. Economically, the Vietnam war challenged the Keynesian premise that war stimulates output, and improvements in productivity, as it did in the Second World War. Because of the relative decline of the American economy, the war led to inflation and greater pressure on the dollar rather than increased trade surpluses and domestic expansion. And, finally, the spectacle of what might be described as a Fordist war machine, an essential prop of the imaginary war, was badly damaged by guerrillas armed with small arms and missiles. Vietnam revealed a chasm between the high-flown rhetoric of imaginary war, drawn from the experience of the Second World War, and the reality of America's declining role.

The decline of Fordism

The decline of the American pattern of industrial development can be observed in a number of different dimensions. First of all, it became harder and harder to sustain productivity growth within the mass production paradigm. From the 1950s onwards, the US rate of productivity growth lagged behind that of other advanced industrial countries. Part of the reason was simply the fact that the United States was the lead country. The diffusion of Fordism meant that other countries were following the American example; it is much easier to catch up than to imitate. But from the mid-1960s, the US rate of productivity growth actually declined and this has to be explained in terms of the trajectory of Fordist methods of production. Sooner or later, all technologies reach a point of diminishing returns, where improvements are harder to achieve. In the case of the Fordist production process, an optimum scale is reached beyond which further expansion in size leads to inflexibility; workers are unwilling to work more intensely and become dissatisfied with the tedium of assembly routines; concern about environmental consequences mounts.[2]

Secondly, the key factor of production, oil, was no longer abundant. The two oil shocks of 1973 and 1979 dramatically raised the price of oil. What is more, the United States became during the 1960s and 1970s a net importer of mineral fuels.

Thirdly, the market for consumer durables became increasingly saturated. In the United States 'in 1979, there was one car for every two residents, compared with one for every four in the early 1950s. Ninety-nine per cent of American households had television sets in 1970, compared with 47 per cent in 1953. Similarly, more than 99 per cent of households had refrigerators, radios and electric irons, and more than 90 per cent had automatic clothes washers, toasters and vacuum cleaners.'[3]

After 1960, trade began to increase much faster than output, as firms sought foreign markets. In the US case, foreign markets were often more easily penetrated through overseas investment than through exports; this was reflected in the increased share of trade consisting of internal transactions within large corporations.

The decline of the American pattern of industrial development was reflected in American performance in manufacturing trade. In 1965, the United States enjoyed a comfortable overall trade surplus; in 1971, the United States experienced its first trade deficit since 1936. With the exception of 1973 and 1975, the US has experienced a continuing and growing trade deficit in every year since 1971. As can be seen from table 9.1, one explanation for the deficit has been the increased dependence on imported mineral fuels since 1970, although this has been partly offset by an increase in the value of exports of agricultural products and other raw materials (excluding petroleum). However, equally important is the growing deficit in manufactured trade which can be treated as an indicator of the

Table 9.1 US foreign trade ($US million)

Year	Total			SITC 0+1+2+4 (food, raw materials, etc.)			SITC 3 (mineral fuels)			SITC 5–9 (manufactured goods)		
	X	M	X/M	X	M	X/M	X	M	X/M	X	M	X/M
1967	31,147	26,816	1.16	8,306	7,787	1.07	1,104	2,250	0.49	21,737	16,778	1.30
1968	33,982	33,114	1.03	8,330	8,818	0.94	1,056	2,529	0.42	24,596	21,768	1.12
1969	37,444	36,052	1.04	8,300	8,904	0.93	1,131	2,794	0.40	28,013	24,354	1.15
1970	42,590	39,951	1.07	10,156	9,696	1.05	1,595	3,075	0.52	30,840	27,181	1.13
1971	43,492	45,563	0.95	10,020	9,957	1.01	1,497	3,715	0.40	31,975	31,891	1.00
1972	48,979	55,563	0.98	12,107	11,418	1.06	1,552	4,799	0.32	35,319	39,347	0.90
1973	70,246	69,477	1.01	22,002	14,506	1.52	1,671	8,175	0.20	46,573	46,796	1.00
1974	97,143	100,972	0.96	27,589	17,159	1.61	3,442	25,350	0.14	66,113	58,643	1.13
1975	106,157	96,941	1.10	27,525	15,905	1.73	4,465	26,404	0.17	74,168	54,633	1.36
1976	113,323	121,793	0.93	29,102	19,173	1.52	4,226	33,929	0.12	79,995	68,692	1.16
1977	117,963	147,848	0.80	30,106	22,350	1.35	4,179	44,198	0.09	83,678	81,300	1.03
1978	140,003	182,196	0.77	37,363	26,951	1.39	3,878	44,685	0.09	98,762	110,557	0.89
1979	173,649	217,462	0.80	46,781	30,711	1.52	5,624	63,735	0.09	121,244	123,016	0.99
1980	212,887	250,280	0.85	55,428	30,987	1.79	7,953	82,204	0.10	149,506	137,089	1.09
1981	225,777	271,213	0.83	55,306	23,737	2.33	10,245	84,261	0.12	160,226	155,214	1.03
1982	206,045	253,033	0.81	47,232	28,413	1.67	12,720	67,424	0.19	146,093	157,195	0.93
1983	194,620	267,971	0.73	76,569	30,489	2.51	9,557	59,999	0.16	138,495	177,483	0.78
1984	212,034	325,726	0.65	49,483	33,404	1.48	9,311	60,980	0.15	153,241	231,342	0.66
1985	206,926	345,276	0.60	40,600	33,440	1.21	9,971	59,917	0.17	156,354	257,918	0.61
1986	205,728	366,064	0.56	38,561	35,616	1.10	8,114	37,310	0.22	159,691	297,036	0.54

X = Exports
M = Imports
SITC 0+1+2+4 = Food, beverages, tobacco, crude materials, excluding petroleum
SITC 5+7+8+9 = Machinery and transport equipment plus other manufactured goods

Source: OECD Economic Outlook, Historical Statistics, 1960–83 (Paris, 1985); OECD, *Monthly Statistics of Foreign Trade*, March 1986, March 1987 and February 1988 (Paris).

performance of US manufacturing industry. In 1965, the ratio of US exports to imports of manufactured goods was 1:6. By 1985, the ratio had fallen to 0:6.

During this period, Japan retained an enormous trade surplus – manufacturing exports were roughly four times the size of manufacturing imports. West European countries, excluding Britain, also managed to retain respectable trade surpluses.

Part of the story was a surge in imports during the early 1980s owing to the Reagan administration's encouragement to private consumption. But the declining US share of the export market was also dramatic. Between 1965 and 1985 the US share of the world market for manufactured goods declined from 21 per cent to 17 per cent. The Japanese share increased from 9 per cent to 18 per cent, while the West German share remained roughly constant at 18 per cent. Whereas 20 years ago, the US still dominated world trade, today, the US is *less* important than Japan or the EEC (whose total exports are approximately three and a half times the total exports of the United States).[4]

The success of Japan, and to a lesser extent Western Europe, reflects in some degree the emergence of a new pattern of industrial development which has been variously described as 'post-Fordism', 'flexible specialization', or 'Fujitsuism'. The characteristic features of this new pattern of development have been widely discussed and debated elsewhere.[5] Here, I shall briefly summarize those that are considered more important.

- First of all, the growth of what is called information technology. This is the combination of large-scale data processing, made possible by the use of microelectronics, with improvements in telecommunications both because of the use of microelectronics for switching and because of new forms of transmission, like fibre optics or satellites. Carlotta Perez-Perez says that the microchip is the new key factor of production.[6] Computers and telecommunications are now the most rapidly growing sectors in the OECD area. According to a recent OECD report, the information technology sector accounted for 25 per cent of the total output of OECD countries. Between 30 and 45 per cent of the total active workforce in the OECD area is now engaged in information-handling occupations; in the US more people are employed in the IT sector than in the automobile industry.[7]

- Secondly, a change in producer–user relations, with greater integration
  – through the use of information – between production and distribution on the one hand, and design and production on the other hand,
  allowing for much greater flexibility in automated production processes. The combination of computer-controlled capital goods, which can
  be modified through a change in design software, and computer-
  controlled distribution, which greatly improves knowledge of the
  market, allows the producer to respond rapidly to changes in taste and
  to varieties of taste. It becomes profitable to adopt a policy of 'market
  niching', that is, to produce small batches of specialized products to
  meet a very specific demand. Piore and Sabel contrast Fordism, as the
  use of custom-built capital goods to manufacture mass-produced
  consumer goods, with flexible specialization, which involves the use of
  mass-produced capital goods to manufacture specialized products.
  The chain of Benetton shops is often cited as an example in which
  computers have been used to coordinate demand in small high street
  boutiques with small units of production in Italy.[8] In fact, the
  technique can be applied to a whole range of industries, including both
  typically Fordist industries like automobiles (Toyota being a leading
  example) and pre-Fordist 'sunset industries' like furniture, clothing,
  footwear, ceramics, etc. (This has been very important in Italy.)
- Thirdly, a change in the production process, involving a reduction in
  the size of units of production. Sometimes this may mean collectivities
  of small enterprises in a particular location, with common research
  laboratories, design centres, advisory or training services perhaps
  supported by a local or regional level of government, as in Italy or
  West Germany or Cambridge, England. An alternative model is teams
  of skilled workers, as at Toyota or Volvo, with knowledge and skills
  relevant to the entire production process, as opposed to the standar-
  dized, assembly-line tasks of the Fordist paradigm. This somewhat
  rosy picture of work after Ford has to be tempered by noting the
  growing duality of the labour market, especially in Japan where
  privileged tenured workers in core enterprises can be contrasted with
  poorly paid labour employed on short-term contracts by subcontract-
  ing enterprises – more often the lot of the elderly or of women of
  minority groups (Korean or Burakumin). Also mass production remains important in the production of electronic components and in
  newly industrializing countries where there are still reserves of labour
  and advantage can be taken of low wage costs.
- Fourthly, a reduction in waste with the introduction of just-in-time
  systems, based on improved information, which allow reductions in

stockholdings and the use of smaller, more widespread retail outlets. Improved information about design and production allows for improved planning and less wastage in the use of energy, raw materials and space. Hence the new pattern of industrial development tends to be resource saving and capital saving as opposed to labour saving (the characteristic feature of Fordism).

- Finally, the new pattern of industrial development is transforming the service sector. This includes the development of new products like home entertainment which substitute for services like cinema and theatre; technical change in services which have hitherto been hardly affected by technology, especially offices, banks and shops; and the possibility of new services or expansion of existing services such as environmental services (monitoring pollution levels), health services (with new diagnostic aids) or education.

This new pattern of industrial development, it can be argued, emerged out of very specific social and institutional conditions that predated the technical revolution in microelectronics. In Japan, it arose from a combination of specific requirements and traditions: the lack of cheap indigenous sources of raw materials, lack of space limiting stockholding, a small domestic market for which mass production was not well suited, traditional gangs of workers rather than skill stratification more typical in the West, and long-term employment guarantees.[9] In addition, the Japanese government, particularly the Ministry of Trade and Industry, played a key role in helping enterprises to adapt initially American technology and later indigeneous technology to the Japanese context; this was achieved through what are sometimes described as horizontal and decentralized relationships with 'family' enterprises, that is, groups of enterprises around a core enterprise.[10] Japan has been at the forefront of the production of information technologies, overtaking the US in the last decade in the production of electronic components, telecommunications and office machinery/data processing, and has applied these new production techniques based on electronics to a wide range of industries. The Japanese success in electronics may be due to an early lead in electronic consumer goods (televisions, radios, etc.) at a time when US electronics output was geared mainly to the military sector.

Although West European countries have not been very successful in the manufacture of electronic products, except for telecommunications, several Western European countries have applied innovative methods of production to their traditional specialisms – West Germany (machine tools and electrical machinery), Sweden (robotics, engineering and vehicles), Switzerland (clocks and watches), Italy (furniture, clothing, ceramics, etc.). These new methods were adopted in the face of Japanese competition, but again were the outcome of favourable indigenous circumstances: pressure for worker participation in Sweden and West Germany, state support for engineering training, local state encouragement and support for research, design and market surveys, and so on. Particularly important in Italy, according to Piore and Sabel, was the decentralization of industry following the strike waves of the late 1960s and the tradition of familiarism, artisanal and merchant activities, combined with positive development strategies by left local governments.[11]

The United States has lost its dominant position in information technology. Its share of the total market for electronics declined from 23 per cent to 19 per cent between 1965 and 1985. (Japan's share increased from 13 per cent to 42 per cent.) Except in computers, owing to IBM's preeminence, the US was experiencing a trade deficit by the mid-1980s in all categories of electronics. Even in office machinery/data processing (this is mainly computers) its export: import ratio declined from 4.27 in 1975 to 1.15 in 1985. More importantly, the United States, like Britain, seems to have had great difficulty in adjusting methods of production in other sectors. This can be explained in terms of the persistence of a Fordist institutional framework and culture: union structures, skill profiles, transport networks, energy extravagance, and especially high levels of military spending.

It would perhaps be wrong to say that a new pattern of industrial development already exists. Rather, the world is in the process of shaping a new pattern of industrial development – its direction and consequences still depend on political decisions that have not yet been taken. It would be more accurate to say that a new set of production processes with some common characteristics have emerged in Japan and some Western countries. This has transformed some aspects of the consumption process, for instance, it has led to greater diversity in consumption and revolutionized some services such as retailing or banking, but by and large this has taken place within the existing framework of household and government demand.

What has happened has been a rapid increase in productivity in some sectors and in some countries, and a decline in productivity growth in other sectors and regions, without a corresponding change in the pattern of demand. This is reflected in a structural imbalance in trade performance between the US, on the one hand, and Western Europe and Japan, on the other hand. And this is the main explanation for the reemergence of mass unemployment in advanced industrial countries, that is, the reappearance of excess capacity, and a slowdown in overall growth rates compared with the 1950s and 1960s.

The problem is not simply how to increase demand but how to shift the geographical and social composition of demand. And this is a political rather than an economic problem. The current composition of demand is determined internationally by the political dominance of the United States among advanced capitalist countries and, domestically, by the political priorities and fiscal structures of the Atlanticist era, in particular the dominance of private consumption and military spending as forms of expenditure.

In other words, as in the 1930s, current economic problems can be described as a mismatch between production and consumption or between supply and demand. And this mismatch is at one and the same time a mismatch between the pattern of industrial development and the institutional framework. It is thus a political problem; it has to do with relations of authoritative reproduction. If we describe the crisis of the post-Stalinist economies as one of shortage, of inadequate and inappropriate production, which is at root a crisis of political relationships, then the current economic problems of capitalist countries can be attributed to inadequate and inappropriate consumption, which is also a problem of political relationships. This is a paradoxical conclusion in so far as it is in East European countries that needs are unfulfilled and it is in advanced capitalist countries that people are unemployed.

This structural explanation for stagnation and for the reemergence of unemployment in advanced industrial countries differs from what might be described as the shock theory of the global slowdown, that is, that the West's economic problems were caused by a series of exogenous shocks: the wage explosion after 1968, the oil shocks, the collapse of the Bretton Woods system, that is to say, the dollar dominated system of fixed exchange rates which lasted until 1971, the rundown of US food stocks, high interest rates, etc. These 'shocks' were either symptoms of the underlying structural problems, or else exogenous events that in other situations might not have caused the perturbations they did.

The breakdown of the Atlanticist compromise

Associated with the decline of the American pattern of industrial development is the erosion of Atlanticism. In chapter 5, I argued that Atlanticism was a kind of concert of advanced capitalist countries, a way of reaching agreement and compromise, a way of providing an institutional framework which could preside over the diffusion of Fordism in four respects: it constituted a political compromise between the United States and Western Europe – a way of creating a common political outlook among elites which combined acceptance of cold war policies with a commitment to managed capitalism; it provided underpinning for the global economic system – the free, or more or less free, trade regime; through the integrated command structure and joint formulation of defence strategy, as well as cultural influence, it favoured the construction of a Fordist infrastructure and Fordist set of governmental priorities within individual countries; and it represented an implicit spheres-of-influence accord among advanced industrial countries. The decline of Fordism was linked to growing strains in each of these four aspects of Atlanticism.

US and European politics

First of all, the Atlanticist political compromise came unstuck. The student revolts and the wave of worker unrest that started in 1968 represented a challenge to the political compromise from the left. On the one hand, 20 years of economic growth and prosperity had raised material expectations. On the other hand, the fact that in the post-war period trade unions had implicitly agreed to confine their role to material demands meant that wage demands were often a way

of expressing deeper dissatisfaction about modern society – dissatis-
factions never properly articulated. Just as workers couched their
angst in wage demands, so students couched theirs in the language of
those left groups which had been excluded from the cold war
consensus. Movements which constitute an outburst of feeling or
emotion are not always able to frame their demands in a politically
relevant way – they often return to the past to seek ways of
expressing themselves, emotion getting diverted by tradition. This is
not to say that there were not relevant demands in 1968; demands
about Vietnam, about the nature of education, and other concerns,
were not only important, they shaped the ideas of a generation. But it
was in the 1970s, with the rise of new single-issue movements, that
concern about women, the environment, the role of the state,
democracy, consumption, militarism and so on came together to
constitute the seeds of a radical critique of Atlanticism.

The wage settlements of the late 1960s or early 1970s nullified the
workers' demands, however. They were passed on along with the rise
in the price of food and oil in price rises, and inflation became the
basis of a right-wing attack on the Atlanticist compromise which
began in the middle 1970s. Attempts by governments to manage the
effects of the 1973 oil shock, the devaluation of the dollar and the
rise in world food prices had led to 'stagflation' – the combination of
inflation and unemployment. This provided an opportunity for the
right to use inflation as well as some of the left concerns about the
role of big government to present a neo-liberal programme of
monetarism – or supply-side economics as it was known in the US –
deregulation and a strong defence sector. It was a programme which
could be used to recapture power. This was particularly important in
north-western Europe, where Labour or Social Democrat parties had
been in power for most of the period since the 1960s. It could also be
used to undermine trade unionism and to spearhead an onslaught on
the new left – 'Marxists in the Labour party', as Mrs Thatcher would
put it, sociologists and philosophers in universities.

It was, in fact, the old Atlanticist left, the Labour party in Britain,
the Social Democrats in Germany and the Carter administration in
the US, that succumbed to these pressures from the right and were
the first to introduce monetary targets and to increase military
spending after a decade or so of more or less constant defence
budgets.

It was a rejection of the original Atlanticist compromise in the sense that it involved the rejection of managed capitalism, of state intervention and welfare. The cold war element of the compromise was maintained: the policies that were introduced by right-wing governments coming to power in the early 1980s therefore had differential consequences in Western Europe and the United States. Because the United States had always placed more emphasis on warfare than welfare and had never adopted policies of nationalization and planning, the United States was able to stimulate the economy through military spending, to adopt what was in effect a policy of military Keynesianism, attracting funds to finance the boom through the high interest rates that resulted from the adoption of monetary targets. In Western Europe, on the other hand, the programmes of right-wing governments were much more deflationary. At the same time, however, West European governments, especially those in West Germany and Italy with their more decentralized state structures, and in the smaller countries, were more responsive to demands from new social movements about the environment, gender, workers' participation, etc.

Liberal Democrats in the United States and social democracy in north-western Europe were thus squeezed in the early 1980s from both right and left. Just as the first cold war had resulted in a rightward shift, so the new cold war had a similar consequence. What is more, the decline of the Fordist pattern of industrial development combined with deflationary policies eroded the social base of these parties – the traditional blue-collar worker – while the attack on trade unionism eroded their institutional base.

The erosion of social democracy was paralleled by the rise of new social movements, especially the peace movement, whose social base was drawn mainly from the growing class of white-collar workers, created partly by the growth of the welfare state (doctors, nurses, teachers, lecturers, social workers) and partly by the growth of information-handling occupations. These movements criticized the original Atlanticist compromise, not for the commitment to managed capitalism, but for the cold war policies. The campaign against cruise and Pershing missiles, which acted as a kind of catalyst for all kinds of single-issue groups which had emerged in the 1970s, was about the Atlantic relationship and about European self-determination.

The main form of political access for these movements was the

Social Democrat or Labour parties and, in the US, the Democrats. (In some countries, particularly West Germany, Green parties emerged.) Hence the collapse of the Atlanticist political compromise was also a crisis of the left. If these parties adopted anti-cold war policies, they did so somewhat halfheartedly and unconvincingly, undermining their electoral credibility. If they failed to adopt anti-cold war policies, they lost the enthusiasm of their supporters and activists.

In southern Europe, the situation was, as in the 1940s, different. There, it was the base of the communist parties that was eroding. In the early 1980s, socialist parties, often greatly influenced by the new social movements, came to power in all the southern European countries, except of course Turkey. The French socialists had been greatly inspired by the new left. The Spanish and Greek socialists had been greatly influenced by the peace movement and came to power on platforms promising withdrawal from Nato as well as Iberian and Balkan nuclear-free zones. Perhaps because the southern Europeans were always subjects rather than participants of the Atlanticist compromise, in almost every case these parties, once in power, sooner or later joined the new cold war, in the sense of not opposing the deployment of Euro missiles, the symbol of the new cold war, and of going along with neo-liberal domestic policies.[12]

Emerging differences of outlook between American and West European elites and within Western Europe were expressed in debates about the nuclear issue. Both West European governments and American administrations insisted that the American nuclear umbrella was an expression of the Atlantic unity. However, West European governments argued that 'flexible response' was a strategy of deterrence – nuclear weapons could not be used without risking escalation to all-out nuclear war, thereby implying a sort of equality between the US and Western Europe. The growing American emphasis on strategies for fighting nuclear war, which implied that nuclear war could be confined to Europe, was a reassertion of US dominance (this is elaborated in chapter 11).

The end of Bretton Woods

The second respect in which Atlanticism had presided over the diffusion of Fordism was that it underpinned the global economic system. Both the Bretton Woods system and the free trade regime began to disintegrate during the 1970s and 1980s.

The immediate cause of the collapse of the Bretton Woods system was the cost of financing the Vietnam war and the cost of President Johnson's 'great society'. But the Bretton Woods system always contained the contradiction that the creation of international liquidity (spending dollars overseas) undermined the role of the dollar as an international currency.[13] As long as the US enjoyed a balance-of-trade surplus, confidence in the dollar was maintained. It was believed that the US could afford the overseas network of military bases, large amounts of military and economic assistance and high levels of foreign investment because the outflow of dollars returned to the United States in the form of purchases of US goods. As the competitiveness of American manufacturers declined, so the dollars were increasingly spent on Japanese and West European goods. In 1950, US gold and foreign exchange reserves amounted to 24.3 billion dollars, while the combined reserves of Germany, Italy and Japan were 1.4 billion dollars. By 1970, US reserves had fallen to 14.5 billion dollars, while the reserves of Germany, Italy and Japan had risen to 23.8 billion dollars.

Essentially, the role of the dollar depended on the willingness of the West European and Japanese governments to tolerate American balance-of-payments deficits and to hold accumulated dollar reserves. De Gaulle talked about the American *privilège exorbitant*, the fact that the system allowed the United States to have large balance-of-payments deficits while the rest of the world had to accept the discipline of fixed exchange rates. This is why in the mid-1960s De Gaulle pushed for a return to the gold standard. By agreeing to hold dollars, the West Europeans and the Japanese were effectively financing the Vietnam war. In the end, it was the refusal of the West German government to buy up billions of dollars flowing speculatively into West Germany that led to Nixon's decision on 15 August 1971 to suspend convertibility of the dollar. By 1973, all major currencies had abandoned fixed exchange rates. At a meeting of leading members of the IMF in Kingston, Jamaica, in 1973, it was agreed to legalize floating exchange rates, reduce the role of gold and increase IMF quotas.

The new system of floating exchange rates is equally open to US abuse, however. With the diminished role of gold, the dollar is even more important as an international currency, although the creation of the European Monetary System has provided a greater role for Western European currencies, especially the deutschmark, and the yen has also become more important. During the 1970s, there was a tremendous growth of world liquidity. The Eurodollar market emerged out of the combination of US deficits and OPEC surpluses and expanded rapidly because of the integration of financial markets through the growth of multinational banks and deregulation, and because of new banking technologies which greatly speeded up the rate of transactions.[14] The growth of liquidity meant an increase in speculative activity, so that capital flows greatly exceeded trade flows, contributing to the instability of exchange rates, and an increase in the volume of world debt, especially that held by Third World countries and East European countries.

Under the system of floating exchange rates, the US continued to enjoy its *privilège exorbitant*. Under Nixon, the balance of payments improved, owing to the rise in food prices (which resulted from the rundown of foodstocks, in part due to Soviet grain purchases, and the replacement of food aid to the Third World by food sales), the rise in oil prices (which affected Western Europe and Japan more than the US because they were more dependent on oil), the increase in arms sales (as a result of both the Nixon doctrine, building up regional surrogates like Iran, and the rundown of military assistance) and the devaluation of the dollar. Hence the cost of improving the American balance of payments was borne by Western Europe, Japan and the Third World.

The Carter administration was greatly influenced by the Trilateral Commission which had been set up by David Rockefeller to bring elites in Western Europe, Japan and the United States together to discuss foreign policy and to reinvigorate West Atlanticism. Therefore some effort was made to stabilize the dollar and to increase overseas aid, but these efforts were not accompanied by domestic deflation. The Carter administration constituted a brief return to the confident epoch of liberal Atlanticism when the conditions for liberal Atlanticism – the dominant role of the American pattern of industrial development – no longer existed. When Europeans and Japanese remonstrated, the Carter administration put forward the 'locomotive theory' of world recovery, the idea that American expansion would pull the world out of recession.

The consequence was renewed deficits, inflation, rising interest rates and gold prices and, after the fall of Iran, the second oil shock. (During the 1970s, perhaps owing to Fordist predispositions, the US government kept domestic oil prices low. Whereas Western Europe and Japan introduced widespread energy-saving measures, confounding predictions of world energy demand, the US became much more oil dependent.)

The Reagan administration's policies of high levels of defence spending, tax cuts and monetary targets led to huge fiscal deficits and ever-growing balance of payments deficits. The trade deficit jumped from $8.4 billion in 1979 to $141.9 billion in 1987. Hence, the American arms build-up and private consumption boom was paid for by foreign loans from Western Europe and Japan and by debt repayment from the rest of the world. The United States was the only country not subject to demands for 'structural adjustment' from the IMF and the international banking community – no one was breathing down American necks asking if the US could really afford the MX, the B-1 bomber, the Strategic Defense Initiative, or the yuppie bonanza. In effect, the Reagan administration presided over a political redistribution of world product in favour of the United States.

During Reagan's second term, especially after the 1987 Wall Street crash, some efforts were made by the G-5, now G-7 (Group of Seven) countries, to stabilize exchange rates. But no one could agree on reform of the system. The US wanted the surplus countries to bear the burden of adjustment – they feared the consequences of deflationary policies. The West Europeans and the Japanese wanted the US to take corrective measures but the US argued, rightly, that this would lead to global recession.

The story of what happened to the free trade regime is somewhat similar. Negotiations under GATT (the General Agreement on Trade and Tariffs) continued during the 1970s at the Tokyo round, and indeed were resumed in the 1980s in the Uruguay round. The Tokyo round did succeed in achieving further tariff reductions, but these gains (if free trade is considered a gain) were overtaken first by the growth of non-tariff barriers, which primarily affected Fordist and pre-Fordist products, and, secondly, by the growth of post-Fordist services – mainly finance and telecommunications – which were not subject to GATT and which are now estimated to account for one quarter of world trade. Non-tariff barriers included voluntary export restrictions (VERs) on textiles, steel, shipbuilding, automobiles and electronic consumer goods; anti-dumping measures; countervailing duties; and various regulations specific to particular countries. Managed trade, that is, trade allowed by agreement between states, rose from 13 per cent in 1974 to 30 per cent in 1982. The Reagan administration adopted what is sometimes described as a policy of 'aggressive unilateralism',[15] demanding from other countries economic concessions such as VERs or the revision of the EEC's Common Agriculture Policy. US insistence on restrictions on high technology exports to the Soviet Union and Eastern Europe affected Western Europe more than the US because Western Europe was more heavily engaged in East–West trade.

Domestic institutions

The third feature of Atlanticism was the influence of the cold war on domestic priorities, social institutions, and material infrastructure. During the 1970s a growing divergence in domestic priorities can be observed between the United States and Western Europe (see table 9.2). In the 1960s, the share of private consumption and military spending in total national income was more or less similar in the United States and Western Europe. During the 1970s and 1980s, private consumption as a share of gross domestic product (GDP) fell in Western Europe, while it rose significantly in the United States. In contrast, West European government consumption, that is, public education, science and technology, health care, environmental spending, etc., rose considerably as a share of GDP, while it remained more or less constant in the United States. In both the United States and Western Europe, military spending (included in the overall figures for government consumption in table 9.2) declined in the early 1970s as a share of gross national product (GNP), although it declined much less in the United States than in Western Europe.

The policies associated with the new cold war of the early 1980s led to increases in military spending and private consumption as a

Table 9.2 Structure of final demand, US and EEC (% of gross domestic product)

	Private final consumption		Govt final consumption (including defence)		Social security transfers		Current govt disbursements		Gross fixed capital formation		Defence as % of gross national product	
	US	EEC	US	EEC	US	EEC	US	EEC	US	EEC	US	Nato Europe†
1960–7	62.6	61.5	17.8	14.7	5.5	11.4	26.3	30.4	18.0	22.0	5.7*	4.5*
1968–73	62.3	59.4	18.7	15.6	7.8	13.4	29.7	34.0	18.3	22.6	5.0	3.3
1974–9	63.3	59.6	18.3	17.8	10.6	16.8	32.1	41.1	18.3	21.1	5.4	3.7
1980–3	64.6	60.5	18.8	19.2	11.7	18.8	35.3	45.9	17.4	19.8	6.1	3.8
1984–7	64.7	61.1	19.3	18.4	n.a.	n.a	36.7	49.4	18.6	21.0	6.5	3.5

† Nato Europe means European Nato countries
* Years 1965–7

Sources: *OECD Economic Outlook, Historical Statistics, 1960–83* (Paris, 1985); *OECD Economic Outlook 44*, December 1988 (Paris, 1988). For defence statistics, US Arms Control and Disarmament Agency, *World Military and Expenditures and Arms Transfers, 1965–74* (Washington DC, 1975) and *World Military Expenditure and Arms Trade, 1988* (Washington DC, 1988).

share of GDP, and stagnation or even decline in social consumption, in both the United States and Western Europe. This reflected the anti-government spending and pro-defence ethos of the new cold war. In other words, the divergent emphasis of the US and Western Europe on warfare and welfare widened during the 1970s. In the 1980s, the policies of the new cold war did temporarily reverse this trend, but not completely. These divergences did not affect all European countries to the same degree; hence Britain and France remained closer to the United States in their domestic priorities, while West Germany, Italy, the Benelux and Scandinavian countries moved further apart.

Similar divergences can be observed in energy policies (the West European countries put more emphasis on energy conservation than the United States), in unionization and in technology policy. Whereas blue-collar unions have declined in both West Europe and the United States, in some West European countries, for instance, West Germany and Italy, there has been an overall increase in unionization owing to the growth of white-collar trade unions. In West Germany, unions account for 46 per cent of the workforce.[16] Likewise, unions have been less economistic in their concerns and have extended their demands to such issues as control over the labour process, arms conversion, the role of female labour, environmental issues, etc. Again the rightward shift associated with the new cold war may have constrained these developments.

There are also growing differences in technology policies. West European countries, except France and Britain, increased spending on civil research and development as a share of GNP and also put more emphasis on policies for technological diffusion than on big military or quasi-military technological projects.[17] In contrast, the renewed American emphasis on military technology in the early 1980s can be interpreted as a sort of industrial policy. Ventures like the Strategic Defense Initiative (Star Wars) can be treated as attempts to confine the new information technologies within a Fordist industrial framework[18] (this is discussed further in chapter 12).

The spheres-of-influence accord

Finally, during the 1970s and 1980s, the spheres-of-influence accord came under pressure. In the late 1960s, Social Democrat and Labour governments reluctantly supported the Vietnam war effort. With the rise of the anti-Vietnam movement, criticism of the United States began to be voiced by West European governments.

The Middle East war of 1973 marked the first serious rift in Atlantic relations *vis à vis* the Third World since the Suez crisis of 1956. West Germany imposed a ban on the transfer of US military equipment from US bases in West Germany to Israel – an action which may not have been technically legal and which prompted the US Secretary of State, James Schlesinger, to threaten a review of American military and diplomatic commitments to West Germany. All European members of Nato except Portugal refused to allow landing rights to American planes airlifting arms to Israel. The nuclear alert announced by Nixon was viewed as a foolhardy attempt to remind West Europeans and others that their lives were dependent on the United States; it called into question the consensual nature of the Atlantic relationship.[19]

The reaction to the Middle East war may have been as strong as it was partly because European leaders were able to express what they had failed to express during the years of the Vietnam war. In general, the 1970s were years of American retreat *vis à vis* the Third World. This was the period characterized by the 'Vietnam syndrome', which was both an anti-interventionist public mood in the United States and a series of restrictions on intervention imposed by Congress.

Revolutions in the Third World during the 1970s, in the wake of the US withdrawal from Indo-China, the Portuguese revolution, the overthrow of Haile Selassie and the Shah of Iran, provided a platform from which the American right could criticize détente policy. This criticism was voiced within the US administration by Brzezinski with his preoccupation with the so-called 'arc of crisis'. The Soviet intervention in Afghanistan constituted a turning point. On 23 January 1980, President Carter announced his determination to defend the Persian Gulf, in terms reminiscent of the Truman doctrine in 1947.

The Reagan administration adopted a much more aggressive policy towards the Third World. Military assistance increased much faster than economic assistance. Covert and overt assistance was provided to 'freedom fighters' in Nicaragua, Cambodia, Angola and

Afghanistan, and to regimes like El Salvador and Guatemala facing radical insurgencies. The capability for military intervention was greatly increased with an expansion of the Rapid Deployment Force created by President Carter, an expanded base infrastructure in the Persian Gulf and Central America, and increased manoeuvres and exercises on the borders of Third World states. The army's new tactical doctrine, AirLand Battle, and the navy's Maritime Strategy integrated conventional, nuclear and chemical warfighting and put increased emphasis on the offensive; they were explicitly designed for intervention in the Third World as well as for the European and Pacific theatres. Finally, the theory of Low Intensity Conflict offered a strategy for dealing with Third World revolutions that was developed out of an appraisal of America's failings in Vietnam.

President Reagan bravely declared that the Vietnam syndrome was a 'temporary aberration'.[20] All the same, actual interventions remained limited and largely confined to aerial and naval bombardment. The domestic popularity of the intervention in Grenada in 1987, which removed a left-wing government, and the US air raids on Libya in 1986, supposedly to punish state-sponsored terrorism, lay in the fact that they were swift and apparently successful. They remained at the level of psychological spectacle. They were aimed at demonstrating the ability to exercise military power. 'What is clear', said US Secretary of State, Charles Schultz, after the raid on Libya, 'is that the US will take military action under certain circumstances. That's established. That's very important.'[21]

The theory of low intensity conflict was claimed to be a more effective method of fighting Vietnam-type situations than direct intervention.[22] But this may have been merely a rationale for indirect, and indeed vengeful, forms of intervention in the Third World. The combination of low intensity conflict and Reaganite economic policies, especially high interest rates, was a primary cause of the tragic cycle of poverty, indebtedness, famine and violence that characterized the Third World during the 1980s.

West European governments distanced themselves from the US 'unilateralism' towards the Third World, although they could have distanced themselves further. France and Britain joined the US in emphasizing 'out of area' roles for their armed forces, and this culminated in the Falklands/Malvinas war and the French intervention in Chad, both implicitly backed by the United States. Moreover, all West European governments, especially Britain and France, were substantial arms exporters.

However, West European countries provided greater economic assistance as a proportion of GNP and were prepared to criticize US policy in Central America. They were critical of the intervention in Grenada and, with the exception of Britain, refused the use of airspace and bases for the raids on Libya; and these public stances received widespread public support. They failed to take any independent initiatives on debt reduction, however.

Détente and new cold war

Détente and new cold war can be viewed as differing ways of jockeying for position in a post-Atlanticist global system. Détente constituted a more equal relationship between Western Europe and the United States; the new cold war was a way of restoring American dominance. (This is not, of course, how these policies or postures were viewed by those that carried them out; rather it is an interpretation based on hindsight, of what these policies actually involved in practice.)

Détente was primarily a European initiative. It was an initiative of those political forces that had been excluded from the original Atlanticist bargain – Gaullism and German social democracy. De Gaulle's overtures to Moscow were part of his concern to reassert French sovereignty. For this reason, De Gaulle also withdrew from Nato's integrated command structure; De Gaulle explained to Kissinger and Nixon on their first visit to Europe that France would be a more reliable partner if it were responsible for its own defence, enabling it, after two defeats, to regain its pride.[23] The German Social Democrats had embraced Atlanticism in 1959 and this was the precondition for joining a coalition government in 1966. Nevertheless, the German question, especially for those who lived in or came from Berlin, remained a central preoccupation. Egon Bahr, in a passionate article written 20 years after the construction of the Berlin Wall,[24] describes how they, the Social Democrats, sought to use the space that existed as a result of the impotence of the two powers 'to create holes in the wall', how they developed a new language to describe the relationship between the two German states, replacing 'the label "zone regime" with the more neutral phrase "the other side"', and how 'responsibility has a twin sister: self-determination.'[25] Up until Willy Brandt's Ostpolitik, German foreign policy was more or less under American control; no initiatives were taken without US approval.[26] The non-aggression pact with the Soviet Union in 1970, the treaty with Poland the same year, recognizing the Oder–Neisse border, the four-power agreement on Berlin in 1971 and finally the Brandt formula of 'two states within one German nation', which amounted to *de facto* reciprocal recognition of the two Germanies and was expressed in the treaty of 1972, more or less cleared up the outstanding European problems left over from the Second World War and constituted an imaginative break-through in the cold war impasse. These agreements paved the way for US–Soviet détente and for the Helsinki agreement.

Détente thus represented a kind of 'rehabilitation' for Europe, to use Willy Brandt's term.[27] The British government and the smaller West European governments were also enthusiastic about détente. They had been influenced by the first post-war wave of anti-nuclear protest which had taken place in the late 1950s and early 1960s and had been particularly strong in Britain and Scandinavia. In effect, détente allowed West European governments to respond to domestic pressures. It was not just that the constraint of military commitments was lessened. It was also that the relaxation of the external confrontation allowed greater tolerance towards radical movements. Marxism became respectable; this was the period of the New Left, the women's movement and the beginnings of the environmental movement. And the emergence of these movements as well as changes in the role of unions do at least in part explain the shift in domestic priorities towards welfare, the environment, education and so on, as expressed in government expenditure.

By the same token, the enthusiastic embrace of cold war policies by the West European right was a reaction to the growth of radical left ideas. Such ideas were still lumped together as socialism, big government and the Soviet Union. Cuts in government spending and renewal of cold war ideology constituted an attack on new social movements, as well as the traditional left.

Détente meant much more for Europe than it did for the United States. Although East–West trade was probably not economically important, except perhaps for West Germany, détente meant increased communication – the reunification of families, the growth of tourism, increased scientific and cultural exchanges – and it meant the reemergence of a sense of European identity. And all this was especially important for the two Germanies. If the Helsinki Act encouraged the formation of human rights groups in Eastern Europe and offered them some hope, it is also the case that the West European peace movement, which emerged in the context of the renewed cold war, was the progeny of the Helsinki Act – a determination to hold on to the gains of the détente period. Both in their different ways could be described as movements for self-determination.

West European governments participated in the new cold war, but, with the main exception of Mrs Thatcher, somewhat more reluctantly than the United States. Despite détente, they remained committed to the alliance, still believing, like Brandt and Bahr, that détente was predicated on a military balance. The decision to deploy cruise and Pershing missiles was thus seen, on both sides of the Atlantic, as a way of restoring the unity of the alliance following the disagreements of the 1970s, even though conceptions of how this was to be achieved sharply differed. The West European governments were thus pulled along by their commitment to Atlanticism as well as, in the late 1970s, by domestic pressure from the right. East–West exchanges were hardly interrupted. (There was some decline in travel between the two Germanies owing to an increase in the foreign currency requirements imposed on tourists by the GDR.)

US–Soviet détente was a much briefer affair, largely confined to the early 1970s. Essentially, Nixon and Kissinger embarked on détente and on a new policy of what might be called economic unilateralism as a way of extricating the United States from Vietnam and from the economic aftermath of Vietnam. Perhaps they really believed that the Soviet Union could restrain revolution in the Third World and, hence, allow the United States to withdraw from Vietnam 'with honour'.

The Kissinger–Nixon formula was détente plus economic unilateralism (the decline in aid and the increased cost of buying

American food and arms) plus continued aggression in Third World, as evidenced by the invasion of Cambodia, the coup in Chile, the show of force in the Bangladesh conflict of 1971 and the Middle East conflict of 1973. It can be described as a policy of political cooperation and economic confrontation, of cooperation with the Soviet Union and confrontation or coercion within the sphere of American influence. It resulted in domestic recovery but growing divisions within the Atlantic alliance and a growing inability to manage developments in the Third World (with the loss of political credibility and the decline of economic and military assistance).

President Carter came to office committed to détente plus a return to economic multilateralism, that is, both political and economic cooperation. He failed to achieve either, partly because economic multilateralism no longer benefited the American economy and partly because of domestic political pressures. As the revisionist histories of the late 1970s demonstrate, the cold war script became a platform from which a right-wing establishment, discredited by Vietnam and Watergate, could regain power.[28] The American right were able to conjure up the spirit of anti-communism and the spectre of the evil empire in their campaigns for reelection.

The Reagan formula was cold war plus economic unilateralism and aggression *vis à vis* the Third World, that is, political *and* economic confrontation. It was a way of reimposing Atlantic unity through coercion rather than consensus. The insistence on nuclear warfighting doctrines and on a nuclear warfighting interpretation of the function of the Euro missiles was a way of reasserting the utility of military power, even if only in psychological terms. The Reagan doctrine constituted a policy of rollback of Third World revolutions and a futile but tragic insistence on the exercise of military power. Both the nuclear warfighting strategy and the Reagan doctrine were ways of renewing the atmosphere of imaginary war.

High interest rates, neo-protectionist policies, the insistence on increased military spending combined with austerity policies, as well as technological ventures like Star Wars, all contributed to a redistribution of the world product in favour of the United States and constrained possible alternative 'post-Fordist' approaches to social and industrial development that were emerging in Western Europe.

The exclusivist Reagan formula was very successful in domestic economic and political terms (although not for the poor, the blacks, and other deprived groups) but it had detrimental consequences for the rest of the world. It led to a polarization within West Europe, between governments committed to Atlanticism and peace movements committed to détente. It contributed to the cultural, economic and ecological catastrophe that now pervades the Third World. It was, in a sense, a new sort of isolationism, an aggressive interventionist sort of isolationism.

After 1985, the new initiatives towards détente undertaken by Gorbachev revealed these growing cleavages within the Western alliance. In particular, the INF treaty, signed in December 1987, removed what were supposed to be the symbols of Nato unity, setting in motion a new heartsearching both about Nato strategy and the future of the alliance itself. Gorbachev became so popular in Western Europe and his policies were so enthusiastically welcomed, not simply because of a sincere concern about the future of the Soviet Union, but because the removal of the missiles, and indeed of the Soviet threat, allowed West European governments, especially West Germany, to adopt a peace agenda and a programme for self-determination in Europe and to renew domestic consensus.

Notes

1 See, particularly, Paul Kennedy, *The Rise and Fall of the Great Powers* (Unwin Hyman, 1988), and David Calleo, *Beyond American Hegemony* (Wheatsheaf, 1987).
2 For a discussion of these factors, see Samuel Bowles, David M. Gordon and Thomas E. Weisskopf, *Beyond the Wasteland: A Democratic Alternative to Economic Decline* (Verso, 1986).
3 Michael J. Piore and Charles F. Sabel, *The Second Industrial Divide: Possibilities for Prosperity* (Basic Books, 1984), p. 184.
4 These trade figures are all taken from various OECD publications.
5 See Piore and Sabel, *Second Industrial Divide*; National Economic Development Council (NEDC), *IT Futures* (London, 1986); Manuel Castells, 'High technology, world development and structural transformation', in Saul H. Mendlovitz and R. B. J. Walker, eds, *Towards a Just World Order* (Butterworth, 1987); Robin Murray, 'Life after Henry (Ford)', *Marxism Today*, October 1988.

6 Carlotta Perez-Perez, 'Structural change and assimilation of new technologies', *Futures*, October 1983.

7 Dieter Kimbel, 'Information Technology: increasingly the engine of growth', *OECD Observer*, 147, August/September 1987.

8 Robin Murray, 'Benetton Britain: the new economic order', *Marxism Today*, November 1985.

9 Andrew Sayer, 'New developments in manufacturing: the just-in-time system', *Capital and Class*, 30, Winter 1986; Martin Kenney and Richard Florida, 'Beyond mass production: production and labour process in Japan', *Politics and Society*, 16:1, March 1988.

10 For a description of the role of MITI, see Erik Arnold and Ken Guy, *Parallel Convergence: National Strategies in Information Technology* (Frances Pinter, 1986); Henry Ergas, 'Technology policy and industrial structure in seven OECD countries', paper presented at the National Academy of Engineering of the United States, February 1986.

11 Piore and Sabel, *Second Industrial Divide*; for different national experiences, see also Scott Lash and John Urry, *The End of Organized Capitalism* (Polity, 1987).

12 President Mitterand of France went so far as to defend deployment in the Federal German Bundestag, to the consternation and bewilderment of his social democratic colleagues. Greece dissented from the decision to deploy the missiles.

13 This was the thesis of Robert Triffin: *Gold and the Dollar Crisis: The Future of Convertibility* (Yale University Press, 1960).

14 For a vivid description of this process, see Susan Strange, *Casino Capitalism* (Blackwell, 1986).

15 See Joan Edelman Spero, *The Politics of International Economic Relations*, 3rd edn (Allen and Unwin, 1985).

16 See Lash and Urry, *End of Organized Capitalism*.

17 See Ergas, *Technology Policy*.

18 For a discussion of Star Wars as a technology policy and as a bid to increase the comparative technological advantage of the US, see Mario Piantia, *New Technologies across the Atlantic* (Wheatsheaf, 1988).

19 The French foreign minister, Michel Jobert, talked about the 'imperious arbitrage' of the United States. According to a US State Department spokesman:

We were in a very critical period, a period which in many ways affected all of us – ourselves and our allies in Western Europe, and we were struck by a number of our allies going to some length to separate themselves publicly from us. It raised questions as to how that action squared with what the Europeans have often referred to as indivisibility on the question of security. (Quoted in Mary

Kaldor, *The Disintegrating West* (Allen Lane, 1978), pp. 151–2).

20 Quoted in Michael T. Klare, 'Marching to a different drummer: US and Soviet interventionism in the Third World', in Daniel Nelson and Roger B. Anderson, eds, *Soviet–American Relations: Understanding Differences, Avoiding Conflicts* (SR Books, Wilmington, 1988), p. 161.

21 Quoted in E. P. Thompson, Mary Kaldor et al., *Mad Dogs* (Pluto, 1986), p. 3.

22 Fred Halliday decribes the formulation of these ideas and how they relate to a reappraisal of American strategy in Vietnam from a right-wing perspective. See *Cold War, Third World* (Hutchinson/ Radius, 1989). It is evident that American leaders were preoccupied with appearance, that Vietnam had damaged the imaginary war story. The Kissinger commission of 1984 talked about the risk that events in Central America would erode 'the worldwide perception of the United States as a country capable of influencing events beyond its frontiers' (p. 63). And Secretary of State Schultz talked about the need for 'steadfastness and endurance' in the 'harder-to-win situations . . . Unfortunately, in the wake of Vietnam, our endurance against any kind of challenge has been open to question' (pp. 71–3).

23 Henry Kissinger, *The White House Years* (Weidenfeld, 1979).

24 Egon Bahr, 'Bearing responsibility for Germany: twenty years of the Wall – ten years of the four-power agreement':

> What our eyes were forced to witness defied all belief. The sense of bitter indignation we felt, compounded by our sense of powerlessness, is still present as if it were yesterday.
> The bewildered, pain-wracked faces of innocent people remain engraved in our memories as sober reminders, beyond even the tears of joy experienced when the first border passes put people in one another's arms once again. The Wall is no pretty sight neither then nor now. (In Rudolf Steinke and Michael Vale, *Germany Debates Defence: The Nato Alliance at the crossroads* (M. E. Sharpe, 1983), pp. 69–70)

25 Ibid.

26 See Angela Stent, *From Embargo to Ostpolitik* (Cambridge University Press, 1981).

27 See Kenneth Dyson's introduction to Kenneth Dyson, ed., *European Détente: Case Studies of the Politics of East–West Relations* (Frances Pinter, 1986).

28 See Jerry Sanders, *Peddlars of Crisis* (Pluto, 1983), and Charles E. Nathanson, 'The social construction of the Soviet threat: a study in the politics of representation', *Alternatives*, 13:4, October 1988.

10

Why Did Détente Fail?

Détente in the early 1970s was undertaken by two very conservative governments – the Nixon administration in the United States and the Brezhnev regime in the Soviet Union.

Perhaps only conservative governments could make the political calculus necessary for détente. But by the same token, their conception of détente was limited, unimaginative and fundamentally flawed. They wanted to maintain their systems intact; they wanted to continue the arms race and retain their hold on power; for them, détente was a strategy of preservation.

Margot Light has pointed out that the Soviet term 'peaceful coexistence' used to describe détente was similar to the Western concept of 'containment', as enunciated by Kennan in the late 1940s:

It presupposes similar sources of imperialist conduct to those identified by Kennan in Soviet behaviour ... Like containment, it does not suggest exporting its own system beyond its borders. None the less, and again like containment, there is an underlying hope and expectation that change will take place. In the case of containment, it was to be democratic change, whereas with peaceful coexistence it is to be progressive change (which is also called democratic by Soviet theorists). In both cases, the emphasis is on firmness of intent and the known ability to respond, rather than the overt use of force.[1]

In other words, détente, at least between the US and the Soviet Union, can be viewed as containment, a way of preserving each social system without threatening the other. Just as in the late 1940s, containment without confrontation was inherently contradictory. Without external confrontation, it was not possible to sustain the high levels of military spending which had become an essential feature of both social systems. Without an 'enemy' it was difficult to maintain the political and social status quo.

The revisionist interpretation of détente – put forward by Soviet thinkers and by those in opposition in Western Europe, especially the West German Social Democrats – holds that détente failed because it failed to tackle the arms race: political détente, in the sense of less threatening behaviour and the settlement of territorial disputes in Europe, was not followed by military détente. And one of the major reasons why détente failed to tackle the arms race was domestic pressure in the United States.

This view is partially correct. A resurgent neo-liberal right criticized SALT II for permitting a Soviet arms build-up (even at the very moment when, for economic reasons, the Soviet arms build-up was slowing down) and criticized the American retreat from military intervention (the Vietnam syndrome) for permitting Third World revolution and an expanded global role for the Soviet Union. These arguments provided the basis of the policies of the Reagan administration.

But the Soviet Union also bore responsibility for the failure to control the arms race. Soviet leaders always insisted that détente was predicated on the achievement of military parity, and that parity, measured in terms of numbers and types of weapons, had to be preserved. Détente was seen as a kind of mutual recognition: the United States had finally accepted the Soviet Union's status as a superpower, although Soviet commentators would have hesitated to use the term.

The problem is that because the arms race is not exactly symmetrical, measurable parity is always open to different interpretations. What is justified by one side as 'catching up' or maintaining parity can be seized on by the other side as gaining an unfair advantage, establishing superiority. The very concept of parity is thus a recipe for an arms race. Only if it is accepted that parity in this sense is meaningless (except in self-imposed psychological terms) and that numbers do not matter in a nuclear age, as it seems to be accepted by Gorbachev, is there any real possibility of arms control and disarmament.

Had the Soviet Union been seriously interested in a military détente, the Soviet leaders should not have turned down Carter's deep cuts proposal so abruptly. Left-wing critics of the deep cuts proposal argue that it was impossible for the Soviet Union to accept because it was so asymmetric, that is, the Soviet Union would have had to make much bigger cuts. But that argument is only correct on the assumption that parity is important. That was the only proposal that Carter was politically able to offer. It might have been wiser to start with SALT II, based on the Vladivostok accord, a tentative agreement negotiated by Kissinger in 1974, and proceed to deep cuts. But had the Soviet Union been willing to consider Carter's proposal (and after all it was not so very different from the US proposal in START – Strategic Arms Reduction Talks – in the late 1980s, which was favourably received by Gorbachev), this could have led to a breakthrough in the arms talks and might have saved détente as well.

A similar argument can be made about the deployment of SS-20s and the overseas Soviet naval role. No doubt the Soviet Union regarded the deployment of SS-20s as a riposte to the fact that American Forward Based Systems (Poseidon submarines assigned to Nato command, F-IIIs in Britain, nuclear-capable aircraft carriers) were not included as strategic arms to be limited in the Vladivostok accord. Moreover, they were regarded as a modernization of already existing SS-4s and SS-5s. (It also seems that there were domestic pressures from the Nadiradze Design Bureau after the failure of the S-16, the technical predecessor of SS-20.)[2] All the same, the deployment of SS-20s provided the perfect pretext for the deployment of cruise and Pershing missiles. It was to prevent this outcome that German Social Democrat leaders argued strongly for negotiations about theatre systems; this was the thrust of Helmut Schmidt's famous speech in London of October 1977, which was later said to be the moment when the Europeans 'asked' for the missiles. The reason for the deployment of cruise and Pershing II missiles had nothing to do with the SS-20; it was about recoupling the United States and Western Europe (to be discussed further in the next chapter). But the deployment of SS-20s provided a public justification that was probably essential.

The Soviet overseas naval combat capability built up in the 1970s was tiny by comparison with the capabilities of Western navies. It was probably viewed by the Soviet Union merely as the attribute of a great power. But again it provided substantiation for the right's charges that the Soviet Union was taking advantage of the American withdrawal from the Third World.

The failure of détente to control the arms race, however, is only part of the story. Indeed it cannot be disentangled from the difficulty of moving away from pseudo-war economy in the East or from the institutional framework that presided over a Fordist pattern of industrial development in the West.

The prevalent view in what were then opposition circles in Eastern Europe is that détente failed because the Soviet Union could not permit reform in Eastern Europe. And this is also partially correct. Détente was viewed as a substitute for reform. Growth was to be achieved through Western credit. By the end of the 1970s, all East European countries were heavily in debt. Moreover, the relaxation of external confrontation had opened political space for new movements, in particular Solidarity. The military build-up in the European theatre, the increased interventionist role *vis à vis* the Third World (in part, merely a response to Third World revolution) and the renewed emphasis on ideological struggle were all part of the re-creation of a wartime atmosphere associated with a reversion to autarky and austerity.

But again it was not only in the East that détente failed because the leadership was not prepared to tolerate fundamental change within the bloc. The new cold war was a method by which the United States could protect its economy in the changed circumstances of the 1970s and 1980s. These circumstances resulted from the exhaustion of Fordism, the American pattern of industrial development, and the emergence of a new pattern of industrial development in Japan and some West European countries.

This is not to say that politicians consciously adopted new cold war policies for economic reasons. On the contrary, there were good political reasons. The combination of neo-liberal economic ideas, increased pressure for military spending and a renewed ideology of anti-communism provided a platform from which the right wing could regain power in both Western Europe and the United States and confront both trade unions, which had grown in strength during the détente years, and new radical movements. Because of the role of the dollar, and because military spending and private consumption could be described as Fordist forms of demand, these policies benefited the United States economically. Essentially, the new cold war allowed the US to use its political and military power to achieve short-term domestic recovery through global redistribution in favour of the United States.

Unlike the first cold war, the new cold war did not result in consensus and prosperity. Unemployment rose dramatically in Western Europe during the 1980s. Cold war policies led to a growing polarization within Western societies. Nor did the new cold war reinvigorate East European economies; this was the period of 'stagnation'. Moreover, the reemergence of civil society in the form of new social movements made it more difficult to reimpose the apparatus of coercion. In both East and West, the cold war story did not make sense when applied to new forms of opposition that did not fit traditional categories – that could not easily be described as tools of the Kremlin or agents of Western imperialism.

All the same, the heritage of the imaginary war cannot be underestimated. It is difficult and slow to change assumptions and ideas except in the context of explosive changes like war or revolution. Ideology not only shaped the views of political leaders but still had a popular resonance as well. A comparison of the memoirs of George Kennan and Henry Kissinger illustrates the point. Kennan was living in one of those moments of ideological flux in history; his views were shaped by direct experience of Europe and the Soviet Union. Kissinger's concepts were drawn from a cold war school of political science; his Pavlovian concept of détente was drawn from theory not experience, from a picture of an imaginary enemy not a real adversary. (This perhaps explains why Kissinger so quickly retreated from détente and joined the Committee on the Present Danger in the late 1970s.) The most enduring consequence of détente in Europe was the ability to penetrate cold war myopia, to learn the reality of each others' political experience – and this changed those in opposition in Europe much more radically than those in power.

The link that was made between parts of the West European peace movement and independent peace, green and human rights groups in the early 1980s undermined the effectiveness of cold war policies as an instrument to subdue opposition. West European peace movements were able, decisively, to establish their integrity and nonalignment. Moreover, the argument that the campaign against missiles was enhanced by the existence of independent groups in the East may have provided more domestic political space in East European countries.

The détente of the 1970s failed both because it failed to tackle the roots of the arms race *and* because it did not permit systemic evolution in *either* East or West. Moreover, détente demonstrated that the impetus for demilitarization and systemic change cannot come from above, especially in the United States. Even if politicians are longsighted and are able to analyse long-term global problems, as Gorbachev may be, they are the prisoners of their political situations, they have to conform to short-term political advantage. But détente did bring about cultural changes, especially in West and East Central Europe, that laid the basis for pressure from below that built up during the 1980s. It was this pressure from below that was to burst forth explosively in 1989.

Notes

1 Margot Light, *The Soviet Theory of International Relations* (Harvester Wheatsheaf, 1988), p. 68.
2 I have speculated about this story in 'Europe after cruise and Pershing II', *Millennium Journal of International Studies*, 13:1, Spring 1984.

PART IV
The Military Confrontation

11

Imagined Strategies

In the period 1945 to 1985, military spending by the great powers was much higher both absolutely and as a share of national income than in any previous recorded period of peacetime. The military confrontation became an important component of the social systems that characterize East and West. It can be described as a form of regulation – both political regulation, that is to say a form of social discipline or psychological coercion, and economic regulation, that is to say a way of matching consumption and production, as well as a form of technology policy. High military spending can be said to have become part of the characteristic mode of regulation (to use the language of the French regulationists) during the Fordist regime of accumulation. That military spending has taken on this role is a reflection of the primitive nature of our methods of social regulation in comparison with our sophisticated technological knowledge.

This chapter is about the role of the military confrontation as a form of political regulation. In the post-war period, discussions about complex political relationships have often been reduced to discussions about military, and particularly nuclear, strategy. Strategies became representations of politics. This has been more important in the West than in the East because, in the East, psychological or ideological forms of coercion were less important than administrative and physical forms of coercion, that is, party control, military intervention, internal security, etc. East Europeans sometimes wonder at the Western preoccupation with strategy, particularly with the nuclear issue. They find it difficult to understand why, for example, grass roots activists should be so obsessed with (boring) technical issues. If politics are to rise above this obsession, then we have to understand the significance of strategy in an imaginary war.

What is strategy?

It is sometimes asked, in both East and West, whether the concept of 'strategy' has any meaning in the nuclear age.[1] Strategy as defined by the classic military theorist Clausewitz means the employment of military forces to achieve political objectives, and Clausewitz was much preoccupied with the need to retain this definition of strategy, given the tendency for 'absolute war', for war to acquire its own momentum and inner logic regardless of the political ends for which it is fought. Surely, goes the argument, nuclear strategy is a contradiction in terms. Nuclear weapons cannot be used; or rather, their use would constitute the final expression of absolute war.

However, this circle can be squared if we redefine strategy in the nuclear age as the way in which military forces would be employed for political ends in an imaginary confrontation. How we expect a future war to happen, and how we plan to fight such a war, have profound political-psychological consequences for the way we view the world and therefore for the way we actually behave. I am not suggesting that planners, wargamers and the like would accept this definition of strategy. On the contrary, strategy in the post-war period developed rather haphazardly out of wartime predilections, technological wizardry, domestic and international expediency. But, over the years, different strategies came to reflect different political positions; they became part of an esoteric discourse which concealed real political differences.

It should be noted that evolving strategies did not necessarily bear much relation to actual military capabilities. The growth of actual military capabilities was probably influenced more by institutional factors such as interservice rivalry, technological innovation or industrial pressure. Strategy provided a rationale for these capabilities that fitted ongoing political concerns. Strategy for an imaginary war was the linkage between the actual disposition of the military confrontation and the politics of the evolving East–West conflict.

There have been real wars in the post-war period in the Third

World and in Eastern Europe, and these wars have contributed to the evolution of strategy. Nevertheless, for the most part, strategy has been addressed not to these so-called 'limited' wars but to the anticipation of an all-out conflict between Nato and the Warsaw Pact, probably centred in Europe.

Nuclear weapons, especially in the West, undoubtedly played an important role in the emergence of a military fantasy. Throughout the period, there was an extraordinary discrepancy between the way in which nuclear war was discussed and the accumulation and use of nuclear weapons contemplated, and our knowledge of the effects of two rather small nuclear weapons in Hiroshima and Nagasaki. With regard to the early years of the cold war, one can only conclude that although scientists and military planners knew objectively what would happen if nuclear weapons were employed, even if only a few, they had somehow not internalized the awesome nature of these weapons.[2] President Eisenhower and Gordon Dean, chairman of the Atomic Energy Commission, as well as others, talked about acquiring numbers and varieties of nuclear weapons as though they were no different from conventional weapons. Samuel Cohen, the physicist who was later to invent the enhanced radiation weapon or neutron bomb, describes how he was sent to Korea to see whether and how atomic weapons could be used. He saw a bridge that had allowed the North Koreans to enter Seoul and he thought: 'What an ideal spot for an atomic bomb . . . What did not cross my mind at that time was what the consequence would have been to the city of Seoul if we had blown up the bridge with a nuclear weapon representative of that period, namely, an atomic bomb of the type we used to destroy Nagasaki.'[3] During the 1950s, the writings of analysts like Herman Kahn or Albert Wohlstetter had the same quality of shocking obliviousness to the reality of nuclear weapons.

Later, it seems that the very unreality of strategic discussions contributed to the imaginary nature of the East–West confrontation, allowing it to become a deep, ongoing, unrealizable fear. In his essay on 'real socialism', Miroslav Kusý describes the 'as if' ideology that characterizes socialist societies. The ideologists of 'real socialism' speak and behave 'as if' what is actually experienced corresponds to an idealized conception of socialism, as if there were democracy, material well-being, equality, freedom, etc.: 'The important thing is not to be a fanatical adherent of the ideology, but to play the *as if* game: and that game always demands an adequate degree of detachedness.'[4]

An analogy can be drawn with the belief in an imaginary war. Those who participate in high-level discussions about international relations behave 'as if' it were possible to conceive of a future war fought along the lines anticipated by war scenarios, exercises, etc. This 'as if' approach to war reached its perfect expression in former President Reagan's astrodome theory of the Strategic Defense Initiative: American schoolchildren drew pictures of their homes protected by an arc off which multicoloured Soviet missiles bounced.

Those who reject the scenarios, who dwell on the actual experience of Hiroshima and Nagasaki, are not, at least in the West, imprisoned or punished as are the critics of 'real socialism'. But they are criticized for their lack of 'detachedness', for their naïveté or sentimentality.

Of course, the discrepancy between the imaginary war and what is likely to happen if there really were a war can be said to be the essence of the concept of deterrence – the paradox proudly proclaimed by the proponents of deterrence. The point of deterrence is to prevent a war. It is presupposed that there is a deep underlying conflict between East and West which has been suppressed by the threat of a hideous and destructive war. The paradox is that in order to prove that the war would really be hideous and destructive, we have to behave, in a cool and detached way, as though we do not quite realize how hideous and destructive the war will be – otherwise the threat of a hideous and destructive war will not be convincing. Anyone who points out that the emperor has no clothes and that war *really* is hideous and destructive has blown the gaffe, as it were, and weakened the effectiveness of deterrence.

But supposing there was *not* a deep underlying clash between East and West. Suppose that the two post-war social systems complemented each other and neither side ever intended to invade the other. Then deterrence, instead of *preventing* war, actually turns out to be a way of keeping the idea of war and the idea of a conflict alive, either to legitimize the growth of military forces or for domestic or intra-bloc purposes.

This argument can be developed by looking at the evolution of strategy in Nato and the Warsaw Pact. Shifts in perception and stated doctrine seem to have come about less through an interactive process than as a result of shifts in government and intra-alliance relations. I do not want to suggest that the military planners did not themselves believe in an East–West conflict or that they did not perceive a threat to which they reacted. What I do want to suggest is that, especially during the 1950s and 1960s, when there was real ignorance on the part of each about the other and when a set of beliefs about the East–West conflict was institutionalized, these perceptions of the threat were shaped by domestic and intra-bloc factors. Another way of putting the argument is to treat the imaginary war as no more than a set of competing perceptions within an established conceptual framework. The belief in an epic struggle between, say, freedom and totalitarianism necessarily colours the way in which we interpret behaviour.[5]

A good example is the way in which the US joint chiefs of staff perceived Soviet forces in Eastern Europe. In 1946, they expected the Soviet Union to retain 3.2 million men in the ground forces and they calculated that this was 'nearly commensurate with occupation and security requirements'. They claimed that the Soviet Union would need 66 divisions in Eastern Europe for occupation duties. In 1948, they estimated that in fact the Soviet Union had only 2.5 million men in the ground forces and 31 divisions in Eastern Europe. However, they estimated that 25 divisions would be available for an attack on Western Europe.[6] In other words, what changed was not the size or nature of Soviet forces, but the way in which they were assessed by the joint chiefs of staff. In what follows, I shall briefly describe these changes of assessment in Soviet and Nato thinking.

The evolution of Soviet strategy

It is possible to identify three distinctive periods in the evolution of Soviet strategy:

- the initial cold war period 1949–53, which involved a rapid build-up of ground forces in Europe, tight bilateral Soviet control over East European armed forces, the creation of the PVO-Strany – the air defence forces – and the development of nuclear-capable bombers aimed at US forward air bases;

- the Khrushchev period, which involved a big reduction in ground and naval forces and an increased emphasis on nuclear weapons, including the creation of the Strategic Rocket Forces; and
- the period from 1962 to 1985, which involved a steady military build-up in all services (although towards the end of the period there was less emphasis on strategic systems, that is, nuclear weapons capable of hitting the United States, and more on conventional weapons, naval forces and theatre nuclear weapons) and the integration of Warsaw Pact armed forces into Soviet strategy and the Soviet command system both through a variety of military and political institutions and through joint exercises which began in 1961.

These periods correspond with domestic political changes and do not exactly parallel the Western evolution of strategy.

Of course, Soviet military developments can be explained in terms of a reaction to US behaviour, and this has been done rather convincingly by Michael MccGwire.[7] Certainly the creation of the air defence forces in 1948 and the initial development of nuclear bombers were a reaction to the American development of atomic air power. It is probably correct to say that reaction is more helpful in explaining Soviet strategy than in explaining American strategy for several reasons. First, as I argued in chapter 6, the West represented more of an ideological threat to the East than vice versa, in the sense that the West represented more of a pull for East Europeans than the other way round. (Arguably, though, the East was more of a military threat owing to the size of conventional forces and Stalin's defensive paranoia.) Secondly, there was greater centralized control over military decision-making in the Soviet Union than in the West. Evangelista argues that decision-making for Soviet military innovation is top-down, in contrast to the United States where decision-making for military innovation is bottom-up – reflecting the different nature of each society.[8] This distinction should be qualified. In a bureaucratically regulated system, there are all sorts of pressures from below. A more appropriate distinction is that between decision-making based on vertical relationships and decision-making based on horizontal relationships that characterize Western society. The more the Soviet economy resembles a war economy, the more these vertical relationships are controlled from the top, the greater the degree of centralized control, and the more the development of military capabilities stems from high-level political strategic decisions.

Thirdly, American society was much more open than Soviet society – the Soviet leaders were able to discover from newspapers, public debates, Congressional hearings and so on much more about what the United States was doing than the other way round. Indeed, until the development of satellite reconnaissance, American planners knew very little about what was happening in the Soviet Union or China[9] – hence the shock of Sputnik in 1957 and the subsequent unfounded alarm about the missile gap.

But to say that there was a reactive element in the determination of Soviet strategy does not explain the form of that reaction: the offensive conventional posture in Europe, the build-up of medium and long-range rockets, the emphasis on numbers, etc. After 1985, Gorbachev began to explore the possibility of defence at much lower levels of weapons and manpower, and this approach always represented a possible alternative.

Three factors are more important in explaining Soviet strategy: the occupation role in Eastern Europe, the heritage of the Second World War, and institutional or ideological pressures. I shall describe these, very briefly, in turn.

First of all, it is important to note that Soviet strategy, in contrast to Nato strategy, was both real and imaginary. The Soviet Union was, after all, engaged in real wars in Eastern Europe – in Hungary in 1956 and Czechoslovakia in 1968. Hence conventional forces, which could be used, were much more important. The Soviet tank was both the image of a Soviet threat to Western Europe and the actual instrument of oppression in Eastern Europe. In the years immediately after the Second World War, occupation control rested in military hands. The military were responsible for forcibly extracting reparations, especially in East Germany, for political repression and for reconstruction: deactivating land mines, rebuilding bridges, railways, industrial facilities, etc. Interestingly, the Soviet armed forces also played a similar role in the western military districts of the USSR, where bands of anti-Soviet partisans were active right up to the early 1950s. The Soviet armed forces were also engaged in the organization of prison camps.[10]

Subsequently, the disposition of Soviet troops in East Germany,[11] the big increase in Soviet troops in Czechoslovakia after 1968, the disproportionately high number of Soviet troops in Hungary given its lack of strategic importance, also pointed to the continuing 'garrison' function of Soviet troops. The offensive nature of the Soviet posture can also be explained in terms of the requirement for intervention; the Warsaw Pact intervention in Czechoslovakia is said to be a perfectly executed example of the kind of 'strategic surprise' Western military analysts anticipated in the event of an invasion of Western Europe. Finally, it has also been suggested that once East Central European armed forces had been integrated into the Warsaw Pact and into Soviet strategy, an offensive style of warfare made sense as a way of minimizing the possibility that national armed forces could defend themselves against a Soviet or Warsaw Pact intervention.[12]

The second influence on Soviet strategy was the experience of the Second World War. Soviet strategists are even today utterly preoccupied with the lessons of the Second World War. And, as in politics generally, debate about strategy often takes the form of debate about the interpretation of particular battles in the last war.[13]

There are two important respects in which the influence of the Second World War can be observed. First, the war reinforced the historical Russian preference for large-scale mobile offensive operations which arose out of a history of combating foreign invasion on flat and open territory. Furthermore, the concern to keep the arena of battle as far west as possible led to a strategy which emphasized the role of East Central Europe as a buffer zone, and anticipated rapid incursions into foreign territory, including the notion of taking Western Europe hostage in the event of a global war.[14] In the Soviet terminology, the political doctrine, that is, the political objective, was defensive, but the military-technical doctrine emphasized the importance of the offensive.

The Second World War also influenced thinking about nuclear weapons. The Soviet Union had no experience of strategic bombing; indeed, Soviet commentators regard strategic bombing as a barbarous legacy of Fascism.[15] The air force was used primarily in support of ground operations. Particular importance was accorded to the role of artillery. Hence, when rockets were developed, they were regarded not as pilotless aircraft as in the West, but as long-range artillery. This also explains the emphasis on short and medium-range rockets as well as long-range rockets. The first commander-in-chief of the

Strategic Rocket Forces was the former Chief Marshal of Artillery, Nedelin, and the Dzerzhinsky Artillery Academy became the Dzerzhinsky Military Engineering Academy, with a curriculum devoted to the study of missile systems.[16] When nuclear-capable tactical aircraft were introduced in the late 1950s, this is said to have been a substitute for nuclear-capable artillery, which had proved technically very difficult to develop.[17]

The emphasis on artillery also explains why nuclear weapons never represented a separate component of Soviet strategic thinking. The use of nuclear weapons was always envisaged in support of conventional ground operations against military targets. Indeed, the Soviet strategic thinkers do not have a separate term for 'deterrence'. They translate deterrence as *ustrashenie*, which means intimidation, and it is only used to describe Western policy. The term *sderzhivanie*, which means holding back or restraining, is used to describe Soviet policy.[18] In the West, Khrushchev's emphasis on nuclear weapons in the late 1950s is often interpreted as a kind of minimum deterrent posture but, in fact, Khrushchev emphasized both tactical and strategic rockets; rather, he envisaged nuclear weapons as a way of increasing the cost effectiveness of Soviet armed forces.[19]

The influence of the Second World War has to be understood both in terms of institutional predilection and in political-psychological terms. Because the experience of the war was shared with the Americans, it contributed to a mutually recognizable conception of the imaginary war. It shored up the memory of Soviet and American victories and sustained the fear of another war.

The third factor which shaped Soviet strategy was institutional and ideological. Khrushchev's policies of cutting conventional forces came up against domestic resistance, and, indeed, this may have been an important reason for his removal in 1964. After the Cuban missile crisis of 1962, a compromise was reached which seems to have allowed a steady increase in all parts of the military budget – input–output conservatism, the process whereby the plan is drawn up through constant additions to the input–output targets of the last plan, especially in the military sector, characterized the Brezhnev years. Input–output conservatism is not just a consequence of mathematical laziness; it is an expression of the static composition of bureaucratic interests. Bargaining power is in practice proportionate to the share of the previous budget. It is difficult to disentangle ideological from institutional pressure. The increased role of the navy and of conventional forces in the late 1970s can perhaps be also explained in terms of the need to reiterate the Soviet Union's revolutionary tasks in the context of renewed cold war.

The evolution of Western strategy

Much more is known about the main phases in the evolution of Western strategy. Western strategy for an imaginary war comprises American nuclear strategy, that is, strategy for US–Soviet nuclear confrontation, and Nato strategy, that is, strategy for the defence of Western Europe. There were also American strategies for real wars in the Third World, for instance, the conventional strategy of the Korean war, Counter Insurgency (COIN) in the 1960s and Low Intensity Conflict (LIC) in the 1980s.

The phases of American strategy can be summarized as: the phase of massive retaliation under Eisenhower; the phase of Mutual Assured Destruction, which was enunciated by Robert McNamara in 1964 when he was Secretary of Defense and roughly corresponded to the détente period; and the increasing tendency for nuclear war-fighting options which began with the Schlesinger doctrine in 1974 and culminated in three major new initiatives in the early 1970s – the Strategic Defense Initiative (Star Wars), AirLand Battle, and the Maritime Strategy. In between, there were short flirtations with different approaches.

Immediately after the war, the emphasis was placed on strategic air power. Then came the Korean war and an expansion in conventional forces as well. Eisenhower's New Look after the end of the Korean war was envisaged as a way of concentrating on nuclear weapons and spending less on conventional weapons. The doctrine of massive retaliation relied on a belief in American nuclear superiority – the idea that any Soviet or Soviet-inspired attack would provoke an American nuclear retaliation. During the Eisenhower period there was a massive build-up of nuclear weapons: the nuclear stockpile grew from 1,200 weapons in 1953 to more than 30,000 in 1961 – subsequently, it declined somewhat. Also during this period the actual use of nuclear weapons was threatened on a number of occasions.[20]

Towards the end of the fifties, at the time of the missile gap furore, concern grew about over-reliance on massive retaliation and there was a growing debate about 'limited' war, both nuclear and conventional. This debate was echoed in the Kennedy campaign. In the early years of the Kennedy administration, McNamara enunciated his city-avoidance strategy, which also involved 'damage limitation'. Attacks were to be concentrated on military targets in the Soviet Union; this would simultaneously limit the 'damage' the Soviet Union could do to the United States. This approach was abandoned after the Cuban missile crisis, which may have helped to bring home the implications of nuclear weapons.

Mutual Assured Destruction (MAD) meant that both sides had the capability to destroy each other. The contradictions of MAD corresponded to the contradictions of détente. MAD actually required some kind of complicity with the Soviet Union; both sides had to agree to allow each side the capability to destroy the other side and not to develop defences against each other's nuclear weapons; hence the 1972 ABM (Anti-Ballistic Missile) treaty. In other words, MAD was a kind of mutual agreement to have an imaginary war. How much was estimated to be enough for Mutual Assured Destruction ingenuously coincided with the size of the US stockpile.

MAD was accompanied by a growing emphasis on 'limited' conventional wars in the Third World, with the growth of naval capabilities and the growth of capabilities for combating revolutions, known as Counter Insurgency or COIN capabilities. The idea was to assert the utility of military power through 'limited' and 'appropriate' responses.

The inability to win in Vietnam contributed to a growing frustration about the inability to make political use of the stockpiles of nuclear weapons. MAD implied a stalemate – an unconvincing and contradictory sort of imaginary war in which both sides would agree on the rules of warfare.

During the 1970s, therefore, there was an increased emphasis on limited nuclear options, on the idea of usable nuclear weapons. This was incorporated into AirLand Battle and the Maritime Strategy in the early 1980s, which envisaged the integration of nuclear and conventional (and chemical) warfighting, and a greater emphasis on mobile offensive operations in the army and navy respectively. The Strategic Defense Initiative protected the United States, at least in the imagination, so that the United States would be more willing to use nuclear weapons in other parts of the world.

As in the Soviet case, an important influence on the evolution of American strategic thinking has been the experience of the Second World War. Most important was the notion of strategic bombard-ment – the idea of terrorizing an enemy population into submission. (Actually, the effectiveness of strategic bombing in the Second World War has been widely questioned;[21] however, the atomic bomb and the development of missiles were expected to overcome some of the limitations of that period.)

The experience of the Second World War also shaped the Amer-ican sense of identity in the world. Subsequent strategies have to be understood in terms of a search for identity – a subjective political-psychological process in which successive American administrations asserted the way in which they believed others should see America.

Strategic bombing and later the doctrine of massive retaliation, were ways of affirming American technological superiority.[22] MAD seemed like an admission of equality. The nuclear warfighting options of the late 1970s and early 1980s were ways of restoring American confidence, overcoming the sense of impotence experi-enced after Vietnam, albeit through a myth of legendary proportions. Even the most avid proponents of limited nuclear options do not claim to believe in real nuclear war, except when, like President Reagan, they get into a muddle, which is easy to do. They talk about 'credibility', about using the idea of limited nuclear war to impress the Soviet Union or others who might be tempted to challenge American power. But the problem of belief and perception has as much to do with America's own behaviour as with the Soviet Union. The point was made by Richard Perle, a key influence on the Reagan administration's nuclear warfighting plans:

I've always worried less about what would happen in an actual nuclear exchange than the effect the nuclear balance has on our willingness to take risks in local situations. It is not that I am worried about the Soviets attacking the United States with nuclear weapons confident that they will win that nuclear war. It is that I worry about an American President feeling he cannot afford to take action in a crisis because Soviet nuclear forces are such that, if escalation took place, they are better poised than we are to move up the escalation ladder.[23]

In other words, because the Soviet Union might do better in an imaginary war, defined in terms of Heath Robinson concepts like the 'escalation ladder', the American president might be fearful of using military force, in, say, Grenada or Libya. That is because the president himself has come to believe the elaborate myth.[24]

Nato strategy can also be roughly divided into three phases, which parallel the changes in American strategy concerning the use of nuclear weapons: the 'tripwire' strategy, associated with massive retaliation; 'flexible response', introduced in 1967; and the increasing emphasis on warfighting (both nuclear and conventional), associated with the deployment of cruise and Pershing missiles, and later with 'deep strike' concepts. All these strategies start from the premise which mirrors the Second World War experience, that Western Europe depends on the technological superiority of the United States for defence against a Soviet blitzkrieg attack across the north German plains.

Michael Howard has made the point that 'reassurance' to the Europeans was as important as 'deterrence' in explaining Nato strategy. He argues that American nuclear weapons provided a form of 'reassurance' in the face of 'widespread fear, not of Soviet military attack on Europe, but of disintegration of the whole political and economic structure'.[25] 'Reassurance' may not be quite the right term. It is certainly true that West European governments were anxious to obtain guarantees about the American political and economic commitment to Europe. But, initially, they were rather nervous about the deployment of tactical nuclear weapons in Europe.[26] The theory of the 'tripwire' was that any Soviet conventional attack on Western Europe would immediately trigger a nuclear response. The deployment of American nuclear weapons would compensate for Nato's conventional inferiority. However, wargames and exercises demonstrated the enormous casualties that would result from the use of tactical nuclear weapons. Lord Mountbatten, who was Chief of the British Defence Staff up to 1965, and Solly Zuckerman, who was chief scientist during the same period, consistently opposed the deployment of tactical nuclear weapons in Europe.[27] It would perhaps be more appropriate to say that nuclear weapons were the price that Europeans paid for 'reassurance'.[28] Europeans literally surrendered control over European lives to an American president. The imaginary war fought in the European 'theatre' was a daily reminder of their dependence. Hence, American nuclear weapons did indeed become the symbol of the American nuclear guarantee to Europe.

'Flexible response' was the outcome of a debate about atomic control in Europe. MAD introduced the problem of 'credibility' and called into question the tripwire strategy. Once the Soviet Union had acquired nuclear weapons, would America use nuclear weapons in Europe? Would an American president risk American lives in order to defend Europe? Behind this question also lay a question about the future relationship between the United States and Europe in the wake of West European recovery. De Gaulle argued that America would not risk Chicago for Paris. France withdrew from Nato's integrated command structure, and the development of independent nuclear forces established French presidential control over French lives. During this period, there were also discussions about the possibility of a multilateral nuclear force (giving a share of control to West Germany), and about the status of British nuclear weapons, which were supposed to be attached, somehow, to Nato.

Flexible response, known as MC-1413, has been described as a 'ladder of escalation options ... from conventional to strategic forces, via the nuclear forces deployed in the European theater, both those for tactical use and those longer range systems assigned to SACEUR [the Supreme Allied Commander Europe]'.[29] It was always an ambiguous doctrine, interpreted differently in Europe and the United States. Americans tend to argue that tactical nuclear and conventional options increased the credibility of the American guarantee to Europe – the imaginary war could be fought in Europe without spreading to the United States. The argument was that if the Americans used short-range nuclear weapons in Europe, the Russians would not necessarily retaliate by using long-range nuclear weapons against American territory. Because the Americans were not risking American territory, their readiness to use nuclear weapons was greater. Because the Russians knew this, they would be deterred from invading Western Europe. The risk that a US president might be prepared to use nuclear weapons underlined the unequal relationship between the United States and Western Europe.

For the Europeans the 'lower level' options were supposed to tie European defence into the strategic arsenal; tactical nuclear weapons could *not* be used without risking retaliation against the United States. In other words, the Europeans argued exactly the opposite. *Any* use of nuclear weapons would immediately escalate to full-scale nuclear war. The presence of short-range nuclear weapons would ensure that Americans regarded any attack on Western Europe as an attack on the United States. Such an interpretation was supposed to establish a more equal Atlantic relationship; European lives could not be risked without risking American lives – the imaginary war would automatically spread to the United States. The European position was not very logical, at least not within the rules of the imaginary wargame. For if the European interpretation was right, there was no reason to suppose that the US would be willing to engage in lower level options; that is to say, there was no reason to suppose the US would ever use short-range nuclear weapons and hence the defence of Western Europe was not 'credible'.

The American interpretation became clear during the decision to deploy cruise and Pershing missiles. This decision was viewed as a way of reestablishing the cohesion of Europe and the United States. The missiles were to be land-based to increase their 'public visibility' and they were to be numerous so that several countries could participate in the deployment programme. The American argument was that an American president would be willing to use these missiles because they would strike deep into Warsaw Pact territory and because he would believe that the Russians would know that they were launched from Europe and therefore would not retaliate against the United States. They would be used in a 'warning shot' mode which would buy time to negotiate. These intermediate-range missiles were said to be much more appropriate than any other option. Short-range nuclear weapons would be used on West European territory and would, therefore, be 'self-deterring'. Aircraft were too vulnerable. Submarine-launched missiles might be mistaken for US strategic forces and might invite retaliation against the United States.

In effect, the deployment of cruise and Pershing II at bases protected against protesters by barbed wire and paratroops was a way of rekindling the imaginary war and reminding Europeans of their psychological thraldom.

The subsequent concepts of 'deep strike' and follow-on force attack (FOFA) put greater emphasis on conventional warfighting. They involved the use of missiles equipped with conventional or chemical area destruction munitions (said to be equivalent in immediate lethality to nuclear munitions) to strike at the rear echelons of an attacking Soviet force. Deep strike was supposed to be reassuring because it raised the nuclear threshold, that is, it was supposed to lengthen the number of days it was imagined that Nato could hold back a Soviet attack by purely conventional means. But by the same token, deep strike made real war more imaginable.

The psychological complexity of American and Nato strategy also had something to do with the need to explain, rationalize or justify the actual growth of military capabilities, which has to be explained in terms of domestic institutional pressures throughout the period. That strategic bombing received such emphasis was not only due to the experience of the Second World War or to the need to impress. It was also due to the air force's search for a separate identity and to the problem of surplus capacity in the aircraft industry. Unlike other sectors of the defence industry, there was insufficient pent-up demand for civilian aircraft immediately after the war. In the late 1940s, American aircraft corporations argued that military procurement was essential to ensure the maintenance of a national capacity for aircraft production in the event of another war.[30] Over the years a variety of considerations, which included the enthusiasms of technologists, the Keynesian beliefs of economists, the rivalry between armed services, and pressure from industrialists – all of which found some expression in the US Congress and the US administration – contributed to a military build-up that was rather independent of strategic thinking. How did it happen that the US accumulated 30,000 nuclear weapons during the 1950s? Targets had to be found for each weapon and some kind of rationale developed for the targets. The difficulty of denting the inexorable process of 'upgrading' and 'modernizing' nuclear and conventional forces was illustrated both during the McNamara years of the early 1960s and the

Carter years of 1977–81. Strategy had to find a political purpose for what actually existed.

The anticipation of conflict

The predispositions of East and West, drawn from their common experience of the Second World War, from their domestic and intra-bloc concerns as well as from their institutional bias, were mutually reinforcing. The Soviet emphasis on conventional offence, arising from tradition and from the requirements of occupation in Eastern Europe, reinforced Western warnings of an imminent Soviet invasion of Western Europe. The Western emphasis on the use of nuclear weapons as a response to a Soviet conventional attack, arising from the American self-identification with technical fixes and with the need for a psychological bond to Europe, reinforced Soviet analyses of the barbarous, inhumane nature of Western 'imperialists'. What is more, critics in both East and West used the same sorts of arguments; they tended to play the imaginary wargame by the same rules. Hence Western critics of the arms race would argue that the Soviet Union did not have conventional superiority and could not invade the West, and that the West was acquiring a first-strike capability to knock out Soviet retaliatory capabilities. They were discredited in the West because they denied Soviet conventional superiority, even though it is true that Soviet conventional superiority has been greatly exaggerated (estimates of the military balance generally failed to take into account the size of Soviet divisions, their lack of readiness, inadequate support, morale problems, the quality of equipment, etc.). At the same time the argument about first strike, which is predicated on an imaginary war scenario, helped to legitimize Soviet perceptions of the West. Opponents of 'real socialism', on the other hand, argued that the West should be strong enough to stop Soviet tanks. This argument legitimized the acquisition of nuclear weapons in the West and could be used in the East to point out that such people were agents of the 'enemy'. The problem was that Western nuclear weapons did not and could not stop Soviet tanks in Eastern Europe; on the contrary, they provided a rationale, a pretext, for the tanks.

Together, governments and opposition contributed to an anticipation of conflict that served to sustain a memory of the Second Word War based on the experience of the victors. Interestingly, the deployment of cruise and Pershing missiles seems to have rekindled other memories – the memories of the victims. I remember in 1982 talking to a group of women in Hamburg. 'How can we accept these missiles,' they asked, 'when we remember the bombing of Hamburg?' (which resulted in more immediate casualties than Hiroshima). Whether because of the time that has elapsed, making long-buried experiences less painful to recall, or whether there are more immediate political reasons having to do with the rediscovery of a European identity and the practice of détente, these alternative memories do seem to have helped to revive reality and to break through the hold of imagined strategies.

Notes

1 See Lawrence Freedman, *The Evolution of Nuclear Strategy* (Macmillan, 1982).
2 An illuminating example of the process of internalization is provided by Herbert York in his memoirs, *Making Weapons: Talking Peace. A Physicist's Odyssey from Hiroshima to Geneva* (Basic Books, 1987). York describes how proud he felt that he had made a small contribution to the Manhattan Project and to the surrender of Japan. He also says that it is important that the bombs *were* dropped on Hiroshima and Nagasaki because it made people aware of the power of these weapons. After the war he planned to resume his career as a college professor. However, with the onset of the cold war he was recalled to the Livermore laboratory to work on nuclear weapons – an intellectually stimulating task. In 1953 he was asked to run a second laboratory. He recalled:

Our working philosophy ... called for always pushing at the technological extremes. We did not wait for higher government or military authorities to tell us what they wanted and only then seek to supply it. Instead we set out from the start to construct nuclear explosive devices that had the smallest diameter, the lightest weight, the least investment in rare materials, or the highest yield-to-weight ratio or that otherwise carried the state of the art beyond the currently explored frontiers. We were completely confident that the military would find a use for our product after we proved it, and that did indeed usually turn out to be true ... In pushing this philosophy, I had in mind two complementary benefits. First, it seemed the best way to assure continuing American superiority in nuclear weaponry. Secondly, it provided the kind of intellectual stimulus and quest for adventure that young scientists usually find only in basic research. (pp. 75–6)

It was only towards the end of the Eisenhower administration, when the US stockpile had grown to some 30,000 nuclear weapons, that he came to be sceptical of scientific and technical solutions and aware of the 'frightful dilemmas and paradoxes that flow from them' (p. 196).

3 Quoted in Matthew Evangelista, *Innovation and the Arms Race: How the United States and the Soviet Union Develop New Military Technologies* (Cornell University Press, 1988), p. 119. Likewise, General Gavin toured Europe for a similar purpose. He concluded:

The Northern Italy area particularly adapted itself to the tactical employment of nuclear weapons since the mountains channelized an attacker ... Admiral Carney had recommended, on a number of occasions, the static use of nuclear weapons in the Alpine passes and they obviously had great merit. The Greek and Turkish areas, with the exception of the area immediately north of the Dardanelles which is rolling open country, likewise offered excellent opportunities for the use of tactical nuclear weapons in defense. (p. 126)

4 Miroslav Kusý, 'Chartism and "real socialism"', in Vaclav Havel et al., *The Power of the Powerless* (Hutchinson, 1985), p. 165.
5 Robert Jervis has explored this relationship between deterrence and perception. One of the most 'significant and pervasive' barriers to accurate perception, he argues, is

the tendency for people to assimilate new information to their pre-existing beliefs, to see what they expect to be present. Ambiguous or even discrepant information is ignored, misperceived, or reinterpreted so that it does minimum damage to what the person already believes ... This tendency is not always irrational and does not always decrease the accuracy of perception. Our environment presents us with so many conflicting and ambiguous stimuli that we could not maintain a coherent view if we did not use our concepts and beliefs to impose some order on it. ('Deterrence and perception', *International Security*, 7:3, Winter 1982–3)

See also Robert Jervis, *Perception and Misperception in International Relations* (Princeton University Press, 1976).
6 This story is told by Matthew Evangelista in 'Stalin's post-war army reappraised', *International Security*, 7:3, Winter 1982–3.
7 See Michael MccGwire, *Military Objectives in Soviet Foreign Policy* (Brookings Institution, Washington DC, 1987) and 'Soviet military objectives', *World Policy Journal*, 3:4, Fall 1986.

8 Evangelista, 'Stalin's post-war army'.
9 For example, Herb York describes predominant perceptions of China in the late 1950s:

> Historically, China had not been expansionist, but it was easy to interpret her lively alliance with Russia and her behavior in Korea as signaling a change. We were wrong, but we had good reasons for being so. One was our own stupid action several years before in eliminating all the knowledgeable 'old China hands' in a fit of political anguish over the question 'Who lost China?'. Equally important was the policy of supersecrecy. Both Russia and China used to hide everything they did. We were, in sum, mainly wrong because of ignorance, although surely a touch of paranoia was there too. (*Making Weapons: Talking Peace*, p. 172)

10 Evangelista, 'Stalin's post-war army'.
11 See John Erickson, 'The ground forces in Soviet military policy', *Strategic Review*, Winter 1978.
12 Christopher Jones, *Soviet Influence in Eastern Europe: Political Autonomy and the Warsaw Pact* (Praeger, 1981).
13 See Gerard Holden, 'After INF: a new Warsaw Pact military doctrine?', *ADIU Report*, 9:6, November–December 1987.
14 Gerard Holden, *The Warsaw Pact* (Basil Blackwell, 1989).
15 Alexander Yakovlev says that the belief 'that possession of a powerful bomber airforce could secure decisive military supremacy over the enemy . . . was based on the barbarous fascist concept of total bombing of civilian populations'. *The Aim of a Lifetime* (Progress Publishers, Moscow, 1972), p. 142.
16 See David Holloway, *The Soviet Union and the Arms Race* (Yale University Press, 1983).
17 Evangelista, *Innovation*.
18 Holloway, *Soviet Union*.
19 'More rubble for the rouble,' as Evangelista puts it (*Innovation*).
20 See Daniel Ellsberg, 'Call to mutiny', in E. P. Thompson and Dan Smith, eds, *Protest and Survive* (Monthly Review Press, 1981).
21 United States Strategic Bombing Survey, *The Effects of Strategic Bombing on the German War Economy* (Washington DC, 1946).
22 This perception was described in 1947 by American columnist Walter Lippman. Atomic bombs and rockets were, he wrote,

> the perfect fulfillment of all wishful thinking on military matters: here is war that requires no national effort, no draft, no training, no discipline, but only money and engineering know-how of which we have plenty. Here is the panacea which enables us to be the greatest power on earth without investing time, energy, sweat, blood and tears, and – as compared with the cost of a great

Army, Navy and Air Force, not even much money. (Quoted in Freedman, *Evolution*, p. 48)

23 Quoted in Robert Sheer, *With Enough Shovels: Reagan, Bush and Nuclear War* (Secker and Warburg, 1983), p. 13.
24 The novelist Salman Rushdie has described this myth as a kind of 'Stalinist theologising', which is embodied in the Strategic Defense Initiative:

It is conceived on a gargantuan scale because God's State must make its designs grand; it places the chosen people (in theory) under God's mighty invincible Shield and it requires of its disciples a colossal leap of faith – because it almost certainly will not work. Positioned half-way between the earth and the infinite, its huge and incompetent weapons will acquire a status which is, if not divine, at last angelic. Star Wars is the guardian angel myth of the nuclear age. ('Yielding to the Force', *European Nuclear Disarmament Journal*, 25, December 1986–January 1987)

25 Michael Howard, 'Reassurance and deterrence', *Foreign Affairs*, 61:2, Winter 1982–3, p. 161.
26 Tactical nuclear weapons were first deployed in 1952 without the knowledge of the allies. As late as 1956, General Gruenther, then Supreme Allied Commander, sent a telegram to the US Secretary of Defense: 'An educational campaign is urgently needed on the subject of fall-out with the purpose of re-establishing confidence in the minds of the Europeans as to the essentiality of our atomic posture and our ability to cope with the associated problems.' Quoted in Evangelista, *Innovation*, p. 227.
27 See Louis Mountbatten, 'A military commander surveys the nuclear arms race', *International Security*, 4:3, Winter 1979/80.
28 I remember an elderly German social democrat saying to me during the height of the debate about cruise and Pershing missiles: 'We have to accept the missiles because the Americans liberated us and we owe so much to them.'
29 *The Modernization of Nato's Long-range Theater Nuclear Forces*, report prepared for the Subcommittee on Europe and the Middle East, Committee on Foreign Affairs, US House of Representatives, by the Congressional Research Service, 31 December 1980, p. 11.
30 See Mary Kaldor, *The Baroque Arsenal* (André Deutsch, 1982), ch. 3.

12

Real Resources

Strategies may belong to the realm of imagination. But preparations for an imaginary war are real enough. The imaginary war consists of real soldiers, weapons, arms manufacturers and scientists pretending to fight a war. And because this drama involves substantial real resources, it constitutes a form of economic intervention; it can be treated as a mechanism for regulation.

How this form of economic intervention works, whether it stimulates or retards industrial development, does not just depend on the quantity of resources involved in preparations for warfare. It also depends on the nature of those resources and how they are reproduced. The term 'military-technological style' can be used to describe a specific pattern of military organization, that is, a military labour-process and a specific mix of military products, both weapons and infrastructure – transportation, communication, food, uniforms, even health care.[1] Just as a pattern of industrial development such as Fordism can be said to involve not just this or that innovation but a pervasive change in the principles of production and consumption produced by a series of interrelated technical, social, cultural and political innovations, so a military-technological style incorporates technological, social, organizational and even geopolitical innovations. Military-technological style is the way in which a particular subset of authoritative resources, namely socially organized means of violence, are reproduced; it could also be described as a mode of warfare.

One of the ways of characterizing a shift in military-technological style is in terms of the classic shift from offensive to defensive modes of warfare, which can be traced throughout the history of warfare.[2]

Hence, for example, the mass armies of the Napoleonic wars constituted a new offensive-military-technological style, based on the revolutionary élan of the soldier. However, the development of lethal, efficient and easily operated guns made people, however brave, highly vulnerable.[3] Courageous infantry offensives were tragically mowed down in the First World War and the stalemate of the trenches typified a changeover to a defensive military-technological style, in which victory was only possible through attrition. The tank and the aeroplane could withstand machine-gun fire, and quick, mobile, offensive operations became the style of the Second World War. Today, improvements in electronics and in materials have greatly increased the accuracy and destructiveness of all munitions so that tanks and aeroplanes and surface ships have become almost as easy to destroy as people were in the First World War. The Iraq–Iran war was reminiscent of the trenches.

Military-technological style changes during periods of major and prolonged wars. New technical and organizational innovations may be introduced as a result of pressure from the civilian economy, from engineers or private manufacturers, or as a result of minor or peripheral wars. But in peacetime or in periods of imaginary war, these by and large do not result in fundamental changes of military-technological style.

There is a critical difference between a real war and an imaginary war. In a real war, the war effort is centralized and focused on the objectives of war. Military-technological style is determined by the necessity to respond to requirements on the battlefield. In an imaginary war, there are exercises, games and scenarios to test out the war effort in the imagination. But what is judged to contribute to victory or defeat, that is, what is regarded as an efficient or inefficient use of resources, is ultimately subjective and depends on the predilections of military planners and politicians and on the institutional environment.

During periods of prolonged warfare, the military sector is often very dynamic and innovations emerging from the experience of warfare may be applied to the civilian sector; this is the process of 'spin-off'. In peacetime or in times of imaginary war, the civil sector tends to be more dynamic than the military sector. New innovations pioneered in the civil sector are pressed upon the armed forces, which tend either to resist them or to incorporate them within the prevailing military-technological style. This process can be termed 'spin-in'.

In using these terms 'spin-in' and 'spin-off' or in arguing that one sector is more dynamic than the other, I am not making a normative judgement. I am not implying that technological dynamism or 'spin-in' and 'spin-off' are necessarily valuable. Such a judgement would presuppose a linear view of technological progress in which all innovations and ideas are somehow useful. Innovations in the civilian sector which increase economic efficiency, for example, or fulfil some unmet need, or are even just interesting or clever ideas, may not necessarily contribute to military utility; on the contrary such innovations may simply lead to a wasteful and extravagant use of resources. Likewise, innovations generated from the forcing-house of war are not necessarily appropriate for civilian goals, however they are defined. Indeed, they may shape or distort patterns of industrial development in ways that citizens might not have considered desirable had they been able to make social choices with different information; an example is nuclear power.

The military-technological style of the imaginary war does not depart significantly from the military-technological style of the Second World War. It involves nuclear weapons employed in ways which are reminiscent of that war, as an extended form of strategic bombardment on the Western side and an extended form of artillery on the Eastern side. It also involves conventional forces, using Fordist forms of transport – tanks and aeroplanes, configured for mobile offensive operations much along the lines of the blitzkrieg.

There has, of course, been some evolution in military-technological style and this evolution has to be explained in terms of the form of regulation in East and West and in terms of differences in civilian style, involving the different methods by which preparation for warfare are reproduced and their relationship to the methods through which civil production is regulated. These differences also explain the differing impact of the military sector on the Soviet system and on Atlanticism.

Soviet preparations for warfare

In the Soviet case, the difference between real war and imaginary war is reflected in the difference between a war economy and a pseudo-war economy which is bureaucratically regulated. What does this imply for the regulation of the military sector?

First of all, centralized political control (top–down decision-making) is eroded in a bureaucratically regulated economy. Vertical relationships still prevail. Administrative directives determine what and how much is to be produced. But, as in other sectors, the military sector is characterized by a process of 'building up' and 'breaking down' the plan, in which military-industrial enterprises, defence ministries (responsible for the military-industries), design bureaux and laboratories, the armed forces and their staffs, the military academies, etc., contribute to the determination of administrative directives. The experience of Gorbachev (and, earlier, Khrushchev) seems to suggest that, because of the framework of vertical relationships, political control can be reestablished – albeit with considerable difficulty.

Secondly, in a bureaucratically regulated system, the privileged nature of the military sector stems both from its role in the bureaucracy and from the political importance accorded to the imaginary war. It is often argued that in the Soviet Union the military sector (that is the armed forces and the military-industrial enterprises) constitutes a privileged sector because the state is both consumer and producer; and there is a good deal of evidence for this argument. The military and the military-industrial enterprises are able to cut through red tape, commandeer scarce materials and insist on high standards through the use of quality inspectors known as *voenpredy*. More importantly, perhaps, the military sector has been the beneficiary of command-style technological development; that is to say, major technological programmes such as the atomic bomb or the rocket programme are initiated from above and pursued vigorously.

However, the military sector is not the only sector where the state is consumer as well as producer. The state is also the consumer of capital goods; why should the armed forces be any more influential, say, than the managers of heavy industries? Both military spending and investment receive priority over consumer spending, where the consumers are powerless households (this is discussed in chapter 8 above). The special privileges of the military sector arise not merely from the fact that the military sector is part of the state apparatus; it also stems, in the absence of real war, from the political or ideological importance accorded to the pseudo-war. To some extent of course, the political importance of the imaginary war depends on how political priorities are established and, in the absence of democracy, this depends on various interest groups within the state apparatus, which includes the military sector.[4]

Thirdly, as in other sectors of the Soviet economy, the military sector retains a bias towards quantity and not quality. Despite top–down technological innovation, military-industrial enterprises are said to exhibit much the same resistances to innovation as other kinds of enterprises. Innovation disrupts routines, established supply lines, etc., and interrupts the fulfilment of quantitative plan indicators. Although there is a certain degree of competition among design bureaux and a stimulus 'from above', these tendencies for technological improvement are contained by the mass production bias of enterprises and the military preference for massed offensives of the Second World War type. Soviet military-technological innovation is 'conservative', that is, incremental or evolutionary, involving modest improvements to existing models.[5] But in terms of numbers, Soviet military programmes very often turn out to be bigger than anticipated in the West, and this provides some basis for alarmist calculations of the military balance, based on 'bean counts'.[6]

If this analysis is correct, it is possible to establish certain propositions about the overall effect on the Soviet economy. The Second World War and preparations for that war were clearly mobilizing, that is to say, they stimulated economic growth. The Second World War style of warfare can be described as 'Fordist', in so far as it required a Fordist labour process (mass production), and Fordist consumption (mass warfare), tanks and aircraft, and the intensive use of oil. The early years of the cold war can be said to have dragged the economy as a whole, in Eastern Europe as well as the Soviet Union, along a military-related pattern of industrial development – involving mass production, mass consumption of armaments, the development of heavy industry, and the intensive use of oil and, later, nuclear power. This is, perhaps, what is meant by the extensive pattern of accumulation. No one knows, not even, it appears, the Soviet government, the true size of military spending in the Soviet Union; estimates vary from 12 to 25 per cent of Net Material Product (NMP – national output).

Even in the 1950s there was talk of the exhaustion of extensive accumulation. But the very existence of a substantial military sector of the type described above constituted an overwhelming barrier to structural change. This was already evident in the Khrushchev years when his reform plans foundered in part on military and heavy industry resistance.[7] Of course, it is sometimes argued – and Brezhnev himself made the argument – that since the military, on account of their privileged position, are technological leaders, a changeover to a more 'intensive' mode of production might be initiated from the military sector through 'spin-off'. This argument has been revived recently. It has been said that the Soviet Union should develop its own 'star wars' programme as a way of introducing information technology into the Soviet economy.[8] However, if it is correct to say that the style of warfare has not significantly departed from that of the Second World War, then there are evidently limits to the degree to which the military sector could assimilate new technologies in ways that might be applicable to a restructuring of the civilian economy. Any 'spin-off' is likely to preserve the existing pattern of industrial development rather than to encourage transformation.

Herein lies the fundamental dilemma of the Soviet economy. Historically, economic change has been stimulated by war. Military-technological style is determined in war and this has a profound influence on industrial development. But in the absence of war, bureaucratic regulation tends to reproduce whatever has been in the past. Gorbachev has proposed to introduce new defensive strategies that could initiate a shift in military-technological style. But how are these strategies to be proved? If they are not tested out, will the armed forces be ready to accept them? Without a war, how can the bureaucracy be shaken up? Can democratization transform the role of the military?

In East Central Europe, military spending and military production are much lower than in the Soviet Union as a share of NMP, although it is impossible to estimate what share of manufacturing output destined for export to the Soviet Union is an input into Soviet military production. Some countries, notably Czechoslovakia, are important arms exporters. Since East Central European armies are tightly integrated into the Warsaw Pact, the military-technological style is Soviet. There are very few indigenous military products – Polish small arms, Czech light aircraft and armoured cars. Even though the military sector is smaller than in the Soviet Union, all the East Central European countries bear the scars of the Stalinist war economy, reproduced through bureaucratic inertia. There is some evidence that countries with relatively low military spending, for instance, Hungary and East Germany, have been relatively more successful economically. All the same, the possibilities for restructuring, even with a move away from bureaucratic regulation, are, even after the political changes in these countries, constrained by military-industrial links with the Soviet Union.

Western preparations for warfare

The American military sector combines bureaucratic and market forms of regulation. There is a parallel with the late nineteenth-century British naval arms build-up. The rise of large quasi-public defence companies, dependent for their survival on the defence budget, combined with the enthusiasms of the technologists and the decentralized nature of American political life, have generated considerable innovatory energy. Nuclear reactors for submarines, integrated circuits, supercomputers, laser X-rays, are but a few of the technological ideas stimulated by the military sector. However, these innovations have been adopted and integrated into military theory and practice only where they conform or can be made to conform to the prevailing military style.

There is one important respect in which the American military-technological style does differ from the typical style of the Second World War. This is the emphasis on quality rather than quantity. Mass production was crucial to the American (and Soviet) success in the Second World War, although there was always a tension between quality and quantity. Tooling up for mass production, as Ford did at his Willow Run factory, limited the ability to make the continuous improvements demanded by the experience of fighting.

In the post-war period, there has been an emphasis on continuous improvement of products rather than on mass production or process improvements. The pressure for improvement comes not from the experience of fighting but, primarily although not exclusively, from the competition between defence manufacturers. Product improvement can be viewed as the Western defence industry's equivalent of 'hooking on to the plan'. Technological improvements invariably cost more than anticipated, thus putting continual pressure on the defence budget. In other respects, the American military-technological style continues to resemble the 'Fordist' style of warfare: the emphasis on weapons platforms (tanks, aircraft, submarines, surface ships, large missiles), the intensive use of oil and the continued stress on the offensive. Hence technical change has consisted of continued improvement to Fordist type products or within a Fordist style of warfare. Elsewhere I have used the term 'baroque' to describe this pattern of technical change.

The military sector, ever since the Second World War, has been an important consumer of electronics. Radar and computers were Second World War spin-offs. During the 1950s and 1960s, the US air force introduced very important new technologies, like numerically controlled tools (that is to say, machine tools controlled by the use of computer programmes) and, CAD/CAM, Computer Aided Design/ Computer Aided Manufacturing (although the aim was to improve the quality of the products not to reduce costs and, on the whole, the equipment developed was too complex for civilian use).[9] The Minuteman and Apollo programmes provided an initial market for integrated circuits.

During the early 1970s, at the time of the Vietnam and Middle East wars, there was much debate about the implications of new electronics technologies on strategy. Essentially the combination of new forms of communication or sensing (lasers, microwaves, sonar, terrain-matching, etc.) and new forms of control or data processing, based on microelectronics, has enormously increased the ability to identify and hit targets. Very high attrition rates were experienced in Vietnam and the Middle East.

Some argued that these new technologies would bring about fundamental changes in strategy, a shift in military-technological style. The vulnerability of weapons platforms has shifted the balance of advantage to the defender. Proponents of this line of thought put forward various proposals for a dispersed, decentralized strategy which would aim to bog down an enemy offensive so as to give time for negotiation. Such strategies have been variously described as the 'chequer board' or the 'attrition sponge'.[10] They would require decentralization of military organization – numerous, relatively autonomous, military units operating in dispersed hiding places. They would be equipped with large numbers of missiles which could be mass produced at low cost and launched by an individual or by a small vehicle (also cheap) which could be easily hidden. A maritime version of this strategy would rely on small submarines and missile-equipped patrol boats.

Others argued, however, that the implications of the new technologies were quite different. Because of increased vulnerability, weapons systems need to be larger and more expensive so as to incorporate complex electronic countermeasures, greater protection, etc., in order to increase survivability. Increased use of area destruction munitions (also widely used in Vietnam and the Middle East), like cluster munitions, incendiaries or chemical weapons, would be used to swamp the defence.[11] Some of these munitions are said to be equivalent to nuclear weapons in their destructive and dispersive effects. More decoys, remotely piloted vehicles, jamming devices, etc., would ensure the continued success of the offensive.

In practice, the second argument prevailed although this was not the result of rational debate or experiment. There has been no test of the alternative approaches. Rather, the second argument has won because it suits political and institutional predispositions. It is consistent with the political objectives of the imaginary war, and with the institutional bias of military planners. In the early 1980s the Strategic Defense Initiative, AirLand Battle and the Maritime Strategy were all hailed as radical new strategic concepts arising out of ET (Emerging Technologies). Both the Maritime Strategy and AirLand Battle put particular emphasis on the importance of offence and manoeuvrability, and both require complex and expensive weapons platforms to improve existing missions: heavily protected aircraft carriers and surface ships capable of carrying cruise missiles for the Maritime Strategy and land-based nuclear, conventional and chemically armed medium-range missiles and aircraft for the 'deep strike' role demanded by AirLand Battle.[12] The Strategic Defense Initiative appears more radical, since it uses the language of the defensive. However, because SDI is not and cannot be 100 per cent effective, its main consequence is to enhance the offensive. *More* offensive missiles have to be built to penetrate SDI. Also, SDI envisages the use of weapons platforms like long-range anti-ballistic missiles, high velocity space guns, laser-firing satellites, even brilliant pebbles. In other words, none of these new strategic concepts displaces the characteristic features of the post-war military-technological style. The emphasis on mobility and offence, the reliance on weapons platforms, the continuation of intensive energy use are all augmented and reinforced by the new technologies.

Within Western Europe, only the British defence industry survived the war. Elsewhere armed forces were dependent on American imports in the immediate post-war period and arms industries were gradually rebuilt, primarily with American help. European arms production was largely based on various forms of transfer of American technology, especially licensed production. Even where indigenous design capability was established, as in Britain and France and, to some extent, in West Germany and Italy, these indigenous efforts had nevertheless to fit conceptions of military utility determined by Nato. Because strategic theories and military missions are determined collectively within Nato headquarters, because Nato shares a common infrastructure (airfields, communications, radar warning, pipelines, etc.), and because Nato countries engage in joint manoeuvres and exercises, the opportunity for an alternative evolution of military-technological style was and is extremely limited.

This conclusion can be modified in two respects. First of all, because national markets for military equipment are so much smaller in West European countries than in the United States, West European defence manufacturers are much more dependent on exports than the United States. West European countries typically export between 20 and 30 per cent of output and, for some companies, this proportion is even higher – Dassault-Breguet exports over 75 per cent of its output. Because of this dependence on exports to Third World countries, military-technological style has been influenced, not just by imaginary conceptions of war in Europe, but by real wars in the Third World. Britain, for example, has successfully developed small missile-firing patrol boats. France has put more emphasis on simplicity and low cost in the design of aircraft.

Secondly, some West European countries have been influenced by ideas of alternative defence linked to the development of information technology. This is especially important in Sweden, which is not a member of Nato and which emphasizes its 'special profile' in defence. But such ideas have also been influential in some military and industrial circles in West Germany. It is worth noting that, in these cases, manufacturers of defence equipment are generally large and successful civilian firms, and their defence sales are a very small share of total output, for instance, Saab and L. M. Ericsson in Sweden, large electronics companies in West Germany. These companies have an interest in challenging the prevailing military-technological style.

During the 1950s and 1960s, the adoption of American military-technological styles encouraged the diffusion of a Fordist pattern of industrial development within Western Europe, influencing the construction of infrastructure and the preferences for oil and nuclear power, certain types of skills, etc. Contributions to Nato's common infrastructure were considered the 'membership fee' of Nato.

However, in the 1970s and 1980s, there was a growing bifurcation of military-technological style and patterns of industrial development.[13] The continued development of Fordist type military products was characterized by sharply diminishing returns (exponential increases in cost for each improvement in performance). Military products became increasingly expensive, complex, energy-intensive and unreliable. This represents a stark contrast to the goals of civilian innovation, which include cheapness, simplicity, reliability, and efficient use of energy and raw materials.

This contrast was particularly significant in the development of the electronics sector. The military have always been important consumers of electronics. But it is only in the last 20 years that the development of electronics, especially components, has had a pervasive influence on all sectors of industry. Military spending has diverted the skills and energies of the electronics industries; everywhere, there are shortages of electronic engineers. More importantly the contrast between military-technological style and the goals of civilian innovation distorted the development of the electronics industry in those countries where the military demands are highest. This is especially important in chip manufacture, the new key factor of post-Fordist production, and in electronic capital goods. For example, the Pentagon's programme for Very High Speed Integrated Circuits (VHIC) calls for specifications like resistance to radiation, or speed (as opposed to scale) of decision-making, which are completely at variance with civilian requirements.[14]

The bifurcation of military-technological style and civilian innovation is one of the main explanations for the changing pattern of manufacturing trade in the last 20 years. There has been a dramatic deterioration in the manufacturing competitiveness of the United States and Britain, especially in electronics. (In Britain the defence industry as a share of total industry is comparable to that of the United States.) France and Sweden have done less badly than might have been expected from the size of their defence industries and this can be explained by the fact that both have modified their military-technological style – in the one case as a response to wars in the Third World, and in the other case as a result of a geopolitical interest in challenging the norms of the imaginary war.[15]

Military spending as an economic regulator

Within the Soviet system, preparations for warfare have been a goal of economic development. Because Soviet-type economies are re-source constrained, preparations for warfare represent a subtraction from what is available for other goals – higher standards of living or economic growth. All the same, military spending has played a mobilizing role in increasing overall resources. War has, in the past, represented a technological stimulus to innovation and increased productiveness in ways that are otherwise not possible in Soviet-type economies. This was especially important during the Second World War and the cold war period when competition with the West encouraged the spread of mass production and the introduction of new technologies. However, the bureaucratic inertia of pseudo-war petrifies military-technological style in the memory of the Second

World War; as the innovatory potential of that period is exhausted, so the military sector becomes a barrier rather than a stimulus to civilian industrial change. Hence the Soviet Union did not adapt its military-technological style, as a consequence of the war in Afghanistan, although Afghanistan, like Vietnam 20 years earlier, may have been important in bringing the role of the military into question.

Capitalist economies, on the other hand, tend to be demand constrained. In periods of excess capacity, any increase in government spending stimulates economic growth in the short run. Whether or not military spending stimulates the expansion of capacity in the long run depends on military-technological style. During the Second World War and the cold war period, military spending did encourage the diffusion of a Fordist industrial infrastructure as well as providing a market for new products, like computers and integrated circuits, that might not otherwise have been developed. However, as the pattern of industrial development has changed, as Fordism has given way to post-Fordism, and as oil has given way to the microchip, the persistence of what might be called a Fordist military-technological style inhibits the creation of new types of industrial capacity. Or to put it another way, military spending sustains traditional types of industrial capacity (Fordist and American) and blocks or distorts the evolution of an alternative pattern of development. It is a way of avoiding decline and, at the same time, postponing recovery.

This is one reason why political choices now being made in Europe, both East and West, will profoundly influence future patterns of industrial development. How far European countries reduce military spending and what kind of military-technological style they adopt will be the consequences of political decisions about the future of Europe, about how to regulate political relationships in Europe, both East and West. But these political choices will also be choices about forms of economic regulation.

Notes

1 The spread of inoculation was an important twentieth-century military innovation. Professional nursing was a spin-off from the Crimean war.

2 See, for example, William H. McNeill, *The Pursuit of Power: Technology, Armed Force and Society since AD 1000* (University of Chicago Press, 1982), and Michael Howard, *War in European History* (Oxford University Press, 1976).

3 Machine guns were used to great effect in the 'scramble for colonies'. Dervishes, Zulus or Matabele were literally wiped out by machine-gun fire. 'There are not tears enough to grieve for all our dead,' said the Zulu chief. And at the battle of Omdurman in the Sudan, 48 Europeans and 11,000 Dervishes were killed. The implications of machine guns were not recognized by the Europeans, however, and they tended to attribute their success to cultural and racial superiority. Military tactics were not adjusted to the new technology and, in the First World War, Europeans met the same fate as Africans had done earlier. John Ellis describes the First World War as a tragic clash between eighteenth-century forms of warfare and nineteenth-century technology. See John Ellis, *The Social History of the Machine Gun* (Pantheon, 1975).

4 Nevertheless, despite the privileged nature of the military sector, various studies seem to suggest that in the Soviet Union, the quality and technical level of military products are not markedly superior to other products. See M. Evangelista, *Innovation and the Arms Race* (Cornell University Press, 1988); David Holloway, 'The defence industry', in Ronald Amann and Julian Cooper, eds, *Industrial Innovation in the Soviet Union* (Yale University Press, 1982); Andrew Cockburn, *The Threat: Inside the Soviet War Machine* (Hutchinson, 1983).

5 See Mary Kaldor, *The Baroque Arsenal* (André Deutsch, 1982), chapter 4.

6 See, for example, the controversial article on this subject by Albert Wohlstetter, 'Is there a strategic arms race?', *Foreign Policy*, 16, Autumn 1974.

7 See Edward L. Warner, *The Military in Contemporary Soviet Politics: An Institutional Analysis* (Praeger, 1977).

8 See Jerry Hough, 'Gorbachev's strategy', *Foreign Affairs*, Fall 1985. Also Matthew Evangelista, 'Economic reform and military technology in Soviet security policy', unpublished.

9 David Noble, *Forces of Production: A Social History of Industrial Automation* (Alfred A. Knopf, 1984).

10 Stephen Canby, 'The Alliance and Europe. Part IV: Military doctrine and technology', *Adelphi Papers* 109, IISS, Winter 1974–5; Horst Ahfeldt, *Defensive Verteidigung* (Rowalt Reinbeck, Munich, 1983).

11 Julian Perry Robinson, 'Qualitative trends in conventional munitions: the Vietnam war and after', in M. Kaldor and A. Eide, eds, *The World Military Order* (Macmillan, 1978).

12 See *The Maritime Strategy*, US Naval Institute, Washington DC, January 1986; and for AirLand Battle, *US Army Field Manual*, FM 100–5, 1982, and Tradoc Pamphlet 525–5, *The AirLand Battle and Corps 86*, 25 March 1981, Fort Monroe, Virginia, US Army Training and Doctrine Command, Department of the Army, 1981.

13 This argument is developed in Mary Kaldor and William Walker, 'Technologie militaire et dynamisme économique', *La Recherche*, October 1988.

14 See Jay Stowsky, 'Competing with the Pentagon', *World Policy Journal*, 3:4, Fall 1986.

15 This argument is explored further in Kaldor and Walker, 'Technologie militaire'. See also Mary Kaldor, Margaret Sharp and William Walker, 'Military R & D and industrial competitiveness', *Lloyds Bank Review*, October 1986.

PART V
Conclusion

13

Beyond Détente?

Mikhail Gorbachev did not spring from nowhere, nor did his enthusiastic welcome in the West. He was the trigger for changes in East and West that were long overdue. He was the first important political leader to admit the bankruptcy of the ideology of imaginary war, something most people were already aware of even if only privately: the emptiness of socialist slogans, repeated with renewed vigour in the early 1980s, long after they had ceased to have any real meaning for ordinary citizens in Eastern Europe and the Soviet Union; and the absurdity of arcane doctrines of nuclear deterrence, enthusiastically elaborated in the early 1980s in the West, despite the fact that anyone who had understood the effects of nuclear war knew that no refinements of tactics or strategy were possible. And without the ideology, the institutional framework that sustained Atlanticism and the Soviet system was bound to totter.

What comes next? Will perestroika succeed? Are the processes of democratization in the East irreversible? Will Western Europe become a distinct political entity? Will we achieve a nuclear-free Europe by the year 2000? Questions abound. But the answers are not predetermined. The most we can do is to describe the contours of change, to think about the kind of outcomes that are implied by the main lines of thought described by this book, and to develop some guiding principles in a situation where particular policy prescriptions are rapidly overtaken by events.

This chapter starts with some preliminary remarks about the economic impasse and political conjuncture that characterize both East and West, recapping the argument of earlier chapters. I then consider four possible directions for change: one is implied by orthodox interpretations of the cold war as a struggle between freedom and totalitarianism, most prevalent among the American right; one is implied by a post-revisionist or a realist view of the world, prevalent in both American and West European establishment circles; one is implied by revisionist interpretations of the cold war and détente that can be found in the Soviet Union and in German social democratic circles and which derives from a mixture of Marxian and realist world views; and finally one is implied by the approach put forward in this book, which draws on thinking developed in opposition in both East and West.

The economic and political context

Gorbachev's reforms were significant because they were the beginning of the far-reaching *political* changes which have taken place in Europe. In both East and West, economic problems have to be explained in terms of the rigidity and inertia of political institutions. Indeed, it has been a theme of this book that what appears to be an economic crisis is, in fact, a crisis of power relations, a crisis in the reproduction of authority.

At the time that Gorbachev came to power, all the East European countries faced a situation of economic stagnation. In varying degrees, the countries of East Central Europe were heavily indebted to the West and all had been forced to adopt austerity policies. In the Soviet Union, standards of living failed to rise after 1980 and suppressed inflation has been expressed in lengthening queues as well as open price inflation. It was impossible for aging autocratic leaders to sustain what little political legitimacy they had through the provision of consumer goods.

All the East European countries had, to a greater or lesser degree, adopted economic reforms. Actually, the Soviet economic reforms began in 1982, under Andropov, when Gorbachev was put in charge of economic policy-making. He remained in that position during Chernenko's brief period of office. Even after 1985, the economic reforms did not go further than the reforms in Hungary, Yugoslavia or China which were introduced many years previously. These reforms involve the use of financial indicators such as profit in place of quantitative indicators, greater tolerance for private enterprise, greater autonomy for state enterprise, less central control over price determination and an end to the monopoly of foreign trade held by the Ministry of Foreign Trade. In other words, the reforms aim at introducing a market mechanism within Soviet-type systems.

The problem was that as in the past there are always limits to economic reform in the absence of political reform. This is not just because economic reform comes up against conservative bureaucratic resistance, which it does. It is also because the market has been conceived as a mechanism for improving central planning. Or rather, it has emerged within a framework determined by central planning. The economic structure is shaped by the inheritance of the Stalinist war economy – the emphasis on armaments and heavy industry, the giant factories, energy intensity, the neglect of agriculture. And this structure is mirrored in the bureaucracy and the planning system. The dynamism of war which propelled industrial development gave way to the inertia of a bureaucratic institutional framework shaped by that same experience. Bureaucratic regulation is, as Hannah Arendt pointed out, rule by nobody. It is a system which reproduces a bias towards investment and military spending and generates perpetual shortages as planned projects invariably cost more than anticipated. This is why, despite centralized planning, it is so difficult to control government spending – the Soviet budget deficit by 1989 amounted to some 20 per cent of net material product – and why consumer spending is perpetually squeezed. Within this framework, markets can mitigate shortage, they can fill lacunae and correct mistakes in the planning system but they cannot reorientate the direction of the economy. Markets are a mechanism; they cannot establish the goals of development. They are always shaped by the social, cultural and political environment.

The so-called second economy has represented, up to now, both legal and illegal forms of market. It is parasitical upon the first economy, that is, the planned economy. It consists of private plots nestling in the security of state and collective farms, leaseholders borrowing their factory equipment after hours, private lorries taking vegetables to the cities when the state distribution system breaks down, repair shops, small restaurants, private doctors and undertakers, black market currency dealers. As Istvan Rev puts it, the second economy 'breeds on the debris' of the first economy. It fosters skills of cunning and deviousness, it exists in the world of legal loopholes, tax dodges and unwritten codes. 'There is no straight path from this part of the economy to the world of bourgeois enterprise.'[1]

In other words, the market does not replace the planned economy and it cannot be used as a mechanism for economic restructuring without a transformation of the public sector: a fundamental shift in political priorities and a transformation of the institutional and infrastructural framework. Even in Western countries, markets develop within a socially determined composition of demand, public infrastructure, skills and specialities.

In the Soviet Union and East European countries, restructuring requires changes in the composition of expenditure including reductions in military spending (especially in the Soviet Union) and increases in spending on consumption, on the environment and on agriculture; changes in infrastructure; changes in the forms of planning and ownership; changes in the composition of skills and attitudes, etc. And it also requires changes in international economic relationships so as to lessen the rigidity resulting from bilateral trading arrangements among the Comecon countries and to increase openness towards the West.

But how is this to be achieved? The only hope is democratization. It is only through the opening up of Eastern societies, that it is possible to develop civic traditions in the Western sense and to overcome inertia as well as graft and corruption. And it is only through a democratic decision-making process that the social goals of economic restructuring be established.

Does democratization require markets? Probably it does, at least in Soviet-type societies where nearly everything is bureaucratically controlled. Markets are necessary to provide political space, independent of the state, for free expression and also to break the stranglehold of the Stalinist economy. But the point is that markets alone can guarantee neither democracy nor economic restructuring. Markets can be both destructive and creative; it depends on the social context. Markets are by no means incompatible with authoritarianism and extreme poverty, as is clear in the Third World. This is why the priority is the democratic transformation of the power structures.[2]

The West, in the middle of the 1980s, also experienced economic problems – slow growth, high levels of unemployment, international economic imbalances. In contrast to the East, a major restructuring of Western economies did take place in the 1970s and 1980s. Fordist methods of production were increasingly replaced by more flexible, decentralized, resource-saving methods of production based on the revolution in what are known as information technologies. The economic problems stemmed from the fact that these fundamental economic changes had not penetrated political institutions. Political institutions still reflected the international economic relations and domestic social priorities of the Fordist era. If centrally planned systems tend to shortage, market systems tend to excess capacity, represented by unemployment. If shortages can only be resolved through markets, the problems of excess capacity can only be resolved by appropriate government policies at both national and international levels.

Internationally, the problem is that political and economic institutions still reflect American dominance. In the late 1940s, the United States accounted for 40 to 45 per cent of world output and enjoyed a huge balance of payments surplus. Today, the US accounts for between 20 to 25 per cent of world output and is experiencing an unprecedented trade deficit. In the late 1940s, Nato provided a mechanism for a continuous transfer of resources from the US to Western Europe, which helped to underpin the international financial system. Today, Nato helps to maintain the privileged role of the dollar, thus relieving the US of pressure to correct its deficit (in contrast to the indebted countries of the Third World and Eastern Europe). The dilemma today is that if the US does take steps to correct its deficit by, for example, reducing military spending, this will cause a global recession unless the surplus countries – Japan, some West European countries and the newly industrializing countries of the Far East – spend an equivalent amount either domestically or through the transfer of resources to deficit countries, those caught in the austerity trap in Eastern Europe and the Third World. If this is to be achieved, it requires a new or reformed international financial system based on a different set of power relations, which include but are not dominated by the United States.

In their domestic economies, neo-liberal governments of the early 1980s reasserted the political priorities of the cold war – higher levels of military spending, private consumption, a preference for oil and nuclear power as a source of energy. The new techniques and forms of work organization that transformed some Western economies were thus devoted to military projects like Star Wars, AirLand Battle or Low Intensity Conflict, and to a dizzy increase in consumerist choice, with the introduction of new information-based products like video recorders and home computers, as well as greater variety in a wide range of consumer products from shoes to kitchen tiles to cars.[3]

The new post-Fordist productive capacities can thus be said to have been reined in by the Atlanticist institutional framework. Decaying urban infrastructure, environmental degradation or Third World poverty were largely excluded from the menu of social choice. Those countries which had more space for manoeuvre, which spent more on education, energy conservation, etc., and less on military spending (or which adopted a different military-technological style), and which responded to new social demands and new patterns of labour relations, do seem to have been more successful economically. In Europe, these countries included Sweden, Finland, Switzerland, West Germany and Italy. All the same, a more far-reaching shift in domestic priorities and institutions is difficult without a change in the political assumptions of Western governments.

What Gorbachev did was to break the political logjam, to break the hold of the imaginary war on political institutions, long after its purpose had been served. He did so through initiating a process of democratization which revolutionized political relations both within the Soviet Union and among the countries of the Warsaw Pact, and a process of disarmament, which is also reshaping political relations between the United States and Western Europe. He was able to do this because profound changes in political consciousness were and are taking place in both East and West.

A number of commentators have pointed out that the Gorbachev phenomenon was the product of a social and cultural transformation which was taking place in the Soviet Union even under Brezhnev.[4] This transformation included the growth of the intelligentsia, the spread of informal intellectual networks and clubs, the growth of *samizdat* publications of both left and right varieties (largely suppressed between 1982 and 1985), the growing reformist discussion in official institutes in major cities centred on the Novosibirsk publication *Eko* edited by Abel Aganbegyan and Tatiana Zaslavskaya, the transformation of youth attitudes expressed by rock groups such as Kino and Aquarium, and later in the monthly television programme *Twelfth Floor* and the film *Is It Easy to Be Young?* Like Vietnam 20 years earlier, the Afghan war expressed many of the pent-up contradictions of Soviet society – the barrenness of ideology, the burden of military spending, the impotence of military power. The war seems to have had a critical impact on informal opinion. More than a million young men had served in Afghanistan by 1988, and the official casualty figures (over 13,000 dead and over 35,000 wounded) are widely considered to be underestimated.[5]

Gorbachev released a cultural and political explosion. The publication of books, films and plays that had previously been banned, the rapid spread of clubs and later popular fronts revealed that Brezhnev, as well as Andropov and Chernenko, had been sitting on a veritable timebomb of suppressed political energy and creativity. And this explosion expresses a bewildering variety of tendencies – national, religious, chauvinist, populist and anti-semitic as well as liberal, socialist, social democratic and green.

This political and cultural transformation was not only a Soviet phenomenon. Indeed, in many ways, the process was more developed in some East European countries at the time of Gorbachev's accession to power. The Hungarian sociologist Elemer Hankiss uses the term 'second society' to describe the *samizdat* publications, informal welfare networks, political and intellectual clubs that grew up outside the framework of state and party.[6] If economic reform consists of the legalization of the second economy, then political reform represents the legalization of the second society – the reemergence of a civil society. The concept of civil society, as developed by East European intellectuals during the 1980s, meant the existence of autonomous social groups, movements, institutions, etc., capable of articulating discontent and negotiating with government. Civil society, in this sense, can also be contrasted with military society since it is only through legally recognized independent forms of expression that social conflicts can be settled democratically without violence.

In several East European countries, the early 1980s marked the transition from the activism of (isolated) dissident intellectuals to social movements. The most important was Solidarity in Poland, which survived throughout the Jaruzelski years despite imprisonment of its members and other persecutions – it was so extensive. Also significant were peace movements in the GDR (Swords into Ploughshares), Hungary (Dialogue) and later in Poland (Freedom and Peace) and Czechoslovakia (the Independent Peace Association) and the green movement (especially in Hungary) as well as embryo democracy movements (for instance, the Democratic Forum, the Network for Free Initiatives, the independent youth movement FIDESZ in Hungary).

The revolutions of 1989 were, of course, an outburst of popular feeling, and involved thousands of people who had never before dared to engage in politics. But the new mass democracy movements, like Civic Forum in Czechoslovakia or New Forum in the GDR, which articulated and organized this outburst of feeling, grew out of the experiences of the peace, green and human rights groups that had been active earlier.

In the aftermath of 1989, however an array of new tendencies can be observed – nationalist or cosmopolitan, religious or secular, liberal democrat or social democrat. Where political parties have been established, as in Hungary, they cannot be defined in the Western language of left and right. Only in the GDR, owing to the intervention of West Germany, have Western-type political parties been established.

The term 'second society' can be applied to the West as well. Mass peace and green movements emerged in the 1970s and 1980s in Western Europe to fill the political gaps of the 'first society', the world of political parties, governments and established institutions which occupy the attention of the media. Precisely because the first society had been coopted by Atlanticism, these institutions failed to absorb or express new concerns for emancipation around issues of democracy, gender, peace and the environment. In particular, the parties of the left seemed caught in the time-warp of the 1940s when socialist ideas were most popular and the manual working classes were the dominant force in society.

The dramatic upsurge in the peace movement in the early 1980s was as important, in its way, as the rise of Solidarity. Five million people or more demonstrated in the capitals of Western Europe in the autumn of 1981 and again in 1983. This experience fundamentally changed public consciousness, not just about nuclear weapons, but about European identity, the need to end the division of Europe and to remove the military presence of the superpowers. The ideas that emerged during this period influenced, at least in part, the thinking of Gorbachev as well as socialist, social democrat, green and even centre parties in Western Europe.

Gorbachev was enthusiastically welcomed by the peace movement because he offered the possibility of implementing their agenda and by West European governments because they could engage in a disarmament process and reestablish a domestic consensus without appearing to give in to the peace movement. The importance of the INF treaty lay in the fact that it removed the kingpin of the flexible response strategy that provided the imaginary tie between the United States and Western Europe – the cruise and Pershing missiles that had become the symbol of the conflict between governments and peace movements. Nothing illustrated the Atlantic relationship so clearly as the fact that four out of five West European countries went ahead with the deployment of cruise and Pershing missiles for the sake of Atlantic unity despite the fact that the majority opinion in *all* five countries was opposed to deployment. (In the Netherlands, the decision to deploy was delayed by two years so that the missiles were never actually delivered.) What this showed was the gap between the first and second societies, the fact that debates in the official political arena did not represent debates in the population at large.

The removal of these missiles has marked, therefore, the beginning of a new political relationship between the United States and Western Europe, a situation in which governments and political parties are more able to act independently. So far, they have responded differently in different countries. The West German government has adopted much of the peace agenda, or perhaps it should be more accurately described as a German agenda. France has reiterated the need for an independent West European entity; Britain has clung to the 'special relationship' with the United States. The late 1980s have witnessed a resurgence of the green movement and indeed the growing success of green parties, of Third World solidarity movements (anti-apartheid, solidarity with Nicaragua and with Palestine, BandAid, etc.) and of movements campaigning for the rights of national minorities (for instance, in Wales and Scotland). As in Eastern Europe, there has also been a more sinister rise of right-wing exclusivist nationalism, represented by the Le Pen movement in France, the Republikaners in West Germany, and by some elements in the British Conservative party. Finally, as the United States floats away and as the implications of the Single European Act (which comes into force in 1992 and will abolish customs barriers within the European Community) are absorbed, there is also a renewed political and cultural interest in the concept of Europe.

These contradictory pressures in both East and West have already begun to penetrate political institutions. Two basic features of post-war political relationships have already been changed, probably irreversibly.

One is the role of the Warsaw Pact and of inter-party relations in regulating political relations between the Soviet Union and East Central Europe. The Brezhnev doctrine is finished. When Gennadi Gerassimov, the Soviet spokesman, announced that the way to characterize relations between the Soviet Union and East Central Europe was the Sinatra doctrine: 'I did it my way', this was the signal for the wave of revolutions that so dramatically overturned communist regimes throughout East Central Europe. Subsequently, the communist parties have renamed and reclothed themselves in a desperate bid to hold on to a diminishing minority of votes in the democratic elections of 1990. Moreover, new non-communist governments have demanded the withdrawal of Soviet troops, so that the Soviet military presence in East Central Europe, except Germany, is declining faster than can be agreed in the CFE (Conventional Forces in Europe) talks in Vienna.

Most dramatic of all is the rapid process of German unification which has resulted from the opening up of the Berlin Wall, the mass migration from East to West, the 1989 revolution and the subsequent elections of March 1990. There will be no GDR any more although Soviet troops may remain on what was East German territory. Whether a united Germany will be part of Nato, neutral, or part of a new European security system is now under discussion, and will be an important factor in determining the future of Europe as a whole.

Even within the Soviet Union, party control is being undermined. The break-up of the Soviet Union into constituent republics is entirely possible. So is a forcible reintegration under military pressure. Most likely is a prolonged and painful process of disintegration.

The second feature of the post-war period that has changed is the dominance of the United States and the role of Nato in ensuring the social and political cohesion of the West. The ambiguous compromise about the modernization of short-range nuclear missiles reached at the Nato summit of May 1989 was the last political gasp of the Atlanticist consensus. The West Europeans no longer need a continuing US economic commitment. And the changing political consciousness, the processes of democratization in the East, as well as the INF treaty, has undermined Atlanticist ideology, perhaps fatally.

This is not to say that the Western alliance will not survive in a different guise: with fewer military forces, a reduced US presence and a more dominant role for Germany; perhaps, even the East Central European countries might join. But it is most unlikely to serve the same function in underpinning a US dominated global system.

These are the contours within which the future is to be decided. It is a situation in which, for better or worse, the European countries have space for political manoeuvre. The primacy of domestic politics in Europe has been restored. What happens in West and East Central Europe no longer depends primarily on Washington and Moscow. It is up to governments, political parties, social movements and civic institutions in Europe whether they take advantage of this space to construct new institutions, new ways of ordering political relations between states. This can no longer be left to the superpowers, although the superpowers are still involved.

What are the possible directions that might emerge from the multiple jumble of diverse political tendencies which characterize Europe today?

The end of history?

The American right, those who viewed the cold war as a moral struggle between freedom and totalitarianism, are triumphant. They claim the changes in the Soviet Union as their victory. Migone has distinguished between sincere and instrumental anti-communism (a distinction which differs from the distinction between progressive and regressive anti-communism used in chapter 5).[7] Reagan was a sincere anti-communist, cheering on the collapse of the 'evil empire'. Kissinger like many realists was an instrumental anti-communist, for whom the Soviet threat has always been an argument for military spending. He was always more concerned with stability than with freedom. This is why he appeared to be less perturbed than others by the brutality of the Chinese in Tiananmen Square.

The orthodox Western interpretation of the East–West conflict derived from both idealist and realist assumptions. It is idealist in so far as it regards the conflict as a struggle between freedom and totalitarianism and the collapse of totalitarianism as the condition for ending the cold war. It is realist in so far as Western military strength is seen as a crucial factor in bringing about the collapse of totalitarianism. In contrast, opposition thinkers in Eastern Europe (or rather those who used to be in opposition), who can be characterized as idealist, regard the collapse of totalitarianism as the consequence of internal contradictions and domestic pressure within the Soviet system; whether this is helped or hindered by Western military strength is a matter of controversy.

The clearest statement of the orthodox position has been expressed by Francis Fukuyama in his article, 'The end of history'.[8] Fukuyama says that the twentieth century is ending with the 'unabashed victory of economic and political liberalism'. Moreover, this phenomenon 'extends beyond high politics and can be seen in the spread of consumerist Western culture in such diverse contexts as the peasants' markets and colour television sets now found throughout China, the cooperative restaurants and clothing stores in Moscow, the Beethoven piped into Japanese department stores and the rock music in Prague, Rangoon and Tehran'. History has ended because of widespread acceptance of the 'universal homogeneous state' which is defined as 'liberal democracy in the political sphere combined with easy access to VCRs and stereos in the economic'. The alternative offered by Marxism-Leninism has totally failed.

Although other Western writers do not talk about the end of history, they too imply that there is only one Atlanticist future. 'There is no third way,' says the American economic adviser to the Polish government, Jeffrey Sachs, or the British reporter, Timothy Garton Ash. And because the second way, the Soviet system, has collapsed, there is only one way – the Western way. Essentially, the emphasis on the Western way confuses 'freedom' with the Atlanticist social system. This confusion is a consequence of the conditioning which results from an orthodox cold war thinking. It is an approach which fails to take into account the differences that have emerged in the 1970s and 1980s between the United States and Western Europe and the differences which always existed between the capitalist West and the capitalist South. Such writers miss the point that freedom means diversity – fourth, fifth, sixth, and many ways.

Fukuyama does not specify what the victory for liberalism implies for military forces, although high levels of military spending have been an important feature of the Atlanticist social system. Generally, orthodox analysts argue that the West needs to maintain its strength both to make sure that the changes are irreversible, and alternatively, in case the changes are reversed.

More importantly, the end of history does not mean that there will be no more conflicts. There will still be some conflicts in the historical part of the world, as well as conflicts between those who have come to the end of history and those who have not. Orthodox thinkers worry about terrorists, drug traffickers, Third World revolutionaries, fundamentalists and fanatics of various kinds who might try to nibble away at the post-historical world. (In other words, they worry about the poor and excluded who are not allowed to participate in the 'universal homogeneous state'.) And these might well live in the Soviet Union and East Central Europe as well as the Third World. According to Fukuyama: 'Palestinians and Irish, Sikhs and Tamils, Catholics and Walloons, Armenians and Azeris, will continue to have their grievances. This implies that terrorism and national liberation will continue to be an important item on the international agenda.' This is lucky for the orthodox analysts. Otherwise, Fukuyama fears that the end of history might be rather boring.

A (West) European bloc?

The post-revisionists view the East–West conflict as a rivalry between great powers. This interpretation derives from realist assumptions about the nature of international relations. The realist view of the future can be extracted from the debate about the decline of empires. The US is suffering from what Paul Kennedy calls 'imperial over-stretch'. It needs to share the burdens of hegemony or else be replaced. Kennedy describes the rise and fall of great powers as an endless cycle stretching indefinitely into the future. Great powers become economically successful by low levels of military spending. As economic success establishes their status as great powers, they increase their military spending and this precipitates their decline. Today Japan and the EEC are on the verge of becoming great powers and they face this age-old dilemma: 'If they neglect to provide adequate military defences, they may be unable to respond if a rival power takes advantage of them; if they spend too much on arma-ments – or, more usually, upon maintaining at growing cost the military obligations imposed on them in a previous period – they are likely to overstrain themselves, like an old man working beyond his natural strength.'[9]

Because they find it difficult to envisage a future in which military power is not a key factor, realists in the United States tend to advocate burden-sharing between the US and Western Europe, a 'bigemony' between the United States and Japan,[10] or 'devolution' from the United States to Japan and the European Community.[11]

This approach also has its adherents in Western Europe. Raymond Aron, that arch-realist, proposed a European defence policy in the postcript to his book on the United States, *The Imperial Republic*.[12] Today, the notion of a West European defence entity, a West European pillar of Nato or a more independent defence posture, is widely supported in establishment circles, especially in France. Defence is seen as a catalyst for political integration, an essential attribute of a European state in the making. Now that the process of German unification is well under way, the French and the British are concerned to integrate Germany into the European Community, to bind Germany to the West, and therefore they are likely to press for a security role for the Community. French leaders sometimes talk about the way in which the *force de frappe* is being held in readiness for all of Europe, that is Western Europe.

Such a notion has been propelled forward by the integration of the European armaments market. In anticipation of 1992, new trans-national alliances are being created by the big European defence companies. In 1988, the IEPG (Independent European Programme Group) which consists of the European members of Nato (excluding Iceland) announced an action plan to create a more open European market in armaments.[13] But is it possible to have an integrated defence market without an integrated procurement policy? And is it possible to have an integrated procurement policy without an integrated defence policy?

The proposal is, thus, for a West European bloc which would include all of Germany or even, more tightly, a kind of United States of Europe. Such a bloc would continue to prioritize military spending and the well-being of its own citizens. It would engage in trade and investment with Eastern Europe and the Third World but it is difficult to envisage any real cooperation. Such cooperation except between the two Germanies would be precluded by the fortress nature of the bloc.

What is proposed, essentially, is a new imaginary war to ensure the cohesion of the varied nations and political tendencies of Western Europe. But against whom? Given the political disintegration of the Warsaw Pact, can the spectre of the Soviet threat be raised again? The Soviet Union is also suffering from 'imperial overstretch'. Perhaps the answer is to be found in the orthodox prognosis of the future – the threat from terrorists, etc., from those who are still in the middle of history. Already, the British Ministry of Defence and French strategic analysts are justifying the British and French nuclear weapons in terms of the dangers of proliferation of nuclear and chemical weapons and medium-range missiles to the 'fanatics' and 'fundamentalists' in the Third World.

This is a future in which the United States, North West Europe, and perhaps Japan, insulate themselves economically and militarily from the surrounding chaos. Already it is possible to detect the rise of competing currency blocs, the yen, the deutschmark or ECU, and the dollar. This could partially and temporarily resolve the problems of the West. It would shift the burden of military spending from the United States to Western Europe and, depending on military-technological style, weaken the latter's competitive performance; and this could help to correct economic imbalances. But it would not shift domestic priorities in the West. And it would imply a new form of militarized political rigidity in Western Europe, a new form of psychological coercion in place of democratic consent, a new resistance to social concerns that could represent the seeds of future crisis.

Nor would it solve the problems of the East and South. At present, Western countries are somewhat reluctant to provide substantial economic assistance to Eastern Europe and the Third World. The 17 million people of East Germany are privileged in that they will receive via a common fiscal system, and more immediately through emergency assistance, a considerable transfer of resources from West Germany. In relation to the rest of Eastern Europe, it is argued that credit should be based on commercial criteria. If East European countries are to avoid the debt problems they experienced in the late 1970s and still experience today, they have, like the Third World debtor nations, to adopt policies of 'structural adjustment'. Credit must be predicated on reform and reform is interpreted as markets and austerity policies. On 1 January 1990, Poland embarked on a drastic capitalist 'shock therapy' which had, within three months, reduced consumption (by as much as 40 per cent for some basic foods like bread and milk) and increased unemployment, although it may well succeed in halting inflation and eliminating shortages. Other East Central European countries and the Soviet Union will follow, perhaps at a slower pace. Such policies will be much more difficult in countries where the Government does not enjoy the widespread trust enjoyed by the Polish Solidarity government. Even with political support, the immediate effects will be destructive, especially in the poorer countries. Even if the introduction of markets does eventually stimulate production, the economic gap between East and West will be huge without a substantial transfer of resources. In other words, we can expect a new economic division of Europe along the Oder–Neisse line.

Poverty, inequality and unemployment could provide a breeding ground for 'fanatics' and 'fundamentalists', for long suppressed national tensions. Discrimination against ethnic, linguistic or other minorities can all too easily be used to divert attention from economic problems. Already, the situations in Transylvania, where Romanians are attacking Hungarians, Kosovo, where Serbs are in conflict with Albanians, or Ngorno Karabakh, where Azeris discriminate against Armenians, are ominous.

There is thus a new recipe for an imaginary war in which the inward-looking nature of the Western bloc fosters uneven economic development and creates the conditions for the rise of new 'threats' to legitimize the imaginary war – a new cosmology of modernism versus fundamentalism, North versus South, West versus East.[14] How plausible is this scenario? It is difficult to see how military power can be used against the fanatics and fundamentalists of East and South. That is surely the lesson of the post-war period. British and French nuclear weapons are not an answer to proliferation; rather they are an example to be copied by aspiring nationalists. It is the very destructiveness of classical military power that channels violence into the indirect, cruel and insidious methods that are typical of terrorism and, indeed, counter-terrorism. Could an imaginary war against fanatics and fundamentalists draw on the same deep buried fears of war and oppression that upheld the epic struggle against totalitarianism? What is military power for, nowadays? How are rivals going to take advantage of the EEC and Japan, as Paul Kennedy puts it?

Jacques Delors, president of the European Commission, has put forward a more modest hypothesis. He prefers the concept of a European village to Gorbachev's concept of a common European home. And in that village there is a big house, the European Community: 'we are its sole architects; we are the keepers of the keys; but we are prepared to open its doors and talk to its neighbours.'[15]

But who are the neighbours? The doctor, the priest and the schoolteacher live in nice middle-sized houses and can be safely invited to dinner – these might be the neutral countries like Austria, Sweden or Switzerland. The rest of the villagers live in tied cottages and are clamouring at the doors of the big house to be allowed in. In a political framework confined to Western Europe, there is something inexorable about the uneven economic development of West and East. The example of North and South America offers a possible parallel. It is possible that some East European countries, for example Czechoslovakia, Poland and Hungary, will be given some associate status; they will be admitted as junior partners, or provinces, of the European Community.

The problem for the realists is that it is difficult for them to envisage a state that is not ultimately based on military power. Their world consists of Weberian states, claiming a monopoly of legitimate violence. Their history is the history of wars. This is not to say that realists cannot envisage mechanisms for peaceful change. Writers like E. H. Carr and Robert Gilpin do give credence to this possibility. A world of competing blocs with less reliance on military power, as implied by the Delors concept, might represent a realist model in which great powers are still important and military power is less important. All the same, there is a certain hesitancy or scepticism about the notion of great powers who do not rely on military force.

Yet it is possible to envisage new state forms that do not rely on military power, and that do not necessarily constitute blocs. This is already implicit in existing institutions at the European level. The Council of Europe has no military power, yet the European Court of Human Rights is recognized by its members as a higher authority. The European Community also has an element of sovereignty on certain issues relating to the Single European Act (consisting of majority voting in the Council of Ministers in place of consensus, and somewhat increased powers for the European Parliament).[16] If such institutions are to be effective, they have to be democratically accountable, to be capable of generating consent for their policies. But this is no longer necessarily a utopian project – no more impracticable than continued reliance on military power. E. H. Carr described the political transition period between the two world wars as the crisis of utopianism. This transition period can perhaps be described as the crisis of realism.

Our common European home?

Gorbachev's concept of a 'common European home' and the German social democratic concept of a 'European peace order' are very similar. Indeed, their similarity was explicitly recognized in the joint communiqué issued after Gorbachev's visit to West Germany in June 1989. Both concepts place a central emphasis on security. They also favour increased East–West cooperation. They can be viewed as extensions of the concepts of détente, as favoured in West Germany, and of peaceful coexistence. They envisage a new all-European security system based on the CSCE (the Conference on Security and

Cooperation in Europe), often known as the Helsinki process, which is regarded as the crowning achievement of détente in the 1970s. Like détente and peaceful coexistence, they presuppose that different social systems can protect themselves while not threatening each other, and while, indeed, maintaining good relations at the state level. Like détente and peaceful coexistence, they derive from a Marxian view of a conflict between social systems which, because it was a conflict about ways of organizing societies, could in principle be demilitarized. But they are also realist concepts, in so far as they deal with state-to-state relations and treat the state as a subjective agent in world affairs.

The failure of détente in the 1970s is ascribed to the failure to control the arms race. According to Horst Emke, one of the SPD's most prominent foreign affairs spokespersons:

In sum, the first phase of détente failed because we were not successful in stopping the arms race or in preventing military competition in the third world from spilling over into East/West relations in Europe. If an improvement in political relations was thought to be necessary for disarmament, we now know that disarmament is also necessary for sustained improvement in East/West relations.[17]

Central to both the notion of a common European home and a European peace order are ideas about alternative defence – variously known as 'reasonable sufficiency' (Soviet Union), 'structural inability to attack' or *Strukturelle Nichtangrifffähigkeit* (SPD) or non-provocative defence (British Labour party).[18] According to Gorbachev: 'The philosophy of the Common European Home concept rules out the possibility of an armed clash and the very possibility of the use or threat of force – alliance against alliance, or whatever. This philosophy suggests a doctrine of restraint should take the place of a doctrine of deterrence.' His proposed doctrine of restraint is 'reasonable sufficiency', which 'rules out the physical possibility of launching an attack and large scale offensive operations'.[19] This approach of defusing the military confrontation by reorienting military forces towards defensive purposes characterizes the proposals of both sides for the Conventional Forces in Europe (CFE) talks in Vienna, and the unilateral cuts so far undertaken by the Soviet Union and other Warsaw Pact countries.

What was intriguing about alternative defence proposals in the early 1980s was the way in which they opened up and engaged with military strategies. They remained within the discourse of the imaginary war. They presupposed an underlying East–West conflict. They were strategies for the employment of military force in an imaginary war and, as such, they had specific political objectives. In effect, they imagined a military stalemate, in which both sides could defend themselves or at least bog down an offensive so as to give time for negotiations, and in which neither side could attack the other. They were indeed the strategic representation of détente, or peaceful coexistence.

For this very reason, alternative defence proposals were and are inherently contradictory. On the one hand, they challenged the political-psychological implications of the imaginary war. The adoption of alternative defence policies would entail the removal of nuclear weapons and 'deep-strike' technologies in the West, that is, the elimination of those elements of Nato strategy that express the West European dependence on the United States. And in the East, 'reasonable sufficiency' necessitates a big reduction in tanks, which were always the expression of Soviet dominance in Eastern Europe. On the other hand, they accept the assumption of conflict. They presuppose a bloc framework while removing the key elements of bloc cohesion.

A parallel can be drawn with the 1970s. MAD was the strategic representation of the 1970s détente. It constituted a military stalemate based on mutual destruction. Alternative defence is the 1980s political equivalent of MAD, although, of course, more radical and less crazy and dangerous. These proposals for 'conventional stabilization', as they are called, are of their nature transitional. Once both sides are purely defensive, what is the rationale for the alliances? Hence, they could be viewed as a staging post towards disarmament, or towards a political framework in which the distinctions between East and West in anything other than a geographical sense have lost their meaning. Alternatively, the very notion of defensive rearmament could reinvigorate the idea of conflict (not necessarily the same conflict, perhaps the new orthodox conflict between the modern liberal world and the backward fundamentalist world). Even the Chinese Wall was considered offensive.[20] Such strategies, for example, are entirely consistent with Delors's 'European house', a way of keeping out intruders. What happens depends not so much on this or that military strategy but on the underlying political conditions that give rise to conflict.

And herein lies the weakness of the Soviet and SPD concepts. Although they stress that conflicts have to be resolved by political means, that cooperation must be increased and that human rights must be respected, they do not offer any analysis of the underlying conflict and, therefore, they offer no solutions. Or rather they appear to presuppose that the conflict is *between* East and West and about capitalism versus socialism rather than about domestic intra-bloc conflicts as suggested in this book. Their solution, if it is a solution, is that social systems must tolerate each other. The implication is a kind of mutual recognition of sovereignty, of non-interference in each other's sphere of influence.

Gorbachev, in his Strasbourg speech, said: 'I know that many people in the West regard the existence of two social systems as the major difficulty. But the difficulty is rather in the very common conviction (or even a political directive) that overcoming the split of Europe implies the overcoming of socialism. This is a course towards confrontation, if not worse. There can be no European unity along these lines.'[21]

And yet overcoming socialism, *as it actually existed*, that is, moving away from Stalinist and post-Stalinist systems, has turned out to be the essential element in overcoming the split of Europe. It is, above all, the democratic revolutions in East Central Europe as well as the process of democratization in the Soviet Union that has undermined the imaginary war, from both Eastern and Western perspectives.[22]

If we are to prevent imaginary wars in the future, we have to tackle the causes of imaginary war. In the West that includes the inward-looking commitment to consumerism, military Keynesianism, Third-World intervention and domestic divisions (like anti-communism or racism) that can be diverted towards external menace. And, in the East, it means reducing the role of the military and avoiding possible future legitimations for menace, like, for example, cracking down on struggles for independence within Soviet republics, which are also rationalized in terms of external menace.

Gorbachev insists on non-interference. 'Any interference in domestic affairs and any attempts to restrict the sovereignty of states both friends, allies or any others, are inadmissable.'[23] But does not the persecution of national minorities, the violation of human rights or ecological destruction or extreme poverty require some form of (non-military) interference? Economic sanctions and/or assistance? The pressure of public opinion? On some other matters, should not the sovereignty of states be constrained by higher bodies within a European framework, which can express, and implement, some common values? Otherwise, are there not endless new sources of conflict?

The Common European Home concept is a half-way house between the continuation of the bloc system, perhaps in a new guise, with an independent or semi-independent West European bloc or even several blocs, and an all-European political framework. The CSCE process and ideas for alternative defence were developed at a time when the two blocs were still intact. It was a mechanism for managing relations between the blocs. In the new situation, it could still provide a mechanism for managing relations between Nato or a West European bloc and the Soviet Union, or alternatively among a set of nations, dominated by the United States, Germany and the Soviet Union. The CSCE, in short, could well become a new Concert of Europe, in which conflicts are settled by the great powers. This could involve lower levels of military spending, a new military-technological style based on defensive electronics technologies,[24] and it might involve some increase in East–West economic cooperation beyond what is taking place in Germany. Hence it could contribute to resolution of economic problems in both East and West. But how and by how much, and whether new divisions emerge, depends on domestic political change in both East and West.

The opening up of the blocs has brought in its wake a new set of conflicts, old and new, long suppressed or about to be created. The next few years are likely to witness new economic divisions, national and religious conflicts, conflicts about resources, or about human rights. Are these conflicts to be settled in the time-honoured way by the great powers? Is the future of Lithuania and Estonia, or Slovenia and Transylvania to be decided by Germany and Russia? Or rather are existing national governments to have sovereignty in deciding these matters – a sovereignty guaranteed by the new European Common House? Or are we going to demilitarize Europe so that these issues can *only* be determined through discussion and negotiation? Can we create an all-European political framework that is more than just a twenty-first-century Concert of Europe?

Alternative defence proposals represent an ingenious mechanism for winding down the military confrontation. The eventual disposition of armed forces may well be along the lines envisaged by the experts on reasonable sufficiency and non-provocative defence. But if this winding down of the military confrontation is to be a continuous and permanent process, then we also have to deal directly with the political, social, economic, cultural and ecological roots of conflict. And this has to do with the evolution of social systems in both East and West, the readiness of the West to reduce military spending and engage in a significant programme of East–West and North–South cooperation, and the extent to which the process of democratization in the East, especially the Soviet Union, can be sustained. To that extent, the idealists who insist that democracy is a necessary condition for disarmament, that 'overcoming socialism [as it actually existed]' is necessary to overcome the split of Europe, are right. But so are Western peace activists, socialists or greens, who insist that Western capitalism has to change as well.

A European civil society?

Idealists have tended to assume that a pacific democratic capitalism is possible. Markets plus liberal democracy seems to be viewed as a formula for peace in Europe both in orthodox circles in the West (though they are worried about those still experiencing history) and in what were opposition circles in the East.[25] This assumption also characterized nineteenth-century liberal thinkers. Gorbachev, in his Strasbourg address to the Council of Europe, quoted Victor Hugo: 'A day will come when markets, open to trade, and minds, open to ideas, will be the sole battlefields.'[26] In support of this claim, it has been argued that no democratic countries have ever fought against each other.

Yet the argument of this book is that the imaginary war was a 'joint venture', a collusion between Atlanticism and Stalinism. The military confrontation was a form of psychological coercion, a way of 'turning outwards' the domestic conflicts of both Atlanticism and post-Stalinism. In other words, it was in part the consequence of a system characterized by liberal democracy plus markets. Far from countering totalitarianism, Western military strength provided an argument, a rationale for oppression – it fed the paranoia of Stalinist ruling parties. It was not Western military strength, as the right would have it, that brought about the changes in the Soviet Union. Rather, it was the internal contradictions and political pressures – the emergence of an embryo civil society. If anything, Western military strength delayed those changes by legitimizing the new cold war mood of Soviet leaders in the early 1980s.

Similarly, it is difficult to describe the various interventions by the United States or Britain and France in the Third World as 'pacific'. Even though it is true that they were generally directed against undemocratic enemies, they could not be said to have contributed to democracy. On the contrary military interventions create a war situation in which any evolution towards democracy is extremely difficult; this has been evident in Central America. The coup in Chile in 1971 represents one clear case in which a US intervention was directed *against* democracy.

So far, Gorbachev's disarmament initiatives have succeeded in removing cruise and Pershing missiles, the symbol of the relationship between the United States and Western Europe. This was possible, however, because these missiles had been the subject of a domestic Atlanticist political struggle – the zero option was originally proposed by the West as a way of dealing with domestic opposition. The talks in Vienna about reducing conventional forces in Europe will bring about big reductions on the Warsaw Pact side, but much smaller reductions on the Western side. There is also likely to be an agreement to eliminate short-range nuclear weapons. If British and French nuclear weapons are to be eliminated or US nuclear-capable aircraft in Britain and if there are to be substantial reductions in conventional forces and defence budgets, this will have to be achieved through domestic political pressure.

Market relations constitute a more peaceful form of economic regulation than feudal or bureaucratic relationships. Markets require the removal of physical violence from the labour contract and they operate best in politically stable conditions. All the same, market regulation is a form of economic coercion. It is preferable to physical or administrative coercion but not to consensual relationships. Markets give rise to extremes of wealth and poverty between classes and between regions; they generate excess capacity, periodicially throwing people out of work. They do not respect nature or culture, or even family life.

If parts of the Western left can be accused of myopia with respect to Soviet-type systems, it is also the case that parts of the East European opposition have failed to comprehend some of the more brutal undersides of Western life – racism, the suppression of minority cultures, job insecurity, urban violence, inner city poverty and, above all, the pillage of the Third World. Indeed the very idea of a 'universal homogeneous state' implied by the assumption of liberal democracy plus markets is inherently coercive. Who says that Beethoven piped to Japanese department stores or rock music played in Rangoon represents a higher form of civilization than indigenous art or music?

Of course, it is better to live in the West than in the East but it is not evident that it is better to live in the South. Atlanticist regulation is characterized by a mix of consent and economic and psychological coercion; relations with the Third World are characterized by a mix of economic and physical forms of coercion. Stalinist and post-Stalinist regulation consisted primarily of physical and administrative coercion with elements of economic and psychological coercion.

If we want to resolve major conflicts without the use of force, we have to explore their economic, social, ecological and cultural roots. We have to establish certain social goals: a minimum standard of economic well-being – security in a material sense, respect for nature, respect for minority cultures, etc. And this can only be achieved through a social and political system characterized by forms of regulation that maximize consent and minimize coercion, especially physical coercion.

Together, citizens' initiatives in both East and West have expressed their (perhaps utopian) goal as 'a fully demilitarized and socially just community, whose economic development will not be at the expense of the environment ... a multi-cultural community, open to the South ... A community which will respect the rights of the individual and the principles of national self-determination ... a Europe of peace, justice, well-being, human dignity, and world-wide solidarity'.[27] This implies, on the one hand, the establishment of certain common values or standards and a framework for implementing those values and, at the same time, maximum autonomy and diversity in order to ensure democratic accountability and the preservation of Europe's rich and very varied cultural heritage. It implies a Europe which gives greater priority to welfare, the environment and global cooperation and much less to defence. And, at the same time, it implies a Europe in which regions, nations, even localities can choose social and private priorities (welfare, environment, consumption) according to local traditions and cultural preferences, and can choose appropriate forms of property (private, state, cooperative, municipal, etc.) and appropriate forms of work organization (workers' councils, codetermination, etc.).

In economic terms, this approach is not as utopian as it sounds. The new pattern of industrial development, 'flexible specialization' or 'Fujitsuism', is much better suited to varied and decentralized forms of production and distribution than the Fordist pattern of industrial development, even though, at present, control of finance and research and development is highly centralized. Moreover, the new technologies are at least as well if not better suited to environmental purposes like resource conservation and recycling, monitoring of pollution, etc., and social purposes like education, health or even planning, than to private consumption and military spending.

It is possible to envisage an ecological and social Keynesianism that would replace military Keynesianism as a way of coping with surplus capacity in capitalist countries. In place of Nato, a new political mechanism would be needed to ensure the automatic transfer of resources from surplus to deficit nations. The US would reduce its deficit by cutting military spending and, in order to avoid a global recession, the surplus countries in Western Europe and the Far East would transfer resources on a continuing basis to Eastern Europe and the Third World. In place of credit issued by banks and international economic institutions, which set conditions of good behaviour, what is needed instead are explicit forms of subsidy (debt reduction, grant aid or long-term low interest credit) to fulfil certain goals – ecological goals such as eliminating acid rain, cleaning up rivers and seas, or social goals, such as sustaining democracy, reducing inequalities or protecting culture – which ideally would be democratically determined by both donors and recipients. Likewise, some kind of democratic international trading regime is required that would discourage the formation of wealthy trading blocs and encourage freer trade, while protecting the interests of the poorest countries.

Is it possible to devise a political framework within which these goals could be achieved? Historically, Europe has always been characterized by a diversity of political institutions. In contrast to the great Asian empires, Europe had a states system, in which sovereignty was divided into multiple centres, based on territory. It was this diversity that gave rise to Europe's creativity, although it also gave rise to Europe's destructiveness – to imperial rivalries and wars. Is it possible to envisage a mechanism for preserving the creativity that arises from diversity while eliminating war and imperial rivalry?

One idea is that Europe should continue to have a diversity of political institutions based on fields of activity rather than territories. Already this exists in embryo, with several Europe-wide institutions – the European Community, the Council of Europe, Comecon, the Helsinki process – and a variety of local, national and regional political arrangements. Naturally, the competences of each institution would overlap, giving rise to considerable but not insurmountable legal complexities.[28]

It is possible, for example, to envisage one set of institutions for security arrangements as traditionally conceived perhaps along the line proposed for the Common European House. These might involve the remnants of Nato and the Warsaw Pact and/or a strengthening and institutionalization of the Helsinki process. The two alliances might remain in truncated form with (diminishing) non-provocative defence postures, or, alternatively, the verification regime associated with CFE (Conventional Forces in Europe) talks might offer another security model, with bands of military inspectors dotted all over the continent. The principle of such a security framework would be to prevent both the return to national armed forces and the restoration of offensive military blocs (in Europe as a whole or in East and West).

Another set of institutions would deal with economic, social and possibly ecological issues. These might include the European Community, perhaps together with Comecon, the UN Economic Commission for Europe, or a new Europe-wide institution for the environment as proposed by Gorbachev. The aim would be to ensure economic openness, minimum social and environmental standards and automatic transfer of resources from rich to poor regions. Delors's 'house' would have to be democratized and extended to include individual East European countries, or the Comecon as a whole, on an equal basis if the uneven development of Europe is to be avoided – that is, if we are to avoid a new division of a rich capitalist West and a poor mixed chaotic East.

A third set of institutions including both the Helsinki process and the Council of Europe would have the task of ensuring compliance with European legislation about human rights.

And as well as these overlapping transnational institutions covering all of Europe, parts of Asia and North America, existing nations would continue and there might be even greater devolution to regional and local levels. Smaller nations like Wales and Scotland might enjoy greater autonomy. In this model, the *länder* would be powerful institutions within a unified confederal Germany, and the Soviet republics might be independent or loosely integrated. And other permutations could arise – a Danubian federation, for example, or a Balkan or an Iberian federation.

And, finally, these various institutions have to be situated in a global context, within the framework of the United Nations and a new set of international economic institutions or, alternatively, the democratization of existing institutions. This is something that European countries are now in a position to bring about in conjunction with Third World countries (for example, East European countries could now take the lead in pressing the international community to introduce debt reduction schemes, in order to ensure the survival of democracy).

But how is the sovereignty of these new institutions to be established? What is the basis of their power? How is the new set of authoritative relations to be reproduced? The answer is, on the basis of consent, through the construction of a trans-European civil society.

The notion of a European civil society is an extension of the notion of détente from below, which arose from the links created between the West European peace movement and the East European independent peace, green and human rights groups. Détente from below meant détente between citizens as opposed to détente between governments. It meant the coming together of new social movements to learn from each other's experiences and to act in mutual solidarity. A European civil society means a set of interrelated autonomous networks of self-organized groups, associations, clubs, movements, initiatives and institutions acting across national and bloc boundaries. It means the creation of new social relationships, new forms of dialogue through which citizens can act together to negotiate with and put pressure on political institutions, and, indeed, to resolve many issues without the direct involvement of governments. It means the expansion of public (non-state, non-private) spheres of activity and the creation of a European public opinion.

Why should it be possible to construct a European civil society now when it was not possible earlier? Why should such an idealist project be any more successful now than it was in the inter-war years when the League project failed so abysmally? There is no satisfactory answer for those with a pessimistic view of human nature who expect human society to degenerate from time to time into barbarism. But, unlike the inter-war period, military power is no longer an answer to barbarism. It is too dangerous for rational politicians to use, and intelligent but mad barbarians, which Hitler was, can take advantage of this. That is why military power is no longer a deterrent. For this reason, there is no long-term alternative to the construction of an international civil society.

But there is also a more positive answer. The last 50 years have prepared us for a new set of relations of authority. We now know that a major war between great powers is unthinkable. The bloc system did eliminate real military conflicts within the blocs and did provide a framework for economic and social interdependence, which provides a material basis for a transnational civil society. Improved communication – faxes, telephones, desktop publishing – facilitates the construction of networks. Satellite transmissions enable us to witness wars, riots, natural and manmade calamities all over the world. We can no longer claim that we do not know about the atrocities of our time.

But even if there is a historical and material basis for a civil society, why should we assume that an active civil society could ensure the observance of a set of common values about political and socio-economic rights, as well as the rights of nature, or can prevent the reemergence of barbarism? Again, there is no satisfactory answer. But there is no more reason to trust the power holders, bureaucrats or experts to ensure the observance of such values. That is what we have learned as a result of the experience of Fabianism and Leninism in the twentieth century – notions of paternalism that characterized both Atlanticism and the Soviet system. Civil society – an ongoing dialogue among citizens and between those within the power apparatus and those without – is the best we can hope for.

Which direction?

It is possible that the final outcome of all this feverish change will be different from all these four directions described above, or more likely, an uncomfortable mix between these different approaches. Then it will be necessary to think again, as the future throws up new problems and issues, new social groups, which require new ways of thinking if they are to be adequately described.

It may be the end of history for those who think in terms of liberal democracy, a limited form of political regulation. But for those who live in Europe and who are hoping to extend and deepen democracy, this is an exciting moment. After an interregnum of 40 years in which European history (perhaps deservedly) was suppressed by those who made universal claims on behalf of American capitalism and Soviet socialism, who attempted to establish two distinct homogeneous social systems in Europe, history has just resumed.

Notes

1 Istvan Rev, 'Uncertainty as a technique in the exercise of power', paper presented at the Seminar on Arms Control and East–West Relations, Moscow, 10–24 July 1989, organized by the Institute for Global Conflict and Cooperation (IGCC) of the University of California, the

Armament Disarmament Information Unit (ADIU) of the University of Sussex, and the Moscow State Institute for International Relations (MGIMO), unpublished.

2 Indeed, it is clear already that democratization has allowed opposition to markets to be expressed. Striking workers in the Soviet Union object to the new inequalities; they oppose the new private profiteering cooperatives.

3 In the late 1980s, all Western countries experienced an increase in private consumer debt – partly rising from the need to circumvent the effects of squeezing public spending, partly from the revolution in financial services, especially credit cards, resulting from the new technology, and partly arising from the readiness of banks to offer attractive credit terms.

4 See, for example, Moshe Lewin, *The Gorbachev Phenomenon* (Radius, 1988); Boris Kargalitsky, *The Thinking Reed* (Verso, 1988); Patrick Cockburn, 'Gorbachev and Soviet conservatism', *World Policy Journal*, Winter 1988–9; Ernest Mandel, *Beyond Perestroika: The Future of Gorbachev's USSR* (Verso, 1989).

5 I have talked to Afghan veterans who told me that they went to Afghanistan believing that they were doing their patriotic duty and increasingly experienced unease and uncertainty. Afghan veterans have great difficulty settling down when they return to the Soviet Union; they say they only feel comfortable with their comrades from Afghanistan. Some veterans formed vigilante groups to hunt out 'anti-socialist elements'; they joined the 'Lybers' who beat up 'metallists' (pop enthusiasts who wear a lot of metal) or those with long hair. For a discussion of the impact of Afghanistan, see Andrew Wilson and Nina Bachkatov, *Living with Glasnost, Youth and Society in a Changing Russia* (Penguin, 1988), pp. 71–6.

6 See Ferenc Miszlivetz, 'Reform, crisis and the second society', paper presented to the conference on Withdrawal of the Developmental State, Institute for Development Studies, University of Sussex, July 1987.

7 Lecture to the IGCC-ADIU-MGIMO Seminar on Arms Control and East–West Relations, Moscow, 10–24 July 1989.

8 Extracted in the *Independent*, 20 and 21 September 1989.

9 Paul Kennedy, *The Rise and Fall of the Great Powers* (Unwin Hyman, 1988), p. 540.

10 C. Fred Bergsten, 'Economic imbalances', *Foreign Affairs*, Spring 1987.

11 David Calleo, *Beyond American Hegemony* (Wheatsheaf, 1987).

12 Aron saw the search for glory and prestige as the motivation for state behaviour, and military power as an essential attribute of the state. He

considered nuclear weapons to be symbols of prestige. 'Tomorrow, other men will live by different passions. French, of Jewish origin, how could I forget that France owes her liberation to the strength of her allies, Israel her existence to her arms, a chance of survival to the resolve of Americans to fight if need be.' See John Hall, 'Raymond Aron's sociology of states or the non-relative autonomy of inter-state behaviour', in Martin Shaw, ed., *War, State and Society* (Macmillan, 1984).

13 For an informative discussion of the process of European defence industrial integration, see William Walker and Philip Gummet, 'Britain and the European armaments market', *International Affairs*, 65:3, Summer 1989.

14 For an argument about the new cosmology of a North–South imaginary war, see E. P. Thompson, Mary Kaldor et al., *Mad Dogs: The US Raids on Libya* (Pluto, 1986); Richard Falk, *Revolutionaries and Functionaries: The Dual Face of Terrorism:* (E. P. Dutton, New York, 1988), and Noam Chomsky, 'The fifth freedom', *The Listener*, 27 March 1989.

15 Address to the European Parliament, 17 January 1989, in *Europe*, 89, April–May 1989.

16 See Vernon Bogdanor, 'The June 1989 European elections and the institutions of the community', *Government and Opposition*, 24:2, Spring 1989.

17 Horst Emke, 'Double-zero and beyond: a second phase of détente', *World Policy Journal*, Summer 1987.

18 For descriptions of these different ideas, see Gerard Holden, 'Soviet "new thinking" in security policy', and Karsten D. Voight, 'The prospects for conventional stabilisation in Europe', in Mary Kaldor, Gerard Holden and Richard Falk, eds, *The New Détente* (UNU/Verso, 1989). See also The Alternative Defense Commission, *Defence without the Bomb* (Taylor and Francis, 1983); Frank Barnaby and Egbert Boeker, 'Non-provocative non-nuclear defence of Western Europe', *ADIU Report*, 5:1, January–February 1983; and Robert Neild and Anders Boserup, 'Beyond the INF Agreement: a new approach to nonnuclear forces', *World Policy Journal*, Fall 1987.

19 Address to the Council of Europe, Strasbourg, 6 June 1989, in *Soviet News*, 12 July 1989.

20 See Laszlo Valki, 'Certainties and uncertainties about military doctrines', *Proceedings of the Thirty-Sixth Pugwash Conference*, Budapest, 1–6 September 1986.

21 Address to the Council of Europe, 6 June 1989.

22 As late as September 1989, just before the removal of Honecker, the

unreconstructed post-Stalinist regime in East Germany was blaming the flight of thousands of East Germans to the West on a capitalist conspiracy. I have before me a pamphlet circulated by the East German embassy, entitled *The Great Coup of the FRG: Orchestrated Provocation against the GDR*.

23 Address to the Council of Europe, 6 June 1989.

24 The proponents of alternative defence often engage in tactical thinking in planning different types of defensive strategies with new forms of military organization and new types of military technology. German defence companies are even developing defensive types of equipment. Obviously this kind of thinking is needed if military planners are to be convinced. But I am doubtful whether there can be a change in military-technological style without a war or near war situation. Military institutions are notoriously conservative and difficult to change. Would not these defensive technologies develop a menacing momentum of their own? And if there were a real prolonged war, would this turn out to be the most effective style? The crazy enthusiasts of AirLand Battle might turn out to be horribly right.

25 See Timothy Garton Ash, Adam Michnik and Janos Kis, 'One thousand words', *Independent*, 7 July 1989.

26 See note 19.

27 Prague 1990. Appeal for a Helsinki Citizens' Assembly, the Helsinki Citizens' Assembly Preparatory Committee, Civic Forum, Prague, March 1990.

28 How this might be achieved through the mutual recognition of different institutions is suggested by Mirielle Delmas-Marty, 'One law versus many', *Liber*, 1, October 1989. She suggests that such a complex system could be the most constructive approach. 'Not a complexity of the kind endured in the Middle Ages, devoted to making proceedings more difficult and eventually leading to a blockage of the entire system but rather deliberate complexity, designed to maintain the openness of the system and organised within the dual perspectives of the relationship between Europe and its member states and that between one legal Europe and the other.' She also suggests that the new technologies provide an opportunity for the democratization of the law (through the use of expert systems and audiovisual aids) so as to avoid the main risk of complexity – the rise of a self-interested legal profession.

Bibliography

This bibliography is intended as a guide for those who wish to delve further into the themes of this book. The book covers a wide range of subjects on each of which there is an extensive literature. I have included books that I have found particularly helpful or that represent an unusual and/or critical perspective on the subject. The bibliography is divided into four sections: cold war and détente; Soviet-type systems; continuities and discontinuities in political, economic and military history; and the military confrontation.

The first two sections cover relatively discrete bodies of literature. The third section is very broad and includes background literature on long political and economic cycles, the decline of empires including the American empire, international economic relations, the theory of regulation, Fordism and post-Fordism, and the economic effects of military spending. The last section includes literature on the military confrontation that is not included in the other sections.

At the end, I have added a list of periodicals for those who wish to keep up with some of the subjects touched on in this book, especially developments in East Central Europe and armament and disarmament issues.

Cold war and détente

Alperowitz, Gar, *Atomic Diplomacy: Hiroshima and Potsdam, the Use of the Atomic Bomb and the Confrontation with Soviet Power*, revised edn, Penguin, London, 1985.

Appleman Willams, William, *The Tragedy of American Diplomacy*, World Publishing, Ohio, 1959.

Aron, Raymond, *The Great Debate*, Doubleday, New York, 1965.

—— *War and Industrial Society*, OUP, Oxford, 1958.

Barnet, Richard, *The Alliance*, Simon and Schuster, New York, 1984.

Bernstein, Barton, 'Les Etats Unis et les origines de la guerre froide', *Revue de l'histoire de la deuxième guerre mondiale*, 3, Presses Universitaires de France, July 1976.

Buchan, Alastair, *War in Modern Society*, C. A. Watts, London, 1966.

Bullock, Alan, *Ernest Bevin: Foreign Secretary 1945–51*, Heinemann, London, 1983.

Brzezinski, Zbigniew, 'The Future of Yalta', *Foreign Affairs*, 63:2, Winter 1984/5.

Carlton, David and Levine, Herbert M., *The Cold War Debated*, McGraw Hill, New York, 1988.

Chomsky, Noam, Steel, Jonathan and Gittings, John, *Super Powers in Collision: The New Cold War*, Penguin, London, 1982.

Cook, Don, *Forging the Alliance, Nato 1945–50*, Secker and Warburg, London, 1989.

Cox, Michael, 'From the Truman doctrine to the second superpower détente: the rise and fall of the cold war', *Journal of Peace Research*, 27:1, February 1990.

Crockatt, Richard and Smith, Steve, eds, *The Cold War: Past and Present*, Allen and Unwin, London, 1987.

Cromwell, William C., 'The Marshall Plan, Britain and the cold war', *Review of International Studies*, 8, 1982.

Davis, Lynn Etheridge, *The Cold War Begins: Soviet–American Conflict over Eastern Europe*, Princeton University Press, Princeton, NJ, 1974.

Deighton, Anne, 'The "frozen front": the Labour government, the division of Germany and the origins of the cold war, 1945–7', *International Affairs*, 63:3, Summer 1987.

Deutscher, Isaac, *The Great Contest: Russia and the West*, OUP, Oxford, 1960.

Dulles, John Foster, *War or Peace*, Macmillan, New York, 1950.

Dyson, Kenneth, ed., *European Détente: Case Studies of the Politics of East–West Relations*, Frances Pinter, London, 1986.

Edmonds, Robin, *Setting the Mould: The United States and Britain, 1945–50*, Clarendon Press, Oxford, 1986.

Emke, Horst, 'Double-zero and beyond: a second phase of détente', *World Policy Journal*, Summer 1987.

European Network for East–West Dialogue, *Giving Real Life to the Helsinki Accords, A Memorandum Drawn up in Common by Independent Groups and Individuals in Eastern and Western Europe*, Berlin, 1967.

European Nuclear Disarmament German–German Working Group, *Voices from the GDR: Documents on Peace, Human Rights and Ecology*, END, London, 1987.

Feis, Herbert, *Between War and Peace: The Potsdam Conference*, Princeton University Press, Princeton, NJ, 1957.

—— *Churchill, Roosevelt, Stalin: The War They Waged and the Peace They Sought*, Princeton University Press, Princeton, NJ, 1957.

—— *From Trust to Terror – The Onset of the Cold War*, Blond, New York, 1970.

—— *Japan Subdued: The Atomic Bomb and the End of World War II*, Princeton University Press, Princeton, NJ. 1957.

Fleming, D. F., *The Cold War and its Origins, 1917–1960*, 2 vols, Doubleday, New York, 1961.

Fontaine, André, *History of the Cold War from the October Revolution to the Korean War, 1917–1950*, trans. D. D. Page, Secker and Warburg, London, 1968.

Furtado, Jean, ed., *Turkey: Peace on Trial*, END Special Report, Merlin Press/END, London, 1983.

Gaddis, John Lewis, 'Containment: its past and future', *International Security*, Spring 1981.

—— 'The emerging post-revisionist synthesis on the origins of the cold war', *Diplomatic History*, 8, Summer 1983.

—— 'The long peace', *International Security*, 10:4, Spring 1986.

—— *Strategies of Containment: Critical Appraisal of Postwar American Security Policy*, OUP, Oxford, 1982.

—— *The United States and the Origins of the Cold War 1941–47*, Columbia University Press, New York, 1972.

Garthoff, Raymond L., *Détente and Confrontation: American–Soviet Relations from Nixon to Reagan*, The Brookings Institution, Washington DC, 1985.

German, Harry, *The Brezhnev Politburo and the Decline of the Détente*, Cornell University Press, Ithaca, NY, 1984.

Graf, William, 'Anti-communism in the Federal Republic of Germany', in *Socialist Register 1984*, Merlin Press, London, 1984.

Grosser, Alfred, *The Western Alliance: European–American Relations since 1945*, Macmillan, London, 1980.

Halliday, Fred, *Cold War, Third World: An Essay on Soviet–American Relations*, Hutchinson/Radius, London, 1989.

—— *The Making of the Second Cold War*, Verso, London, 1983.

—— 'The new cold war', *Bulletin of Peace Proposals*, 14:2, 1983.

—— 'Vigilantism in international relations: Kubalka, Cruickshank and Marxist Theory', *Review of International Studies*, 13, 1987.

Hinton, James, *Protests and Visions: Peace Politics in 20th Century Britain*, Hutchinson, London, 1989.

Horowitz, David, *From Yalta to Vietnam*, Penguin, London, 1967.

Kaldor, M. and Falk, R., eds, *Dealignment: A New Foreign Policy Perspective*, Basil Blackwell, Oxford, 1987.

Kaldor, M., Holden, G. and Falk, R., eds, *The New Détente: Rethinking East–West Relations*, Verso, London, 1989.

Kavan, Jan and Tomin, Zdena, eds, *Voices from Prague: Documents on Czechoslovakia and the Peace Movement*, END/Palach Press, London, 1983.

Kennan, George, F., *The Cloud of Danger: Some Current Problems of American Foreign Policy*, Hutchinson, London, 1978.

—— *Memoirs, 1925–50*, Hutchinson, London, 1968.

—— *Memoirs, 1950–63*, Little, Brown, Boston and Toronto, 1972.

—— *Russia, the Atom and the West*, BBC Reith Lectures 1957, OUP, Oxford, 1958.

Kissinger, Henry, *Nuclear Weapons and Foreign Policy*, Harper, New York, 1957.

—— *The Troubled Partnership: A Reappraisal of the Atlantic Alliance*, McGraw-Hill, New York, 1965.

—— *The White House Years*, Weidenfeld, London, 1979.

—— *Years of Upheaval*, Weidenfeld, London, 1982.

Kolko, Joyce and Kolko, Gabriel, *The Limits of Power: The World and United States Foreign Policy, 1945–54*, Harper and Row, New York, 1972.

Konrad, George, *Anti-politics*, Quartet, London, 1983.

Khrushchev, N., *Khrushchev Remembers*, André Deutsch, London, 1971.

Kuznetsov, V., *Détente and the World Today, 26th CPSU Congress: The Peace Offensive Continues*, Progress Publishers, Moscow, 1981.

Lafeber, Walter, *America, Russia and the Cold War, 1965–71*, John Wiley, New York, 1972.

Light, Margot, *The Soviet Theory of International Relations*, Harvester Wheatsheaf, Brighton, 1988.

Mark, Edward, 'American policy towards Eastern Europe and the origins of the cold war, 1941–46: an alternative interpretation', *Journal of American History*, 68, September 1981.

Mastny, Vojtech, *Russia's Road to the Cold War: Diplomacy, Warfare and the Politics of Communism, 1941–45*, Columbia University Press, New York and Guildford, 1979.

May, Ernest R., *'Lessons' of the Past*, OUP, Oxford, 1973.

Migone, Giangiacomo, 'The decline of the bipolar system, or a second look at the history of the cold war', in Kaldor, Holden and Falk, eds, *New Détente*.

—— 'Understanding Bipolarity', in Kaldor and Falk, *Dealignment*.

Moray, J. P., *From Yalta to Disarmament: Cold War Debate*, Merlin Press, London, 1961.

Nathanson, Charles E., 'The social construction of the Soviet threat: a study in the politics of representation', *Alternatives*, 13:4, October 1988.

Nitze, Paul, 'NSC 68 and the Soviet threat', *International Security*, Spring 1980.

Nove, Alec, *East–West Trade: Problems, Prospects, Issues*, Washington Papers 532, Sage, London and Beverly Hills, 1978.

Palmer, John, *Europe Without America: The Crisis in Atlantic Relations*, OUP, Oxford, 1987.

Platt, Alan A. and Leonardi, Robert, 'American foreign policy and the postwar Italian left', *Political Science Quarterly*, Summer 1978.

Reynolds, David, 'The origins of the cold war: the European dimension', *Historical Journal*, 28:2, 1985.

Rostow, W. W., 'On ending the cold war', *Foreign Affairs*, Spring 1987.

Sanders, Jerry W., *Peddlars of Crisis: The Committee on the Present Danger and the Politics of Containment*, Pluto, London, 1983.

Sanguinetti, Antoine, *Le Devoir de Parler*, Fernand Nathan, Paris, 1981.

Saville, John, 'Ernest Bevin and the cold war 1945–50', in *Socialist Register 1984*, Merlin Press, London, 1984.

Simes, Dimitri, 'The death of détente', *International Security*, 5:1, 1980.

Smith, Dan and Smith, Ron, 'The new cold war', *Capital and Class*, 12, Winter 1980/1.

Smith, Dan and Thompson, E. P., *Prospectus for a Habitable Planet*, Penguin, London, 1987.

Sokolov, George, *The Economy of Détente: The Soviet Union and Western Capital*, Berg, Leamington Spa, 1987.

Stent, Angela, *From Embargo to Ostpolitik*, CUP, Cambridge, 1981.

Taubman, William, *Stalin's American Policy: From Entente to Détente to Cold War*, W. W. Norton, New York, 1982.

Thomas, Hugh, *Armed Truce: Beginnings of Cold War*, Hamish Hamilton, London, 1986.

Thompson, E. P., *Beyond the Cold War, NOT the Dimbleby Lecture*, Merlin Press/END, London, 1982.

—— *Exterminism and the Cold War*, New Left Books, London, 1982.

Thompson, E. P. and Thompson, Ben, *Star Wars, Self Destruct Incorporated*, Merlin Press/END, London, 1985.

Tucker, Robert, 'The purposes of American power', *Foreign Affairs*, Winter 1980/1.

Volten, Peter, *Brezhnev's Peace Program: A Study of Soviet Domestic*

Political Process and Power, Westview, Boulder, Colorado, 1982.
Wolfe, Alan, 'American domestic politics and the Alliance', in Kaldor and Falk, eds, *Dealignment*.
—— 'The irony of anti-communism: ideology and interest in postwar American foreign policy', in *Socialist Register 1984*, Merlin Press, London, 1984.
—— *The Rise and Fall of the Soviet Threat: Domestic Sources of the Cold War*, Institute for Policy Studies, Washington DC, 1979.
Yanov, Alexander, *Détente after Brezhnev: The Domestic Roots of Soviet Foreign Policy*, Institute of International Studies, University of California, Berkeley, 1977.
Yergin, Daniel, *Shattered Peace: The Origins of the Cold War and the National Security State*, Houghton Mifflin, Boston, 1977.

The nature of Soviet-type systems

Aganbegyan, Abel, *The Challenge: Economics of Perestroika*, Hutchinson, London, 1988.
Amalrik, Andrei, *Will the Soviet Union Survive until 1984?*, Penguin, London, 1970.
Amann, Ronald and Cooper, Julian, eds, *Industrial Innovation in the Soviet Union*, Yale University Press, New Haven, Conn., 1982.
Arendt, Hannah, *The Burden of our Time*, Secker and Warburg, London, 1951.
Artman, Danielle, ed., *Samizdat 86, The Moscow Trust Group*, END/UK– USSR Trustbuilders/SOK Berne, London and Berne, 1986.
Bahro, Rudi, *The Alternative in Eastern Europe*, New Left Books, London, 1978.
Bauer, Tamoás, 'Investment cycles in planned economies', *Acta Oeconomica*, 21:3, 1978.
Bernend, I. T. and Ranki, G., *Economic Development in East-Central Europe in the 19th and 20th Centuries*, Cornell University Press, Ithaca, NY, 1974.
—— *The European Periphery and Industrialization*, CUP, Cambridge, 1982.
Brus, W., Kende, P, and Mlynar, Z., *'Normalization' Processes in Soviet-dominated East-Central Europe*, Research Project, Crises in Soviet-type Systems, Study no. 1, 1982.
Brzezinski, Zbigniew, *Totalitarian Dictatorship and Autocracy*, Harvard University Press, Cambridge, Mass., 1956.

Carr, E. H., *A History of Soviet Russia*, Penguin, London. Includes: *The Bolshevik Revolution, 1917–23*, 3 vols, 1950–3; *The Interregnum, 1923–24*, 1954; *Socialism in One Country, 1924–25*, 3 vols, 1958–64.

Carr, E. H. and Davies, R. W., *Foundations of a Planned Economy, 1926–29*, 2 vols, Penguin, London, 1969 and 1971.

Claudin, Fernando, *The Communist Movement: From Comintern to Cominform*, Penguin, London, 1975.

Cockburn, Patrick, *Getting Russia Wrong: The End of Kremlinology*, Verso, London, 1971.

—— 'Gorbachev and Soviet conservatism', *World Policy Journal*, Winter 1988–9.

Cohen, Stephen, *Rethinking the Soviet Experience*, OUP, Oxford, 1985.

Comisso, Ellen and D'Andrea Tyson, Laura, 'Power, purpose and collective choice: economic strategy in socialist states', special issue of *International Organization*, 40:2, Spring 1986.

Conquest, Robert, *The Great Terror: Stalin's Purges of the 1930s*, Pelican, London, 1971.

Dawisha, Karen, *Eastern Europe: Gorbachev and Reform*, CUP, Cambridge, 1988.

Deutscher, Isaac, *Stalin* (1949), Penguin, London, 1982.

Djilas, M., *Conversations with Stalin*, Hart-Davis, London, 1962.

—— *The New Class: An Analysis of the Communist System*, Unwin, London, 1966.

—— *The Unperfect Society: Beyond the New Class*, Methuen, London, 1969.

European Nuclear Disarmament, Hungary Working Group, *Documents on the Peace Movement in Hungary*, END, London, 1986.

Fehér, Ferenc, Heller, Agnes and Markus, György, *Dictatorship Over Needs: An Analysis of Soviet Society*, Basil Blackwell, Oxford, 1983.

Fejto, François, *A History of the People's Democracies* (1969), Penguin, London, 1977.

Garton Ash, Timothy, *The Uses of Adversity: Essays on the Fate of Central Europe*, Granta Books, Penguin, London, 1989.

Haraszti, M., *The Velvet Prison: Artists under State Socialism*, I. B. Tauris, London, 1988.

—— *A Worker in a Workers' State: Piece Rates in Hungary*, Penguin, London, 1977.

Harman, Chris, *Bureaucracy and the Revolution in Eastern Europe*, Pluto, London, 1974.

Havel, Vaclav et al., *The Power of the Powerless: Citizens against the State* in *Central-Eastern Europe*, Hutchinson, London, 1985.

Hegedus, Andras et al., *The Humanisation of Socialism: Writings of the Budapest School*, Allison and Busby, London, 1976.

Holmes, Lesley, ed., *The Withering Away of the State? Party and State under Communism*, Sage, London and Beverly Hills, 1981.

Jahn, Egbert, ed., *Soviet Foreign Policy: Its Social and Economic Conditions*, Allison and Busby, London, 1978.

Joint Economic Committee, US Congress, *East European Economies: Slow Growth in the 1980s*. 3 vols, 90th Congress, 1st Session, Washington DC, 1985–7.

Kargalitsky, Boris, *The Thinking Reed: Soviet Intellectuals from 1917 to the Present*, Verso, London, 1988.

Kaser, Michael, *Comecon: Integration Problems of the Planned Economies*, OUP, London, 1967.

—— ed., *The Economic History of Eastern Europe, 1919–1975*, vol. 3: *Institutional Change within a Planned Economy*, Clarendon Press, Oxford, 1986.

Kaser, M. and Radice, E., eds, *The Economic History of Eastern Europe, 1919–75*, vol. 1: *Economic Structures and Performances Between Two Wars*; vol. 2: *Interwar Policy: The War and Reconstruction*, Clarendon Press, Oxford, 1985 and 1986.

Konrad, George and Szelényi, Ivan, *Intellectuals on the Road to Class Power*, Harvester Press, Brighton, 1979.

Kornai, János, *Contradictions and Dilemmas*, Corvina, New York, 1985.

—— *Growth Shortage, and Efficiency*, Basil Blackwell, Oxford, 1982.

—— 'The Hungarian reform process: visions, hopes and reality', *Journal of Economic Literature*, 24, December 1986.

Köszegi, Ferenc and Thompson, E. P., *The New Hungarian Peace Movement*, Merlin Press/European Nuclear Disarmament, London, 1983.

Köves, Andras, 'Problems and prospects of East–West cooperation: an East European view', in Kaldor, Holden and Falk, eds, *New Détente*.

Lange, Oskar, ed., *Problems of Political Economy of Socialism*, People's Publishing House, New Delhi, 1962.

Lewin, Moshe, *The Gorbachev Phenomenon: A Historical Interpretation*, Radius, London, 1988.

—— *The Making of the Soviet System: Essays in the Social History of Interwar Russia*, Methuen, London, 1985.

—— *Political Undercurrents in Soviet Economic Debates*, Princeton University Press, Princeton, NJ, 1984.

Mandel, Ernest, *Beyond Perestroika: The Future of Gorbachev's USSR*, Verso, London, 1989.

Michnik, Adam, *Letters from Prison and Other Essays*, University of California Press, California, 1985.

Nove, Alec, *An Economic History of the USSR*, 3rd edn, Penguin, London, 1984.

—— *The Soviet Economic System*, Allen and Unwin, London, 1977.

Rev, Istvan, 'The anti-ecological nature of centralisation', in M. Kaldor, G. Holden and R. Falk eds, *The New Détente: Rethinking East–West Relations*, UNU/Verso, London, 1989.

—— 'Local autonomy or centralism – when was the original sin committed?', *International Journal of Urban and Regional Research*, 8:1, March 1984.

Sandford, John, *The Sword and the Ploughshare: Autonomous Peace Initiatives in East Germany*, Merlin Press/European Nuclear Disarmament, London, 1983.

Šimečka, Milan, 'From class obsessions to dialogue: détente and the changing political culture of Eastern Europe', in M. Kaldor, G. Holden and R. Falk, eds, *The New Détente: Rethinking East–West Relations*, UNU/Verso, London, 1989.

—— *The Restoration of Order: The Normalization of Czechoslovakia, 1969–76*, Verso, London, 1984.

Stead, Jean and Grueneberg, Danielle, eds, *Moscow Independent Peace Group*, END Special Report, END/Merlin Press, London, 1982.

Steele, Jonathan, *The Limits of Soviet Power*, Penguin, London, 1984.

Szelényi, Ivan, 'The prospects and limits of the East European new class project: an auto-critical reflection on the intellectuals and the road to class power', *Politics and Society*, 15:2, 1986–7.

Szücs, Jenö, 'The three historical regions of Europe', in John Keane, ed., *Civil Society and the State*, Verso, London, 1987.

Terry, Sarah Meiklejohn, *Soviet Policy in Eastern Europe*, Yale University Press, New Haven and London, 1984.

Trotsky, Leon, *Revolutions Betrayed: What is the Soviet Union and Where is it Going?*, Faber, London, 1977.

Ulam, Adam B., *A History of Soviet Russia*, Praeger, New York, 1976.

Vajda, Mihály, 'East-Central European perspectives', in John Keane, ed., *Civil Society and the State*, Verso, London, 1987.

—— *The State and Socialism*, Allison and Busby, London, 1981.

Warner, Edward L., *The Military in Contemporary Soviet Politics: An Institutional Analysis*, Praeger, New York, 1977.

Wilson, Andrew and Bachkatov, Nina, *Living with Glasnost: Youth and Society in a Changing Russia*, Penguin, London, 1988.

Continuities and discontinuities in political, economic and military history

Aglietta, Michel, *The Theory of Capitalist Regulation: The US Experience*, New Left Books, London, 1979; revised edn, Verso, 1987.

Anderson, Perry, *Lineages of the Absolutist State*, New Left Books, London, 1974.

—— *Passages from Antiquity to Feudalism*, New Left Books, London, 1974.

Armstrong, Philip, Glyn, Andrew and Harrison, John, *Capitalism since World War II*, Fontana, London, 1984.

Ashley, Richard K., *The Political Economy of War and Peace*, Frances Pinter, London, 1980.

Ashworth, William, *A Short History of the International Economy since 1850*, 2nd edn, Longman, London, 1970.

Barraclough, Geoffrey, *Introduction to Contemporary History*, Penguin, London, 1964.

Berghahn, V. R., *Militarism, the History of an International Debate*, St Martin's Press, New York, 1982.

Bergsten, C. Fred, 'Economic imbalances', *Foreign Affairs*, Spring 1987.

Blackburn, Phil, Coombs, Ron and Green, Kenneth, *Technology, Economic Growth and the Labour Process*, Macmillan, London, 1985.

Block, Fred L., *The Origins of International Economic Disorder*, University of California Press, Berkeley, 1977.

Block, Ivan Stanislavovich, *The Future of War in its Technical, Economic and Political Relations: Is War Now Impossible?*, Ginn, Boston, 1899/1903.

Bowles, Samuel, Gordon, David M. and Weisskopf, Thomas E. *Beyond the Wasteland: A Democratic Alternative to Economic Decline*, Verso, London, 1986.

Bridge, F. R. and Bullen, Roger, *The Great Powers and the European States System, 1815–1914*, Longman, London and New York, 1980.

Bull, Hedley, *The Anarchical Society: A Study of Order in World Politics*, Macmillan, London, 1977.

Bull, H. and Watson, A., eds, *The Expansion of International Society*, Clarendon Press, Oxford, 1984.

Buzan, Barry, *People's States and Fear: The National Security Problem in International Relations*, Wheatsheaf, Brighton, 1983.

Calleo, David, *Beyond American Hegemony: The Future of the Atlantic Alliance*, Wheatsheaf, Brighton, 1987.

Carr, E. H., *The Twenty Years Crisis, 1919–1939: An Introduction to the Study of International Relations*, Macmillan, London, 1940.

Castells, Manuel, 'High technology, world development and structural transformation', in S. Mendlovitz and R. B. J. Walker, eds, *Towards a Just World Order*, Butterworth, Guildford, 1987.

Chase-Dunn, Christopher, 'International economic policy in a declining core state', in William P. Avery and David P. Rapkin, eds, *America in a Changing World Political Economy*, Longman, New York and London, 1982.

Cipolla, Carlo M., *The Economic Decline of Empires*, Methuen, London, 1970.

—— *Guns, Sails and Empires*, Pantheon, New York, 1965.

Clark, Ian, *Reform and Resistance in the International Order*, CUP, Cambridge, 1980.

Cox, Robert W., 'Social forces, states and world orders: beyond international relations theory', in Robert Keohane, ed., *Neo-Realism and its Critics*, CUP, Cambridge, 1986.

Day, Richard B., 'The theory of long waves: Kondratiev, Trotsky and Mandel', *New Left Review*, 99, September–October 1976.

Degrasse, Robert W., jun., *Military Expansion, Economic Decline*, Council on Economic Priorities, New York, 1983.

Dosi, G., 'Technological paradigms and technological trajectories', *Research Policy*, 11:3, June 1982.

Dosi, G., Freeman, C., Nelson, R., Silverberg, G. and Soete, Luc, eds, *Technical Change and Economic Theory*, Pinter, London and New York, 1988.

Dumas, Lloyd Jeffrey, *The Overburdened Economy: Uncovering the Cause of Chronic Unemployment, Inflation and National Decline*, University of California Press, Berkeley, 1986.

Edelman Spero, Joan, *The Politics of International Economic Relations*, 3rd edn, Allen and Unwin, London, 1985.

Ellis, John, *The Social History of the Machine Gun*, Pantheon, New York, 1975.

Falk, Richard, *The End of World Order: Essays on Normative International Relations*, Holmes and Meier, New York and London, 1983.

—— *The Promise of World Order*, Wheatsheaf, Brighton, 1989.

Fieldhouse, D. K., *Economics and Empire, 1830–1914*, Cornell University Press, Ithaca, NY, 1973.

Foreman-Peck, James, *A History of the World Economy: International Economic Relations since 1850*, Wheatsheaf, Brighton, 1983.

Freeman, Christopher, ed., *Long Waves in the World Economy*, Frances Pinter, London, 1984.

Freeman, Christopher et al., *Unemployment and Technical Innovation: A Study of Long Waves and Economic Development*, Frances Pinter, London, 1982.

Gathy, Vera, ed., *State and Civil Society*, Hungarian Academy of Sciences, Budapest, 1989.

Giddens, Anthony, *A Contemporary Critique of Historical Materialism*: vol. 1, *Power, Property and the State*, Macmillan, London, 1981; vol. 2, *The Nation-State and Violence*, Polity Press, Cambridge, 1985.

Gilpin, Robert, *The Political Economy of International Relations*, Princeton University Press, Princeton, NJ, 1987.

—— *War and Change in World Politics*, CUP, Cambridge, 1981.

Goldstein, Joshua, *Long Cycles: Prosperity and War in the Modern Age*, Yale University Press, New Haven and London, 1988.

Gordon, D. M., Weisskopf, T. E. and Bowles, S., 'Long swing and the non-reproductive cycle', *American Economic Review*, 73, 1983.

Gough, Ian, *The Political Economy of the Welfare State*, Macmillan, London, 1979.

Habermas, J., *Legitimation Crisis*, Heinemann, London, 1976.

Hobsbawm, E. J., *Industry and Empire*, Penguin, London, 1969.

Hopkins, T. K. and Wallerstein, I., *Processes of the World System*, Sage, Beverly Hills and London, 1980.

Howard, Michael, *War in European History*, OUP, Oxford, 1976.

Kaldor, Mary, *The Baroque Arsenal*, André Deutsch, London, 1982.

—— *The Disintegrating West*, Allen Lane, London, 1978.

——, Sharp, Margaret and Walker, William, 'Military R&D and industrial competitiveness', *Lloyds Bank Review*, October 1986.

—— and Walker, William, 'Technologie militaire et dynamisme économique', *La Recherche*, October 1988.

Keane, John, *Democracy and Civil Society*, Verso, London, 1987.

—— ed., *Civil Society and the State: New European Perspectives*, Verso, London, 1988.

Kennan, George, *The Decline of Bismarck's European Order*, Princeton University Press, Princeton, 1979.

Kennedy, Paul, *The Rise and Fall of the Great Powers: Economic Change and Military Conflict 1500 to 2000*, Unwin Hyman, London, 1988.

Kenney, Martin and Florida, Richard, 'Beyond mass production: production and labour process in Japan', *Politics and Society*, 16:1, March 1988.

Kenwood, A. G. and Longheed, A. L., *The Growth of the International Economy, 1820–1980: An Introductory Text*, Allen and Unwin, London, 1984.

Keohane, Robert, *After Hegemony: Cooperation and Discord in the World*

Political Economy, Princeton University Press, Princeton, 1984.

Keohane, Robert O. and Nye, Joseph S., *Power and Interdependence – World Politics in Transition*, Little Brown, Boston, 1977.

Kindleberger, Charles, *The World in Depression*, Allen Lane, London, 1978.

Kissinger, Henry A., *A World Restored*, Gollancz, London, 1974.

Kondratiev, N., 'The major economic cycles', *Review of Economic Statistics*, 18, November 1935.

Kurth, James R., 'The political consequences of the product cycle: industrial history and political outcomes', *International Organization*, 33:1, Winter 1979.

Landes, David, *The Unbound Prometheus, Technological Change 1750 to the Present*, CUP, Cambridge, 1969.

Lash, Scott and Urry, John, *The End of Organized Capitalism*, Polity Press, Cambridge, 1987.

Liepetz, Alan, *Mirages and Miracles: The Crises of Global Fordism*, Verso, London, 1987.

McNeill, William H., *The Pursuit of Power, Technology, Armed Force and Society since A.D. 1000*, Chicago University Press, Chicago, 1982.

—— *The Rise of the West*, Chicago University Press, Chicago, 1963.

Maddison, Angus, *Phases of Capitalist Development*, OUP, Oxford, 1982.

Mandel, E., *Late Capitalism*, New Left Books, London, 1980.

Melman, Seymour, *The Permanent War Economy: American Capitalism in Decline*, Simon and Schuster, New York, 1974.

—— *Profits Without Production*, University of Pennsylvania Press, Philadelphia, 1987.

Milward, A. S., *War, Economy and Society, 1939–45*, University of California Press, Berkeley and Los Angeles, 1979.

—— and Saul, S. B., *The Development of Continental Europe 1780–1850*, Allen and Unwin, London, 1973.

—— *The Development of the Economies of Continental Europe, 1850–1914*, Allen and Unwin, London, 1977.

Modelski, George, 'The long cycle of global politics and the nation state', *Comparative Studies in Society and History*, 20:2, April 1978.

—— 'Long cycles, Kondratievs and alternating innovations: implications for US foreign policy', in Charles W. Kegley and Pat McGowan, *The Political Economy of Foreign Policy Behaviour*, Sage, Beverly Hills, 1981.

—— 'Long cycles and the strategy of US international economic policy', in William P. Avery and David P. Rapkin, eds, *America in a Changing World Political Economy*, Longman, New York and London, 1982.

Murray, Robin, 'Benneton Britain: the new economic order', *Marxism Today*, November 1985.
—— 'Life after Henry (Ford)', *Marxism Today*, October 1988.
Nairn, Tom, ed., *Atlantic Europe? The Radical View*, Transnational Institute, Amsterdam, 1976.
Nef, John O., *War and Human Progress*, Harvard University Press, Cambridge, Mass., 1950.
Nelson, R. and Winter, S., *An Evolutionary Theory of Economic Change*, Harvard University Press, Cambridge, Mass., 1982.
Noble, David, *Forces of Production: A Social History of Industrial Automation*, Alfred A. Knopf, London, 1984.
Offe, Claus, *Contradictions of the Welfare State*, Hutchinson, London, 1984.
Parboni, Riccardo, *The Dollar and its Rivals*, Verso, London, 1986.
Perez-Perez, Carlotta, 'Microelectronics, long waves and world structural change', *World Development*, 13:3, 1985.
—— 'Structural change and assimilation of new technologies in economic and social systems', *Futures*, 15:4, October 1983.
Piantia, Mario, *New Technologies across the Atlantic*, Wheatsheaf, Brighton, 1988.
Pijl, Kees van der, *The Making of an Atlantic Ruling Class*, Verso, London, 1984.
Piore, Michael J. and Sabel, Charles F., *The Second Industrial Divide: Possibilities for Prosperity*, Basic Books, New York, 1984.
Polanyi, Karl, *The Great Transformation: The Political and Economic Origins of our Time* (1944), Beacon Press, London, 1957.
Rich, Norman, *The Age of Nationalism and Reform, 1850–1890*, Weidenfeld and Nicolson, London, 1970.
Rosencrance, Richard N., *Action and Reaction in World Politics: International Systems in Perspective*, Greenwood, Westpoint, Conn., 1977.
Rostow, W. W., *The World Economy: History and Prospect*, University of Texas, Austin and London, 1978.
Sayer, Andrew, 'New developments in manufacturing: the just-in-time system', *Capital and Class*, 30, Winter 1986.
Schumpeter, J. A., *Business Cycles: A Theoretical, Historical and Statistical Analysis of the Capitalist Process*, 2 vols, McGraw Hill, New York, 1939.
Sen, Gautam, *The Military Origins of Industrialisation and International Trade Rivalry*, Frances Pinter, London, 1984.
Shaw, Martin, ed., *War, State and Society*, Macmillan, London, 1984.
Strange, Susan, *Casino Capitalism*, Basil Blackwell, Oxford, 1986.

—— *States and Markets: An Introduction to International Political Economy*, Pinter, London, 1988.

Therborn, G., 'The rule of capital and the rise of democracy', *New Left Review*, May–June 3:10, 1977.

Thompson, W. R. and Zuk, R., 'War, inflation, and Kondratieff long waves', *Journal of Conflict Resolution*, 26, 1982.

Tilly, Charles, *The Formation of Nation-States in Western Europe*, Princeton University Press, Princeton, 1975.

Toynbee, Arnold J., *A Study of History*, OUP, Oxford, 1961.

Vayrynen, Raimo, 'Economic cycles, power transitions, political management and wars between major powers', *International Studies Quarterly*, 27:4, 1983.

—— 'Economic fluctuations, technological innovations and the arms race in historical perspective', *Cooperation and Conflict*, 18:3, 1983.

Wallerstein, Immanuel, *The Politics of the World Economy, the States, the Movements and the Civilizations*, CUP, Cambridge, 1984.

Wee, Herman van der, *Prosperity and Upheaval, 1945–80*, Pelican, London, 1987.

Wight, Martin, *The System of States*, Leicester University Press, Leicester, 1977.

Winter, J. M., ed., *War and Economic Development: Essays in Memory of David Joslin*, CUP, Cambridge, 1975.

Wright, Quincy, *A Study of War* (1942), University of Chicago, Chicago, 1965.

The military confrontation

Ahfeldt, Horst, *Defensive Verteidigung*, Rowalt, Reinbeck, Munich, 1983.

Alternative Defense Commission, *Defence Without the Bomb*, Taylor and Francis, London and Philadelphia, 1983.

Barnaby, Frank and Boeker, Egbert, 'Non-provocative non-nuclear defence of Western Europe', *ADIU Report*, 5:1, January–February, 1983.

Canby, Stephen, 'The Alliance and Europe, part IV: military doctrine and technology', *Adelphi Papers*, 109, IISS, London, Winter 1974–5.

Cockburn, Andrew, *The Threat: Inside the Soviet War Machine*, Hutchinson, London, 1983.

Evangelista, Matthew, *Innovation and the Arms Race: How the United States and the Soviet Union Develop New Military Technologies*, Cornell University Press, Ithaca, NY, 1988.

—— 'Stalin's post-war army reappraised', *International Security*, 7:3, 1982–3.

Freedman, Lawrence, *The Evolution of Nuclear Strategy*, Macmillan, London, 1982.

Galtung, Johann, *There are Alternatives: Four Roads to Peace and Security*, Spokesman, Nottingham, 1984.

Garnett, John C., ed., *The Defence of Western Europe*, Macmillan, London, 1974.

Holden, Gerard, *The Warsaw Pact: Soviet Security and Bloc Politics*, Basil Blackwell, Oxford, 1989.

Holloway, David, *The Soviet Union and the Arms Race*, Yale University Press, New Haven and London, 1983.

—— and Jane Sharpe, eds, *The Warsaw Pact: Alliance in Transition*, Macmillan, London, 1984.

Holm, Hans-Henrik and Petersen, Nikolaj, *The European Missile Crisis: Nuclear Weapons and Security Policy*, Frances Pinter, London, 1983.

Hough, Jerry, 'Gorbachev's strategy', *Foreign Affairs*, Fall 1985.

Howard, Michael, 'Reassurance and deterrence', *Foreign Affairs*, 61:2, Winter 1982–3.

Howarth, Jolyon and Chilton, Patricia, eds, *Defence and Dissent in Contemporary France*, Croom Helm, London and Sydney, 1984.

Johnstone, Diana, *The Politics of Euromissiles: Europe's Role in America's World*, Verso, London, 1984.

Jones, Christopher, *Soviet Influence in Eastern Europe: Political Autonomy and the Warsaw Pact*, Praeger, New York, 1981.

Kaldor, Mary and Smith, Dan, eds, *Disarming Europe*, Merlin Press, London, 1982.

Lewis, William J., *The Warsaw Pact: Arms, Doctrine and Strategy*, McGraw-Hill, New York, 1982.

Lifton, Robert Jay and Falk, Richard, *Indefensible Weapons: The Political and Psychological Case Against Nuclearism*, Basic Books, New York, 1982.

MccGwire, Michael, *Military Objectives in Soviet Foreign Policy*, Brookings Institution, Washington DC, 1987.

—— 'Soviet military objectives', *World Policy Journal*, 3:4, Fall 1986.

Mountbatten, Louis, 'A military commander surveys the nuclear arms race', *International Security*, Winter 1979–80.

Myrdal, Alva, *The Game of Disarmament: How the United States and the Soviet Union Run the Arms Race*, revised and updated, Pantheon, New York, 1982.

—— et al., *The Dynamics of European Nuclear Disarmament*, Spokesman, Nottingham, 1981.

Neild, Robert and Boserup, Anders, 'Beyond the INF Agreement: a new approach to non-nuclear forces', *World Policy Journal*, Fall 1987.

Sheer, Robert, *With Enough Shovels: Reagan, Bush and Nuclear War*, Secker and Warburg, London, 1983.

Steinke, Rudolf and Vale, Michael, eds, *Germany Debates Defence: The NATO Alliance at the Crossroads*, M. E. Sharpe, New York and London, 1983.

Stockholm International Peace Research Institute, *Policies for Common Security*, Taylor and Francis, London and Philadelphia, 1985.

Stowsky, Jay, 'Competing with the Pentagon', *World Policy Journal*, 3:4, Fall 1986.

Wohlstetter, Albert, 'Is there a Strategic Arms Race?', *Foreign Policy*, 16, Autumn 1974.

York, Herbert, *Making Weapons: Talking Peace. A Physicist's Odyssey from Geneva to Hiroshima*, Basic Books, New York, 1987.

Regular publications

East Central Europe

Across Frontiers, quarterly, Berkeley, California

Bulletin of the European Network for East–West Dialogue, occasional, West Berlin

Critique, quarterly, Edinburgh

Detente, bi-monthly, Leeds

East European Reporter, quarterly, London

Economist Intelligence Unit, *Country Profiles*, annual, and *Quarterly Report*, London

END Journal, bi-monthly, London, discontinued

Joint Economic Committee, US Congress, occasional reports and hearings, Washington DC

Labour Focus on Eastern Europe, quarterly, Southsea, Hants

Nato Colloquia, annual compilation of papers on various aspects of East–West relations, Brussels

Peace and Democracy News, bi-monthly, New York

Survey, a journal of East–West studies, occasional, New York

Telos, quarterly, New York

United Nations Economic Commission for Europe, *Economic Survey*, annual, and *Economic Bulletin*, annual

Armament and disarmament issues

ADIU Report, bi-monthly, Sussex

Arms Control Reporter, regular updates of arms control talks, Boston, Mass.

Arms Control Today, bi-monthly, Washington DC

Council for Arms Control Bulletin, bi-monthly, London

Focus on Vienna: Developments at the Vienna CSCE meeting and Related Events, newsletter published by the Austrian Committee for European Security and Cooperation in Vienna, bi-monthly, Vienna

International Defence Review, monthly, Geneva

Jane's Defence Weekly, weekly, Horley, Sussex

Nato's Facts and Figures, annual, Brussels

Nato's Sixteen Nations, bi-monthly, Brussels

Non-offensive Defence, quarterly, Copenhagen

RUSI Journal, bi-monthly, London

SIPRI Yearbook on Armament and Disarmament, annual, Stockholm

Survival, bi-monthly, London

US Arms Control and Disarmament Agency, *World Military Expenditures and Arms Transfers*, annual, Washington DC

World Military and Social Expenditures, annual, Washington DC

General

Atlantic News, weekly, Brussels

Bulletin of Atomic Scientists, bi-monthly, Chicago

Bulletin of Peace proposals, bi-monthly, Oslo

Disarmament Campaigns, bi-monthly, The Hague

Europe, the European Community news magazine, monthly, London

European Journal of International Affairs, Quarterly, Rome

L'Évènement Européen, monthly, Paris

Foreign Affairs, quarterly, New York

Foreign Policy, quarterly, New York

International Affairs, quarterly, London

International Affairs, monthly, Moscow

International Organization, quarterly, Stanford, California

International Security, quarterly, Cambridge, Mass.

Journal of Peace Research, quarterly, Oslo

Peace Magazine, bi-monthly, Toronto

Peace Review, quarterly, Stanford, California

Review of International Studies, quarterly, Guildford, Surrey

Soviet News, weekly, London

World Policy Journal, quarterly, New York

Index